THE PARADOX OF AFRICA'S POVERTY

D1112048

THE PARADOX OF AFRICA'S POVERTY

The Role of Indigenous Knowledge, Traditional Practices and Local Institutions— The Case of Ethiopia

TIRFE MAMMO

The Red Sea Press, Inc.

Publishers & Distributors of Third World Books

11-D Princess Road   **RSP**   P. O. Box 48
Lawrenceville, NJ 08648   Asmara, ERITREA

The Red Sea Press, Inc.

Publishers & Distributors of Third World Books

| 11-D Princess Road | P. O. Box 48 |
| Lawrenceville, NJ 08648 | Asmara, ERITREA |

Copyright © 1999 Tirfe Mammo

First Printing 1999

Book design: Krystal Jackson
Cover design: Jonathan Gullery

Library of Congress Cataloging-in-Publication Data

Mammo, Tirfe.
    The paradox of Africa's poverty : the role of indigenous knowledge, traditional practices and local institutions—the case of Ethiopia / Tirfe Mammo.
        p. cm.
    Includes bibliographical references and index.
    ISBN 1-56902-048-5 (hc). -- ISBN 1-56902-049-3 (pbk)
    1. Poverty--Ethiopia. 2. Indigenous peoples--Ethiopia--Eonomic conditions. I. Title.
HC845.Z9P625 1997
362.5'0963--dc21
                                          97-46979
                                            CIP

To Gemal Yassin & Tekle Gebru

*In memory of our true friendship, which was far
beyond ethnic barriers and religious affiliations.*

CONTENTS

List of Tables, Charts, and Figures ix

List of Abbreviations. xi

Preface. xiii

Part One
FEATURES OF AFRICAN POVERTY

Chapter One
General Introduction 3

Chapter Two
The Paradox of African Poverty 29

Chapter Three
Deepening African Poverty. 53

Part Two
FOCUS ON ETHIOPIA

Chapter Four
Poverty Aggravated by Internal Factors. 83

Chapter Five
The Attempt to Escape from Poverty 113

Chapter Six
Lessons of Experience from the
Ethiopian Revolution 141

Part Three
WHICH OPTIONS REMAIN?
OUTLOOK FOR THE FUTURE

Chapter Seven
  The Role of Indigenous Knowledge,
  Traditional Practices and Local Institutions 173

Chapter Eight
  Participation as a Method of
  Attacking Poverty 215

Glossary 239

Bibliography 241

Index 259

TABLES

2:1   Africa's Mineral Production, 1988 30
2:2   Africa's Cash-Crops Production, 1978 31
2:3   Africa's Share of Books and Mass Media, 1988 32
3:1   Aid Dispense as Percentage of GNP, 1990 56
3:2   MNCs in Africa's Mineral Production, 1988 63
3:3   Average Hourly Wage for Manual Workers, 1988 64
3:4   Distribution of Economic Output
      by Sector, 1960 & 1980 75
4:1   Absentee Landlords and Absentee Held Land, 1970 88
4:2   Owner-Farmed, *Gabbar* and Mixed-Farmed
      Holdings in Northern Ethiopia, 1966 91
4:3   Owner-Farmed and *Gabbar* and Mixed-Farmed
      Holdings in Southern Ethiopia, 1966 91
5:1   Peasant Associations, 1976 121
5:2   Distribution of Total Cultivated Area,
      1979-80 & 1985-86 130
5:3   New Sites or Centers Villagized Households
      and Total Population, 1987 132
6:1   Average Size of Landholding Percentage of Land
      and Oxen Holdings, 1977 144
6:2   Cost of Production, Government and Free Market
      Prices, 1985-86 149
6:3   Government Involvement in the Economy, 1974-84 159
7:1   Monthly Contributions to *Equb*, 1986 191
7:2   Enabling Facilities to Grow into
      Semi-Formal Organizations 193
7:3   Average Yield Per Hectare, 1982 201

CHARTS

5:1   Organizational Structure of Peasant Associations 120

FIGURES

8:1   Level of Integration Between Top-down
and Bottom-up 225

ABBREVIATIONS

AEPA	All Ethiopia Peasant Association
AMC	Agricultural Marketing Corporation
BHN	Basic Human Needs
BMN	Basic Material Needs
COPWE	Commission for Organizing the Party of the Working People of Ethiopia
EPRP	Ethiopian People's Revolutionary Party
FAO	Food and Agricultural Organization
GDP	Gross Domestic Product
GNP	Gross National Product
ILO	International Labor Organization
IMF	International Monetary Fund
LDC	Less Developed Countries
AESM/*meison*	All Ethiopia Socialist Movement
MNCs	Multinational Corporations
NIC	New Industrial Countries
OAU	Organization for African Unity
OLF	Oromo Liberation Front
PMAC	Provisional Military Administrative Council
PMAG	Provisional Military Administrative Government/*derg*
POMOA	Provisional Office of MassOrganization and Agitation
UN	United Nations
UNDP	United Nations Development Program
UNESCO	United Nations Educational Science and Cultural Organization
WHO	World Health Organization
WPE	Workers Party of Ethiopia

PREFACE

During my earlier days of primary and secondary school, except for brief, sporadic visits to the countryside, I lived in Addis Ababa, the capital city of Ethiopia. After I had finished high school, though only for a short period, I was assigned to work within rural development under the then Ministry of Finance of Ethiopia. This gave me an opportunity to travel in rural parts of Ethiopia and to learn more about the deepest poverty and hard living conditions of the peasants. This was, in fact, the very first activity which triggered my interest in rural development problems.

This experience in the rural areas further consolidated my earlier understanding of urban poverty, and having this in mind I began to study at the University of Addis Ababa, then Haile Selassie I University. During my stay there, myself and many other friends often discussed the poverty in our country. This later became awareness with the help of political education by the then dynamic university students' movement. To be honest, the inspiration from these days has influenced my life and still dominates my heart.

In the early seventies the political turmoil in Ethiopia reached its peak, the Haile Selassie regime's tolerance of any criticism went up in a puff of smoke and many students were arrested en mass—many young people especially from the capital, Addis Ababa, fled. I also left my country and came to Europe, namely Sweden.

The repression at home forced many young Ethiopians to open political fora in exile and Sweden was one of the centers for such activities, and hence I came to be involved. The intensive debates on Ethiopia together with my studies in Sweden, mainly of a social science nature including national economics, sociology and other development oriented courses helped me to consolidate my area of interest in development studies.

Later, I was assigned to work in rural areas in India, Sri Lanka and Bangladesh (a United Nations program, supported by the Swedish

International Development Authority). During these years, I also learned that though there are differences underpinning development problems in many developing countries, the poverty that prevailed in my country is not totally different from the poverty of many other Asian or African countries. Hence I gradually developed an interest in looking into the problems of other developing countries.

In the light of this background, this study summarizes my earlier theoretical trainings, in different disciplines, and practical experiences. It also summarizes the field experience that I have in Ethiopia and South-East Asia. It summarizes the main debates among my Ethiopian colleagues; the literature referred to in our debates.

I pause here to pose the questions that readers often ask before studying the text of any work. Questions such as what is the study about? Why did the author choose such a subject? What specific message does the author address?

The answer to such questions, and many others raised in the course of reading the study, could only be found by looking into the whole text. In short, however, the study is about poverty. Due to many factors discussed in this study, poverty has deepened in many countries of Africa rather than lessened and as a consequence many perish daily. Such counter-development made me curious to investigate further the features of poverty.

In order to understand the features of poverty, I think, there is no better continent than Africa. However, Africa is a big continent to address the points in detail and therefore, I have been forced to focus on one place where I can examine the features of poverty in detail. For such study there are a few countries that have absolute poverty, measured by any standard, like that of Ethiopia. Therefore, by citing some countries of Africa in general, and by especially focusing on Ethiopia, I feel that I have obtained a fair picture of poverty and gained a good overview for making some proposals.

Though the final product of this study is mine, I thank all the people from whose work I have benefited as it was their work which has enabled me to mould and sharpen my ideas.

During the long process of this study there are many people and organizations that have helped me through. The Department of Sociology, University of Uppsala, has provided me with financial and material support and for this my sincere thanks goes to all members of the staff of that department.

My special thanks go to Docent Mats Franzén who critically studied my drafts at various stages and provided me with advice on many occasions. His peerless academic talent, his gentle method of advising and discussing issues has indeed helped me to finish this study. My thanks also go to Rolf Bucht who helped me to obtain different provisions from the University and encouraged me to finish this study. In the early days of my introduction to the use of a Personal Computer (PC) my neighbor Göran Boström, who has an incredibly generous heart, helped me a lot, and for this I owe him many thanks.

Some friends of mine have read the manuscript and have also contributed constructive criticism and my many thanks that I made in the earlier version of this study still stands. I also have benefited from the reviews and suggestions made by Professor Sigfried Pausewang, Chr. Michelsen Institute, Bergen, Norway. I sincerely appreciate his help.

I extend my sincere gratitude to the staff members of the Library of the Scandinavian Institute African Studies, Uppsala, and to the Royal Research Library, Stockholm. Both libraries provided me with study desks and whole-hearted service. The Swedish International Development Authority (SIDA) library staff also deserves sincere gratitude for their cooperation.

Last but not least, my partner in life, Terfenesh Hagos, and our children, Fasil and Yared, deserve special thanks for their understanding of my situation over the long period of my involvement in this study.

Part One

FEATURES OF AFRICAN POVERTY

Chapter One

GENERAL INTRODUCTION

STUDY DISPOSITION

What is this study about? This study is the anti-thesis to the present pessimistic introspection of African post-colonial existence. Currently, it has become fashionable to state that Africa does not have any chance of recovery. The central issue that this study would like to address, however, is that, though the continent is experiencing many problems and crises, the situation is not irreversible. The continent has a bright future and numerous chances but, for this development to occur, many sacrifices must be made and unpopular measures taken.

The attempt of this study, by and large, is about how to attack poverty. However, before discussing the strategy to tackle this problem, the causes of poverty and the forces that entrench it must be identified. Among the causes of the multiple problems of poverty in Africa, this study particularly investigates whether the neglect of indigenous knowledge, traditional practices and local institutions has influenced poverty levels. Thus poverty in relation to the neglect of indigenous knowledge, traditional practices and local institutions is the central theme of this study.

The questions to be answered are: Do these phenomena have impacts on poverty? How has their neglect aggravated poverty? So as to properly expound these central questions, I present first the positions of these phenomena in some African societies past and present. Secondly, I examine if there are periods and places where indigenous knowledge and practices with the help of local institutions have served African societies. After establishing the last point, finally, I will attempt to point out what measures could be taken to reconsider and reconfirm their roles.

However, this may not be enough to employ them as instruments to further development. In order to use traditional activities in development they must be capable of absorbing innovations and open for adaptation to improved technologies. In short, what is called the modernity of tradition is the other key aspect of this study.

One could argue that preservation of traditional activities, *per se*, may not be an advisable instrument with which to attack poverty. This is shown by taking examples from Ethiopia, whose traditional practices and cultural heritage were not that much affected by foreign intervention and yet is a country affected by extreme poverty due to the lack of adaptability and openness to innovation.

This study also attempts to show the route to positive improvements through elaborating on the capacities of local institutions as vehicles for sustainable development.[1] However, prior to employing local institutions as instruments of development, I have to examine the traditional knowledge and practices of a society. This is because local institutions' activities are circumscribed by the extent of traditional knowledge and practices available in a given society. Moreover, it is also essential to note if these traditional practices and knowledge are adaptable to modernity and innovation. The understanding of which local institutions are open to change and in which way they may be used as vehicles for further development also ought to be clearly described.

Therefore, before suggesting the options available in the future, the study focuses first on the major problem itself, namely poverty. The objective towards which all efforts are directed is the amelioration of this poverty, which I consider to be one of the basic factors that hinders further political and socio-economic transformation on the continent in general.

Based on this statement, the focus of this study is on poverty minimizing efforts rather than on development *per se*. This is because, today, the term development has become too attached to Westernization. Many African development activists also seem to conceive development as inter-changeable with Westernization and thereby concentrate their efforts on industrialization and consumption of industrial products. Instead of focusing on poverty reduction, we could help basic human (day-to-day) needs, like availability of food, safe drinking water, sanitation and roofs over the peoples' heads to become central. The understanding here is that the starting point for any development is poverty-reduction efforts and unless poverty is minimized development becomes utopia. What then, are the features of African poverty?

African poverty, according to one version of history, emerged from the competition between pre-capitalist African civilization and European domination. To arrest this indigenous civilization and win everything in their favor, the Europeans labeled Africa as a continent without any roots of civilization. For example, seventeenth and eighteenth century European "learned men,"[2] characterized the people of Africa as pseudo-humans, totally unable to learn new things, incapable of improving their situation and unable to reach the level of a "human race" (Davidson, 1984). Such labeling, firstly, enabled Europeans to increasingly indulged in the most malevolent phenomenon known to human history, the slave trade, through which Africans were forced to work and live under inhuman conditions. Secondly, such notions were also advanced to negatively affect African confidence and clear the way for European domination, as was manifested not only in the slave trade but also in colonialism and racism.

It is true, perhaps, to say that the civilization of one nation could be built on the ruins of another, and the well-being of the former may directly relate to the poverty of the latter. Guided by this principle, Europeans forced Africa and other nations to decline into poverty in order to make themselves rich. Failing the acceptance of this particular interpretation of history, there are many falsified explanations given as to why the economic and social development of Africa has stagnated today.

The reason why attempts to improve the material well-being of African societies are not effective even today, and why efforts from both inside and outside have failed to bring about remedies that can cure Africa from its chronic material poverty, to a considerable degree, lies in Africans being the victims of the misappropriation of its human and material resources by the slave trade, colonialism and neo-colonialism.

It is tempting to contest the statements made above, however, to cover the periods of the slave trade and colonialism, a history of over five centuries, is a task beyond the scope of this study. Instead, I have limited myself only in indicating some of the damages done by them, and pointing out how these damages brought determinant consequences from which Africa still suffers.

Though the slave trade and colonialism are mentioned as a background to my discussion, the primary focus here is post-colonial African poverty.[3] During this period, poverty in Africa has been exacerbated from two fronts—external and internal. The external influences exhibited through development assistance or aid programs have made many African countries heavily dependent on external factors; financial institutions have accelerated African debt; imbalance in international trade has forced prices of primary goods to fall; and multinational corporations use African cut-price labor and natural resources to their advantage. In these processes Africa stands as a loser and is exposed to further poverty.

Internally, in the post-colonial period, the African political elite (the political elite is here defined as decision makers) has also contributed to the poverty of the continent. The policies of the political elite in power can be distinguished by three characteristics, (a) negative political development, (b) lopsided economic priorities and (c) neglect of indigenous knowledge, traditional practices and local institutions—and these points are the crucial elements of this study.

Considering political issues, we often see that in post-colonial Africa, political power does not generally emerge through democratic processes but through twisting of arms. The rule of law, for example, is often replaced by the rule of the gun.[4] A new government that claims political power by force today has to demolish what has been achieved to date and begin to write its (new) history claiming the past is "obsolete." This continues until the day the next party succeeds in grabbing power and begins the same process anew. The question is, how to stop such a series of negative political developments on the continent of Africa and instead establish a tradition of legitimacy, accountability and transparency, which perhaps may lead to stability and the formation of a common front against Africa's common enemy—poverty.

Post-independence Africa's lopsided economic priorities, especially in relation to poverty reduction, are another area of concern for this study. It is often stated that Africa should be modernized and this modernization has been equated with industrialization, which again is associated with Westernization. Because of such fixations the predominant sector of African society, the peasants, and the fundamental life-line of the African people—agricultural activities—were pushed aside. Such a priority, not only hampered economic betterment and social change but, *per contra*, become responsible for millions of lives lost in famine. As a counter-response to the proponents of modernization/Westernization the argument put forward in this study is that the greatest resource present in African societies are the peasants and that their livelihood depends on agriculture. Therefore, any development sought to give results should start by benefiting the rural poor. African development efforts diverted from focusing on peasants necessarily encounter problems in implementing sustainable development.

In poor countries where options are limited, it is true, government as a social organization plays a central role. However, when African decision-makers try to practice development, they normally attempt to implement it in isolation, sealed off from the people's indigenous knowledge, traditional practices and outside of their local institutions. This study however, attempts to consider in detail if the idea that internal forces, such as the participation of the local people and their indigenous knowledge would have significant impacts for ameliorating poverty.

Lastly, while it should unequivocally be stressed here that external factors such as the slave trade and colonialism are indeed decisive for the present underdevelopment of Africa in many respects, this study goes one step further and questions what has been done in post-colonial Africa, an era that has extended over nearly four decades.

Points of Departure
The appropriate backdrop for this study in which one will be able to make inquiries into the subject of poverty is the examination of the features of African poverty in general and then, the substantiation of this general information with an actual case study. Based on the data collected and the arguments put forward it may be possible to arrive at reliable conclusions.

However, from the outset, it has to be clearly stressed that the African part mentioned is to provide a more general perspective in order to be able to understand the different features of poverty and therefore, should simply be taken as a profile and not, by any means, as dealing with the whole range of African problems. Africa is a continent comprised of fifty three countries, accommodating nearly 600 million people with varieties of languages, cultures and historical backgrounds and, under such circumstances a choice must be made irrespective of how inconvenient it is. I made my choice and focused on sub-Saharan Africa but, even here, I limit myself to a few countries to show diversities, contrasts and also use as comparative examples.[5]

More generally, with regard to the causes of African poverty there are at least three main theoretical schools. One system of opinion strongly argues that the present African poverty's *starting-post* was the slave trade, colonialism and neo-colonialism (Rodney, 1972; Inikori, 1979). The second, while accepting the damage done by the slave trade and colonialism, further argues that even without colonialism African poverty was made possible because of the European enforcement of the integration of Africa into the world economy (Amin, 1974; Wallerstein, 1974). This school considers colonialism as one of those methods of integrating peripheral areas into the world economy. In this integration process the center absorbs surpluses from the periphery which in turn accelerates their poverty.

The interpretation of history by the second school of thought, to repeat, is that the integration of peripheral areas into the world economy was unavoidable with or without colonialism. To illustrate the point some rich and poor, but non-colonized, Far Eastern Asian countries are given as examples. To summarize the arguments put forward by this school, the poverty of Africa is caused by the European process of integrating Africa into the world economy, which has been shallow rather than deep; the kind of capitalism that was transferred to Africa was itself lopsided. As Mazrui (1986:14) states, in Africa,

> Western consumption patterns were transferred more effectively than Western production; Western tastes were acquired more quickly than Western skills; the profit motive was adopted without ethics and capitalist greed was accepted rather than its discipline.

In short, the point of departure of this school is that colonialism in Africa neither fully destroy the economy of traditional society and replace it with Western capitalism (as in Singapore), nor adapt and integrate with the local culture (as in Japan), nor leave African indigenous knowledge and traditional practices free to develop in their own ways. The third school, though not yet succeeded in articulating itself clearly, attempts to focus on the African fixation of becoming Westernized (Ake, 1990). In so doing, Africa neglected to sustain the development of its indigenous capacity.

8

General Introduction

All these schools, however, agree on the negative development of post-colonial Africa, and if there are distinctions between them they rest only on the level of emphasis. For example, for the first school, what is happening today in Africa is neo-colonialism while the second stresses the process of integration into world economy, which in my opinion, is not vastly different from the first school.

The third school is very close to my primary involvement. This study also accepts the factors that contributed to African poverty as dealt with above, and yet, attempts to examine in depth in which ways these factors affected African poverty. Among those identified as negative—the neglect of African indigenous knowledge, traditional experiences and utilization of local institutions as instruments to attack poverty are found to be crucial. This sidelining of African heritage was accentuated by the slave trade, colonialism and neo-colonialism. In this manner, this study attempts to add more understanding to the features of poverty in Africa. Moreover, while the schools named above mainly focus on external factors, this study makes an attempt to add the local dimension into it post-colonial African governments.

The factors behind poverty in Africa generally vary. For example, the major causes of poverty in Kenya, Tanzania, Ghana, etc., were external, i.e., colonialism as a common denominator. However, we cannot say that poverty in Kenya is similar to that of Tanzania or Ghana because Kenya was much more of settler-colony and is agriculturally richer than Tanzania. Ghana is rich in gold and other mineral resources and thus, attractive to colonialism from a different perspective. Even after independence these countries followed different paths of development. Kenya stayed within a capitalist sphere of influence, while Ghana and Tanzania adopted a socialist oriented path—yet, their "socialism" differs widely. Additionally, and in contrast to what has been stated above, poverty in Ethiopia is, by and large, internal, being based on the feudal system of misappropriation of arable land, and, therefore, presents another aspect of the causes of poverty. Due to such diversities generalization becomes difficult.

The distinction made above, namely, between internal and external causes of poverty, should not be taken as a rift. In fact, emphasis on internal causes of poverty, as stated earlier, has a central place in this study. In order to make my focus on this issue clear I took Ethiopia as a case.

In the pre-capitalist era of Africa, Ethiopia was one of the many established kingdoms having direct links to other African civilizations

9

for which the Nile River was the center-piece. Ethiopia shared this civilization with the Egyptians, the Nubians, Meroe and the life-styles of West Africans infused by the masters of the desert, the Berbers, who amalgamated the cultures and the civilization of West and East Africa. Much evidence left behind by the Axumite kingdom of Ethiopia (ca 350 AD) proves this connection. In the era of the slave trade, Ethiopians were sold (though comparatively few) east-bound to many neighboring Arab countries and as far as India. In the colonial period, there were devastating wars against the expansionist Ottoman Empire, colonial Britain and fascist Italy (Pankhurst, 1961; Taddesse Tamerat, 1972; Davidson, 1984). From such interpretation of Ethiopian history it could be said that though Ethiopia was for-mally free from colonial domination it was deeply entangled in the world capitalist system like many other African states.[6]

Moreover, the focus on Ethiopia will clearly illustrate that Ethiopia has experimented with both the capitalist and the socialist path of development for nearly five and then two decades respec-tively. These routes are also the major routes of transformation uti-lized by many African countries and are subjects of scrutiny in this study. Secondly, Ethiopia, for long historical periods experienced a feudal social structure, unbroken tradition, etc., which is not common in African countries. Precisely this point is found to be useful for con-trasting with other African countries which lack this historical epoch because of early colonial attack on their past. This in turn, sheds light on the hypothetical discussion—if Africa had passed through a feu-dal epoch like that in Europe, then the situation would have been dif-ferent from what it is today. However the Ethiopian feudal social sys-tem, as presented in this study, does not support this postulate.

One more essential issue has to be clarified here, that is, Ethiopia is a country not colonized, and her indigenous knowledge and tradi-tional practices have not been destroyed or arrested by Western pow-ers, and yet it is an extremely poor country. How is this to be explained? Firstly, it is precisely this point that may support the argu-ment that it is not external forces alone, but also internal forces which may retard development and deepen poverty. Secondly, the focus on Ethiopia could also enable us to realize that keeping tradi-tions *per se* without adapting them better could also be anti-develop-ment.[7] Adaptability, innovation and flexibility of traditional knowl-edge and practices, in order to achieve further betterment and thereby reduce poverty, are not only important but essential (Hobsbawm and Ranger, 1983).

To sum up, as the above schools of thought argue, post-independence models of development thus far applied by foreign agents as well as governments, have not brought about the anticipated results, i.e. the improvement of Africans' living conditions. Furthermore, when the capitalist oriented path of development was found not to bear fruit as expected, the socialist path was taken in its place, forgetting that the very foundation of socialism is erected on capitalism. This does not mean, however, that these models are undesirable. The point rather is, when post-colonial African countries made their decisions to adopt a certain path of development they simply followed Western footsteps—without thorough examination of the model(s) adopted to ensure that they could address the desires of African societies. The argument which is often presented here is therefore, not whether this system is better than that one, but when one or both systems were applied, many African countries failed to use their cultural heritage as a precondition for their political and socio-economic transformation and thereby deepen their poverty.

The Structure of the Study
More generally, this study consists of three parts. *Part One* tries to properly investigate the multiple causes of poverty, by taking two broader aspects into account. These are: poverty, mainly influenced by foreign factors, and that influenced by internal events. The external factors are identified with the help of historical epochs such as the slave trade, colonialism and neo-colonialism. These external and internal factors, especially in post-colonial Africa, are presented from Chapter One to Chapter Three.

Chapter One begins with an introduction, which presents the study's disposition in its first half, followed by a background and a general overview of pre-capitalist indigenous knowledge and traditional practices in Africa. The task of the latter part is to explain how traditional African social and economic organization, once in full operation, were disrupted by the slave trade and colonialism. Chapter Two deals with post-colonial periods. In this chapter first, the paradox of African poverty, then the main development theories introduced to reduce this poverty are presented. Chapter Three attempts to focus on the deepening of African poverty through the efforts of external agencies viz. aid agencies, multinational corporations, financial institutions and international trade agreements. The second half of the chapter, critically assesses African governments' priorities.

11

The second part presents empirical study and it begins with Chapter Four. This chapter explains how feudalism augmented the scope and depth of poverty in Ethiopia. It also summarizes the efforts of five decades of capitalist development which ended in creating a semi-feudal and semi-capitalist system in Ethiopia.[8] The last part of Chapter Four examines the long-standing and the immediate causes of the Ethiopian revolution. Chapter five illustrates the nearly two decades of socialist development under military rule, it also summarises the main achievements and constraints of the 1974 Ethiopian revolution. In the last part of this chapter the socialist path of transformation as applied in Ethiopia is illustrated. Chapter Six attempts to draw lessons from the Ethiopian revolution.

The third part of this study attempts to examine the extent and depth of utilizing indigenous knowledge, traditional practices and local institutions as preconditions for development. This section also concludes the study by seeking options and indicating strategies concerning how to attack poverty at its roots, and attempts to show what it believes to be the proper route to sustainable development. Chapter Seven examines options open for the future. Here African cultural heritage and local institutions are indicated as useful vehicles for transformation and to that end a catalogue of African traditional knowledge and practices is presented. The heart of the discussion here is, how improved and better knowledge and democratic traditions could be integrated with the African traditional knowledge and practices, which according to this study, is not only vital but also essential. Chapter Eight attempts to answer the main question of the study—What is to be done? It suggests the participation of the people as a mechanism for attacking poverty. The last part of this chapter in the concluding remarks, reflects on the search for balanced options and points out the challenges ahead when attempting to reduce poverty. Finally a study project for the future is proposed.

CONCEPTUAL FRAMEWORK

Theoretical definitions of many of the concepts used in this study are given as they appear i.e., within the context of the discussion. However, some concepts like, development, underdevelopment, transformation, poverty and economic growth are frequently used, and below are presented working definitions and the problems faced when utilizing these conceptual instruments.

12

More generally, development has so far been defined as a process of change towards material well-being. The factors that contribute to this increase in material well-being are considered to be rise in output, positive increase in skills, maximum utilization of capacity etc. and consequently an increase in income—all of course, measured by the standards of the industrial societies of Western Europe and North America.

Development, in this study, though it is part of economic growth, it also differs. Economic growth, in its conventional definition, is a rapid and sustained rise in real output per capita with attendant shifts in the technological, economic and demographic characteristics of a society (Mobounije, 1982). In contrast, development is a multidimensional concept which consists of many disciplines and makes a satisfactory definition difficult. On these grounds I prefer to give some interpretations rather than attempting a definition.

(a) Development is conceived here as incorporating both economic growth and non-economic factors ranging from institution building to cultural uplift manifested in the general socio-economic transformation of a society.

(b) Self-reliance and above all greater freedom to stimulate free individual initiative-taking are also incorporated within my conception of development. In line with this, development here also implies a democratic milieu in which people participate in all activities concerning their lives and express their thoughts without any sort of fear. These interpretation resembles Himmelstrand's (1993:4-5) criteria of development in which he identifies,

> Development as the capacity of a given society, increasingly, to use its own resources of land, minerals, and man-power to feed its own people;...without indigenous entrepreneurs and labor there is no further development. A considerable measure of autonomy, self-rule and democracy [are essential components of development].

(c) In order for the named factors to meet their targets, development efforts should include the use of indigenous knowledge and traditional practices as a preconditions.

Finally, the term development here implies what is called sustainable human development or people-oriented or people-centered development. The interpretation of sustain-able development is well summarized by the UNDP's Human Development Report (1994:iii),

Sustainable human development is development that not only generates economic growth but distributes its benefits equitably; that generates the environment rather than destroying it; that empowers people rather than marginalizing them. It is development that gives priority to the poor, enlarging their choices and opportunities and providing for their participation in decisions that affect their lives. It is development that is pro-people, pro-nature, pro-jobs and pro-women.

People-oriented or people-centered development is also sustainable development and it is used here to denote the ideal goals "where no child goes without an education, where no human beings is denied health care and where all people can develop their potential capabilities" (Human Development Report, 1994:13). It also meant creating enabling conditions to protect basic human rights—in short, it means focus on human beings.

The conventional definition of underdevelopment implies less economic growth, inferior skills, low levels of capacity utilization and lower material well-being, again measured by the standard of the industrial societies. Such a definition fails to emphasize that low income breeds lower material well-being which leads to lower individual status that in turn causes loss of self confidence and self reliance completing a process called the vicious cycle of poverty.

In finding remedies for poverty through the mechanisms of development and economic growth, it is important to establish clear distinctions between them. However, the underlying problem here is that these two terms, in practical application, go hand-in-hand and are integral parts of the struggle against poverty. Therefore, to avoid such conceptual overlapping, I am forced here to employ another key concept namely, *transformation*, which connotes both economic growth and social development geared to attacking poverty and improving living conditions.

In order for societies to acquire basic change structural transformation is essential. In line with this, for example, Hettne (1990b), discusses development in terms of transformation. By structural transformation he meant, *cultural, political social and economic change.*

Moreover to Godelier, (1987) transformation denotes a step towards structural change and he suggests that a period of transformation is a period when the old ways die and the new emerge. It may be helpful to note that the concept of transformation here is a process and does not imply to spontaneous or dramatic social change such as a political coup in favor of a certain economic policy. On the contrary, it is understood as thorough, well-rooted and sustainable social development through social agencies, which are referred to as agents of transformation such as societies using their indigenous knowledge, traditional practices and local institutions as preconditions and at the same time utilizing their adaptability to new phenomena.

In short, the definition of transformation here is more similar to its definition in natural science i.e. a change of format at *metamorphosis*—e.g. a transformation of limestone into marble. In this case poverty being replaced with sustainable food supply and better living conditions, dictatorship replaced by sustainable democratic rule, the creation of civil society through the establishment of rule of law, encouragement of independent institutions through broader participation of the people with the use of their accumulated, indigenous knowledge.

The interpretation of development, as earlier referred to, incorporates the use of indigenous knowledge and traditional practices. As Chambers (1983) argues, indigenous knowledge means a stock of local knowledge prevailing in a certain area and derived from that specific milieu. The term indigenous is used here not to indicate, by any means, a glorious past but rather to imply what may also be useful in the present. The understanding of indigenous knowledge here is that, it is a body of experience which could be culturally and regionally specific, adaptable to new and useful innovations, cumulative and supportive to sustaining survival.[9]

Before moving into more working definitions of other concepts, I would like to stress the inter-relationship between poverty, development and the role of indigenous knowledge, traditional practices and local institutions.

Development and poverty are inversely related, i.e. positive efforts contribute to the minimization of poverty. If development is to mean satisfaction of basic human needs, availability of food, safe drinking water, health care, shelter, clothing and basic education facilities—such positive steps (development) negatively affect poverty.

If development and poverty are inversely related, therefore, underdevelopment is directly related to poverty. Impoverishment or underdevelopment is well described by Chamber's (1983:103-139) as showing *powerlessness, physical weakness, vulnerability and isolation*, which in turn deepens and widens poverty even farther. Poverty is also defined in Galbraith (1979) in which he describes mass poverty, especially in underdeveloped countries, to a great extent as a rural problem. In both the works named above, the message is that the efforts and/or achievements of socio-economic development ought to be measured by the level (increase/decrease) of poverty, of the rural population especially.

It is also stated that the instruments of survival available to the poor are their indigenous knowledge, traditional practices and participation in their local institutions. Development for the poor seems to have no other option than to investigate the potential of these traditional practices to adapt better technologies, and examine their openness for any innovation that may minimize poverty.

Other main concepts used in this study are tradition, traditionalism and modernization. Traditional values, as many assume, do not necessarily exclude change or introduction of new ideas. In fact, many aspects of modern industrial societies are based on traditional norms. Moreover, traditional norms are used to filter the negative sides of modern values with the positive old ones and in so doing, they mould, shape and make the new ideas acceptable to the society concerned. In this sense tradition has a characteristic of modernity (Weber, [1920], translated in 1961).

In addition, as Hobsbawm and Ranger (1983:4) note, tradition does not "preclude innovation and change up to a point." They argue that a new tradition can be born from the old—a dynamic process which they refer to as "the invention of tradition," and emphasized how in some African countries colonial traditions have now become fused into local ones.

In contrast to tradition, traditionalism is conservative resistance to new things. It may originate from a conscious revival of past glorious days, from an ideology which looks back to the past as providing a set of norms whose revival would again lead to greatness. Such revivalist ideologies often have a tendency to reject any foreign or newly introduced values and instead warmly advocate the revival and vitalization of old values.

Moore (1963) emphasizes the relationship of being traditional and modern in a different manner. According to him the concept of modernization denotes a total transformation of traditional society into the types of technology and associated social organization that characterizes the advanced, economically prosperous and relatively politically stable nations of the Western world. His description of modernization includes Western rationality, economic growth, planning and institutional arrangements. In light of such working definitions given to this concept, many took modernization as synonym for Westernization.

In this study modernization *per se* is not taken as negative. For example, modernization, e.g., with connotations of improvement in technology, better living conditions etc. is always welcome. In fact, modernization of tradition is the unifying concept utilized throughout this study. However, modernization connoting Westernization or coupling Western life-styles to Africa is seen as problematic. This is because such undertakings have pushed aside African traditions, cultural heritage, accumulated knowledge, indigenous practices and the use of their local institutions. Westernization appears not to promote the sense of self-dependency and in short is a process of self-denial.

Contrary to Westernization, this study however, emphasizes the use of traditional experience, indigenous knowledge and local institutions as prerequisites for African social transformation. The point is that when Africa copied a path of development from the West, it copied wrongly. That is to say, Africa tried to duplicate the civilization of the capitalist nations without first studying the stages of development of the West in relation to the stages of development in Africa. For example, it appeared to ignore the agricultural transformation of the West or the early capitalist stages, which led to present day Western societies. As Hyden (1983:29) correctly observed, Africa has jumped or by-passed "studying the early phases of transition to capitalism."

In dealing with the Ethiopian case, commonly used concepts include land reform, agrarian reform, socialism and peasants. Land reform is a term very much used in development studies, always with a different meaning depending on the specific question at hand. In some cases, it implies distribution of plots to landless peasants, or legal procedures to determine the rights of landless peasants and landlords, while agrarian reform has a broader meaning often accompanied by further poverty reduction measures such as welfare programs (Alemneh Dejene, 1987; Dorner, 1972).

With regard to the use of the term socialism, it is difficult to give one general definition. Socialism in its classical meaning implies a system higher than capitalism i.e. a social development stage after fully-fledged capitalism, which is so far absent in any part of Africa. African socialism, it is often said, is adapted to social conditions and thus blended. Some blended socialism with religion or what they call African traditional beliefs, some others combined it with nationalism, and in yet other countries they simply found slogans that could be enough to mobilize large numbers of people. Therefore, to avoid such confusion, socialism here is referred to as a social system that requires proper capitalist development as its base (Marx and Engles, 1969:489-504). What took place in many countries of Africa, though often referred to as socialism, were nationalistic movements resulting, at best, in social revolution where the old political system was replaced by another. Therefore, many of the attempts at socialism, in this study, are referred as socialist orientation.[10]

THE ISSUE: ROOTS OF AFRICAN POVERTY

Under this title, first, I would like to present in brief, the pre-capitalist development of Africa using its own traditional practices and then move on to show how the slave trade and colonialism suppressed the use of African indigenous knowledge, traditional practices and local institutions. In describing the nature of poverty Galbratith (1979:17) states, "Explanation of poverty has most often been made by people in the rich countries of the poor. But a lesser current of explanation has run from the poor countries to the rich. Of these explanations the legacy of colonialism is the most important." And it is to this explanation that I now turn my attention.

Poverty may be seen from different angles and at different levels. There is poverty, which mainly stems from poor natural resources and/or too large a population in a given country; there is poverty arising from misappropriation of the country's wealth, there is mass poverty arising from total crisis, disjointed stabilization and where the majority of the people are left in despair—all these are the features of African poverty.

Though the main focus here is to concentrate on the post-colonial era of African poverty, it becomes difficult to assess this period in isolation from earlier periods, namely the legacy of the slave trade and colonialism. Indeed, the post-colonial period of African poverty is the facade built upon the foundation of the slave trade for nearly 400 years (1400-1800) and colonization for over 150 years (1800-1950) which together defined African society for over five hundred years.

It is disturbing, for instance, to hear the undervaluation of present Africa without considering the historical fact that Africans were sold as commodities or used as mere tools of production and how their natural resources as well as the surpluses from their labor were systematically transferred to the present developed countries over centuries. On this line, for example, Rodney (1972) strongly argues that the root causes of African poverty were set in motion through the disruption of African indigenous political and socio-economic development by colonial powers. Before this disruption, as much evidence shows, African indigenous economic, political and social developments were not as inferior as people tend to believe today.

According to Iliffe (1983), for example, in the mid-nineteenth century, red leather products that were sold in European markets by the name of *Moroccan leather* were products of Hausa (N. Nigeria) and Madinga (Mali) people. They were tanned and dyed by West African city-states and sold in European markets.

Iliffe further noted that indigo-dyed cotton cloth production was the most important craft industry in sub-Saharan Africa. The same source indicates that from the mid-nineteenth century onwards, sub-Saharan Africa experienced relatively developed pre-capitalist economic performances. This was clearly demonstrated in the merchant capitalism that flourished between the Islamic world of North Africa and West Africa. The business centres of Jenne (Niger), Timbuktu (Guinea), Kano (Nigeria) Asanti (Mali) etc. were renown commercial centres or African city-states.[11]

According to Ayittey, (1990) pre-capitalist West African business centres enjoyed early capitalist mode of production characterized by hiring of labor, exchange in kind and money-like payments. Commercial trade was first carried out by barter, then developed to payments specifically in cloth, salt, iron hoes or cowry shells. In some places payments against expensive exchanges were made in gold and copper and relatively developed credit systems existed. This early commercial activity is sometimes referred to as *bazaar capitalism* (Iliffe, 1983). Ayittey, also names Lozi, as the main commercial center of southern Africa and the city-states around Zambezi River and Sabi Valley as well, known for their indigenous agricultural knowledge and commercial activities.

Adedeji, (1981) and Davidson, (1984), also confirm that West African gold production (in Ghana, Mali, Nigeria etc.) played a central role in laying the basis not only for colonial powers but even for the Mediterranean and Indian Ocean economies.

With regard to East African civilization Pankhurst (1961) states that the Axumite kingdom of Ethiopia dominated trade across the Red Sea and had used coin money since the second half of the third century AD.[12] Furthermore, the same source revealed the commerce that flourished in Axum had contacts not only across the Red Sea but also covered the Indian ocean.

Sub-Saharan African indigenous knowledge and traditional practices were not limited to businesses and agriculture, but were also to be found in local administration and political organization. Africans were not stateless and without kingdoms as it is presented in many (colonial) history books. The Axumite kingdom (Ethiopia—about AD 350) was strong and in close touch with the civilizations of Alexandria and the Byzantine Empire (Trimingham 1976); the kingdom of Nubia over the land of Kush or Meroe of the Middle Nile; the kingdom of Buganda (E. Africa), the kingdom of Asanti (Ghana), Dahomey, Yoruba, Ibo, etc. were states older than modern European states having highly organized societies (Davidson, 1984, Sandbrook, 1985).

With regard to Africans' knowledge of social organizations Ayittey (1990:22) says,

> In fact, there were highly organized systems in Africa before the arrival of the Europeans. Indigenous economic systems were, contrary to popular belief, capitalistic, and indigenous political systems were democratic.

Ayittey strongly argues that African political systems, though basically tribal, were by and large democratic because local leaders were often chosen, power ultimately emanated from the village assembly and most importantly the source of power and wealth, namely land, was the property of the village.

The question that may be posed here is what happened to all this indigenous entrepreneurship that extended from bazaar capitalism to agricultural commercialism? What happened to those functioning social organisations from village leadership to local government or simply what happened to African political and socio-economic development?

Of all the colonized areas of the world, Africa suffered longest and most severely, a suffering evidenced in all historical epochs from the periods of slavery and colonialism to that of neo-colonialism. Through all these eras the continent was, and remains, fated to arbitrary division and resource misappropriation as dictated by the powerful European nations (Hunton, 1957; Inikori, 1979).

According to Inikori the total amount of slaves exported via the Trans-Atlantic slave route from 1701 to 1810 amounted to nearly five million and in the year 1860 it reached eleven million. With regard to the slave trade that took place through the Trans-Saharan, Red Sea and Indian Ocean routes the same source estimates for the period 1451-1870 a total of ten million were sold through Trans-Sahara and the Red Sea; and two million across the Indian Ocean, from Zanzibar and other small ports. Despite differences among historians with regard to the estimates of the volume, the number often referred to is about twenty-two million people exported from black Africa to the rest of the world (Inikori 1992:102).

The numbers given above are only indicative. The exact number of slaves deported from Africa will be difficult to settle. This is because, due to the tariff paid per slave the merchants never declared the exact number.[13] My point of departure is not to quantify the number of slaves exported from Africa but how these numbers affected the development of Africa in many respects or to put in perspective what Himmelstrand (1993:12) referred to as "a gigantic demographic drain, the brutalization of political culture" by Europeans. Since the people sold as slaves were mostly men and women of a productive age, it is not difficult to imagine the damage done to the entire socio-economic development of Africa. For any development, especially pre-capitalistic development, the determinant factor was a labor force. This is more apparent when one considers the surpluses the African labor force generated in the British, Spanish and the Portuguese colonies, the results of which contributed to the fundamental disparities between developed and African nations (Dumont, 1966).

As Malowist (1992:9) correctly puts it, "from 1550, Africa played an extremely important though undesirable role as a supplier of labor and some gold to the developing world economy."

Additionally, Inikori's (1979) study on the slave trade and the Atlantic economies from year 1451 to 1870 presents the extent and the magnitude of the slave trade and its contribution to the development of the capitalist world. His findings suggested that the slave trade helped Europe to develop not only marine technology—i.e. shipyards for the building of slave vessels—it also helped them even to develop marine insurance and bank credit systems. In addition to these, ammunition, gun and liquor manufacturing were the direct beneficiaries of the slave trade. In fact it could be asserted that thanks to slave trade business activities in London, Bristol and above all Liverpool were put on a firm footing.

According to Inikori, it was not only Europe that benefited from slave trade, but slave labor helped America to produce more cotton, which again helped European textile production on a mass scale. West Indies sugar produced with the help of slave labor also turned a lucrative profit to the slave owner states. In short, the slave trade was the vehicle that helped what was known as the triangular or tri-continental trade between Africa, Europe and the Americas to flourish, and then brought prosperity to the slave trading nations.

What did Africans get in return from this "triangular trade?" In this trade Africa lost twice. First, Africa lost a magnitude of human resources which could have produced large surpluses for the continent. Second, Africa sold her "human commodity" not only for an extremely low price, buts also in exchange for worthless and shameful returns such as liquor from Bristol and Liverpool; or/and muskets from Germany. With the guns they obtained in this fashion, some African local chiefs and Arab *dellals* raided for more slaves. Arguing along the same line, Dumont (1966) notes that for the loss Africa suffered from the slave trade, precious ivory, gold, iron ores etc. in urn the continent got *knick-knacks and trinkets* i.e. glittering ornaments, tobacco, gunpowder, old firearms and more alcohol.

Hunton's (1957) statement that, "it was the price of [African] human flesh and blood that gave us [Europeans] a start" rings true both figuratively and literally. Marx also observed not only the brutality but also the significance of slavery in the rise of industrialism, as he indicated in one of his letters as follows;

> Direct slavery is as much the pivot of our industrialism today as machinery, credit, etc. Without slavery no cotton; without cotton no modern industry. Slavery has given value to the colonies; the colonies have created world trade; world trade is the necessary condition of large-scale machine industry (Marx letter to Annenkov in 1884, quoted in *Colonialism Old and Modern*, 1966:20).

The impact of the slave trade is negative to Africa in all respects. The argument that from this trade Africa benefited in the introduction of new food crops such as maize, cassava, groundnuts, sweet potatoes, tobacco, etc. have little support. On the contrary, M'Bokolo (1992) finds evidence that some of these crops have limited nutritional values and the people who relied on them (e.g. Tio and Mbosi people), suffered from malnutrition. The strong fact that remains is that this forced human trade had depopulated the continent of Africa and thereby hampered its development.

While many European countries and North America agreed in principle to stop slave trading, some European countries, however, arbitrarily divided up Africa among themselves entering into a new epoch of African suffering and deep poverty. This direct partition of Africa by the then powerful countries of Europe was officially confirmed at the Berlin Conference of 1885, (widely known as the Scramble for Africa) and this partition was the beginning of the present political, ethnic, social and economic problems in many parts of Africa.[14]

The partition of Africa in many cases forced ethnic groups to be divided into a number of countries under different colonial administrations. The Makonde people of East Africa for example, were portioned into the German (later British) colonies of Tanganyika (present day Tanzania) and the same people again appeared in the Portuguese colonial territories of Mozambique. The Mandinka people of West Africa were divided between the French and the British. The Mandinka people under French rule became Senegal, and those under the British rule were again divided as Sierra Leone and the Gambia. The same procedure was applied to the Hausa people who were divided as Nigeria and Niger under British and French rules respectively (Davidson, 1989).[15]

As it is argued above, the continent was divided according to the interests of the colonial powers rather than according to the African peoples' social, cultural, linguistic and historical realities, the consequences of which are still being felt today as was recently revealed in the tragic events which took place in Somalia. The present problem in Somalia was exacerbated by colonial powers long ago, i.e. when the people were divided into four—those of Britain (Somalialands), Italy (Somalia), France (Djibouti) and Ethiopia (Ogaden).[16]

As a result of the partition of the continent, colonialism damaged the socio-political fabric of African society by intermingling different ethnic groups under a single colonial administration. The argument underlined here is that today, much criticism is directed at Africa due to the ethnic-based civil wars. It also appears to be a widely held belief that Africans cannot live without such wars and disputes of ethnic character. This, of course, is not true. Such conflicts are the effects of colonial rule rather than the choices of the peoples of Africa.

As a net result, colonialism hampered the development of indigenous (pre-capitalist) economic activities carried out by Africans. The imbalance in trade which started with the slave trade helped these European powers to gain control over the sea. They controlled Africa from the Mediterranean in the North, the Cape of Good Hope in the South and the Atlantic to the West. Having secured these strategic routes, the Europeans, over centuries sold African people as simple commodities. Additionally, under colonialism they took African ivory, iron ore, gold, precious gems and metals. Africa's precious wealth was traded in the Middle East, Europe, Imperial China, India etc. In exchange European merchants brought cloth from India, spices and perfume from China and unsold industrial products from Europe.

CONCLUSION

According to one school of thought, the colonial legacy is responsible for African underdevelopment, the primary cause of African poverty and all the crises which followed was the exploitation of human as well as natural resources by the colonizers. The other school maintains that colonialism's unwillingness to fully integrate Africa into a world capitalist economy also contributed to African poverty. According to the former, no continent was colonized by so many different European powers for so long, and no civilization, culture, indigenous tradition and social formation was ruined like that of Africa.

In this chapter it is historically demonstrated that in the pre-colonial era the development of Africa, in general, was not inferior to that of the rest of the world. It was only after the beginning of the slave trade, and especially after the introduction of direct colonialism that African development began to lag behind the rest of the world in all aspects.

During the period of colonization Africa served Europe by supplying the necessary raw materials such as cotton from the Nile valley, wool from the Cape, copper, gold and diamonds from West and South African colonies. Clearly, then, present day African poverty is fundamentally crisis rooted in the underdevelopment of economic, political and social structures historically destabilized by the slave trade and colonialism and not counterbalanced or altered for a period of about five centuries. At this point, I feel, Inikori (1992:112) summarizes my points,

24

It can be validly said that the twentieth century world economic order was constructed originally with the sweat and blood of Africans. Because the population of Africa was forcefully transferred to the Americas for this purpose at a time when Africa needed a growing population and external commodity trade in order to develop commodity production and transform its pre-capitalist social transformation, all the latter development were arrested. Between the late nineteenth and mid-twentieth century, colonial rule contributed immensely to the maintenance of this position of Africa ... Hence, Africa entered the twentieth century as the most economically backward major region of the world.

The point that I would like to stress here is that it is not the intention of this chapter to review African history. The attempt here is to lay down the base for my further understanding the features of African poverty, which to a considerable extent is affected by these historical events. Now, I leave the history of the slave trade and colonial acquisition at this point and attempt to concentrate on the period of neo-colonialism or post-colonial Africa. However, what I have to remind the reader is that even in this post-independence period one encounters the continuation of the legacies of colonialism in different forms. The major difference being between those who were inspired by the new ideas and supported Westernization and those who were uncertain as to what the benefits of such modernization might be. The generation brought up during the post-colonial period accepted the new life style without questioning the nature of the society in which this new system was to be fostered. As a consequence, Africa found itself at a cross-roads and was undecided as to which route to take.

This confusion and uncertainty left the door open for many social, political and economic experiments by foreign agencies in collaboration with local elites. As a result, most of the recent experiments in social, economic and political transformation, that took place on African soil became not only foreign in their nature but also proved to be incapable of curing the people of Africa of their chronic poverty. The seriousness of the matter becomes alarming when one is aware of how Africa is forced to depart from its origins and how many new concepts, new strategies and new practices for eradicating its poverty (without significant impact) have been introduced over the past several decades by both outsiders and African governments.

NOTES

1. Sustainable development is development that not only focus on economic growth but also development that gives priority to the poor.

2. Frederick Hegel of Germany, Richard Bertle and Samuel Baker of England, as referred in Davidson, 1984, *The Story of Africa.*

3. In Africa, the context of the term post-colonial or post-independence, apart from its political and economic connotations, indicates a historical epoch, i.e., the period after the 1960s—a decade of independence.

4. The rule of law is defined here as obedience and respect for the commonly accepted law and human rights, independent judicial system, the creation of free media and independent institutions that have real power (under the law) to ensure public accountability.

5. Note that this study makes on pretension of dealing with poverty existing in all Africa. It rather attempts to identify certain common features of poverty pertaining to some countries of Africa. Though the African part is referred to as general, as far as it is possible, the arguments forwarded are supported by concrete data and take a country or countries as example to qualify statements made.

6. Ethiopia has been dragged into wars against European colonial powers throughout her history. Many wars had been fought directly and indirectly against Italian and British domination in northern Eritrea; and in the S. West region of Ogaden of Ethiopia. Colonial wars in Ethiopia had cost many lives and material resources that could have been used for human development. Detailed information is obtained in Pankhurst, 1961; Triminham, 1976; Tekle Sadek Mekuria [1981, Ethiopian calendar]; Tekeste Negash, 1987, Bahru Zewede, 1991).

7. The other question may be that Ethiopia had contacts with European powers for a long time but why the situation in the country, by and large remained unaffected. The point here is that all these contacts did not strongly influence the country as they were too brief and at times too sporadic in their nature. However, after the 1960s , global economy showed some interest in integrating Ethiopia into its system, but the old political and socio-economic structure could not fully absorb the new influence. As a result the capitalist oriented path of development practiced for

some times led to a revolution and a shift into a socialist oriented path.

8. Capitalist oriented political, social and economic reforms were implemented as the fundamental relationships of production remained to be feudal.

9. Note also here, the conceptualizations of indigenous knowledge differ from other terms such as indigenization, nationalization or Africanization. The differences area as follows: Firstly, indigenization is a process by which some post-colonial African governments limit foreign influence over firms and investments (especially those occupied during the colonial period). In many cases, these are transferred to the natives and is defined as the transfer of ownership from colonial remnants to the inhabitants of a country often also referred to as Africanization (Adedeji, 1981). The term indigenization often is used interchangeably with nationalization. However, strictly defined nationalization is a transfer of ownership from local or foreign owners to the state. Nationalization by some African countries, is understood and executed simply as economic decolonization—a follow up (or extended) programme of political decolonization. Secondly, the understanding of the use of indigenous knowledge and traditional practices here also differs from some opinions that advocate the indigenization, which is mean, "modernization" in Africa. To international forces, indigenization is merely to popularize and empower native political elites. But the argument drawn here goes beyond that and advocates the revival of historical, cultural and traditional bases for anchoring sustainable development to secure survival with the broad participation of the people.

10. In aggregate, African socialism is more rhetoric than in substance. Therefore, wherever such references to socialism are made it is more egalitarian that what is termed "scientific socialism" in the strict sense of its Western meaning.

11. According to the same source, these businesses of West Africa stretched to South and East Africa, the Islam world of the Middle East and as far away as Imperial China.

12. In supporting his statement Pankhurst cited a French author by the name of Kammerer who recorded the golden age of the Axumite kingdom having some 513 different types of coins of which 173 were gold, 18 silver and 322 bronze (1961:30-31).

13. This is documented in a number of incidences, for example, Inikori (1992:95) cited a letter by a treasurer of Marta, wrote to the king testifying that "from every ship that arrived with blacks carried 400 'pieces.' Duties were only paid on 100"; another document from San Domingo, proved that "laving vessels going to Cartagena with 150 registered, in reality carried 300." The same source stated that "the boats arrived with 15, 25, 37 'pieces' actually had on board 200, 300 and 400 'pieces,' " etc.

14. The Partition, or the Scramble for Africa took place between 1884-85, at a conference in Berlin. At this conference, European powers, i.e., Britain, France, Germany, Italy, Belgium, Spain and Portugal agreed in principle to divide the continent of Africa among themselves.

15. I have to stress here this partition of Africa gave the Europeans large colonial territories in a short span of time. In the year 1876, for example, only 11 percent of African territory was colonized by Europeans. A quarter of a century later, however, over 90 percent of the continent was occupied by the colonial powers.

16. This is a clear illustration of the human disaster taking place today in Somalia.

Chapter Two

THE PARADOX OF
AFRICAN POVERTY

This chapter concentrates on the post-colonial (or post-independence) period and an effort is made to illustrate features of African poverty with the help of some socio-economic indicators. A brief overview of the remedies prescribed, thus far, to cure Africa from its chronic poverty is also presented. Even if the remedies prescribed failed to attain their anticipated goals, it would be simple to say that all efforts to help Africa were (are) not consciously aimed at keeping Africa in poverty. Much external assistance is positively motivated, but their results by and large remain insignificant.

THE POVERTY OF POST-COLONIAL AFRICA

> The essence of neo-colonialism is that the state, which is subject
> to it, is, in theory, independent and has all the outward trappings of
> international sovereignty. In reality its economic system and thus
> its political policy is directed from outside (Nkrumah, 1965:2).

Since the end of the 1950s Africa has possessed formal independence, but in many countries ties to their former colonial powers has remained strong. Thus, for post-independence Africa, though it had succeeded in becoming politically decolonized, freedom from what is called neo-colonialism became almost impossible. There are still many hindrances to the achievement of economic decolonization in Africa. Therefore, one may say, although the decolonization of Africa has been achieved, freeing Africans from their colonial legacy and enabling them to embark on the application of African indigenous knowledge and practices remains.

The task of gaining this freedom for Africa has become problematic in many respects due to the severe poverty prevailing on the continent at present. Africa as a whole is currently associated with extensive malnutrition, recurrent famine, rampant disease, high levels of illiteracy and acute shortages of goods to fulfil basic needs. A number of African countries are also ruled by dictatorial governments, where little, if any, respect is paid to fundamental human rights. The paradox is that the potential wealth and rich culture of Africa do not justify a crisis of such dimensions. As the saying among Africans goes, "Africa is poor because she is potentially rich," and with regard to the total crisis facing the continent, there appears to be a lot of truth in this saying (Onimode, 1988; Fantu Cheru, 1989).

Africa is a continent rich in mineral resources, having over 75 percent of world's gold, nearly 70 percent of its cobalt, about 40 percent of world's reserves of platinum and Vanadium, around 30 percent of its diamonds, etc. (Table 2:1). The leading industrial nations, the USA, Western Europe and Japan depend (up to 50 percent) on imports of bauxite, phosphate, cobalt, uranium ore and aluminum from Africa. Despite being endowed with all this wealth, Africa remains incapable of utilizing its own resources for its own purposes and consequently continues to be plagued by poverty (Mazrui, 1986:162).

TABLE 2:1
AFRICA'S MINERAL PRODUCTION AS PERCENTAGE OF WORLD PRODUCTION, SELECTED EXAMPLES, 1988

MINERAL	COUNTRY	PERCENTAGE
Industry Metals		
Chromium	S. Africa	22.0
Cobalt	Zaire	68.9
Vanadium	S. Africa	42.4
Precious Metals & Stones		
Diamonds	Zaire	29.3
Gold	S. Africa	75.4
Platinum	S. Africa	36.8
Nuclear & Chemicals		
Antimony	S. Africa	22.3
Phosphates	Morocco	17.3
Uranium	S. Africa	13.7

Source: Onimode, 1988.

Additionally, Africa enjoys a climate well suited to the cultivation of a wide variety of cereals for food, has many types of seed oils, extensive animal husbandry and an abundance of vegetable resources including rubber, cotton, timber, etc. It has more than 40 percent of the world's potential hydroelectric power.

TABLE 2:2
AFRICA'S CASH-CROPS PRODUCTION AS PERCENTAGE OF WORLD PRODUCTION, SELECTED CASH CROPS, 1978

Cash-crops	Percentage
Cocoa	62
Palm oil	34
Groundnuts	27
Coffee	26
Tea	11

Source: *African Target*, Vol., No.1, 1979.

Some African countries are leading exporters of consumer cash crops such as cocoa from Ghana; cotton from Sudan; palm oils from West Africa; coffee, tea and pyrethrum from East African (Table 2:2). In spite of all these, the continent obtains no benefit from its under-priced products and is unable to feed, clothe, give shelter and nurse its own people (Tedros Kiros, 1992).

According to the UN, *World Population (1992)* statistics, Africa has a large and industrious population base of about six hundred million (10 percent of world's population), of which well over 65 percent are economically active (under 65 years of age). The continent covers 23 percent of world's landmass having over six hundred and twenty million hectares of arable land i.e. enough *per capita* for cultivation. In spite of all this potential, Africa is suffering from poverty.

INDICATORS OF AFRICAN POVERTY

Poverty could be measured by the level of income, malnutrition, the availability of a roof overhead, clean drinking water, child mortality rate, the quality and quantity of heath services, educational enrollment, and, in short, by the living standards of the people.

According to the International Labor Organization (ILO) and the World Bank, of the total world population, one-third of it—i.e. one and half billion peoples live in poor or less developed countries (LDC)—earning about USD 120 per year against approximately USD 20,000 in some industrialized countries. Out of the total poor in what is referred to above as LDCs, between 650 and 710 million peoples are termed very poor or destitute—with an annual income of less than USD 75. Out of a total of twenty-five countries identified as very poor, all except two are sub-Saharan African countries (ILO, 1977; World Bank Report, 1990).

Poverty is generally underdevelopment and underdevelopment, in its turn, is associated with many factors. One among these factors is the level of education. The gaps in literacy level between Africa and the better-off countries are remarkable. For example, the United Nations Education, Science and Cultural Organization's (UNESCO, 1988) statistics describe that in many African countries over 90 percent of the population are unable to read and write—while the developed countries have insignificant numbers of illiterates.

TABLE 2.3
AFRICA'S SHARE OF BOOKS AND MASS MEDIA, PERCENTAGE, 1988

CONTINENT	BOOKS	DAILY PAPERS	RADIO	TV
Africa	1.2	1.9	3.5	0.9
Asia	23.5	33.5	27.9	20.1
L. America*	5.8	14.1	7.7	8.5
N. America	12.6	20.6	28.8	28.3
Europe	54.6	27.1	28.1	38.2
Other	2.3	2.8	4.0	4.0

Source: UNESCO, *Statistical Yearbook*, 1990.

* - Including Caribbean.

The gap in education is clearly seen when the level of enrolment in primary and secondary schools, in teacher training institutes, in colleges, universities and different professional institutions are examined. For example, the developed countries spend on average 2.4 percent of their Gross Domestic Product (GDP) in research and development while African countries spend only 0.3 percent. Moreover, if we take the circulation of books and newspapers, and the availability of radio and TV receivers in Africa compared to other outside nations, they clearly demonstrate how Africa lags behind the rest of the World (UNESCO, 1990; Table 2:3).

The socio-economic crisis of African poverty may also be illustrated by the state of life expectancy and health facilities prevailing on the continent. The World Bank Report (1990) states that life expectancy in sub-Saharan countries is around fifty years (Japan, Sweden, etc. have reached over seventy-five years) and this means that millions of Africans are doomed to die twenty to thirty years earlier than many people in industrial countries.

According to the United Nations Health Organization (WHO, 1990), out of the one thousand children born in developing countries, the infant (under five years) mortality rate is between hundred and two hundred. The corresponding figure for developed countries is between six to ten infant deaths per thousand live births. The disparity in the number of physicians per inhabitant is similarly striking. While one medical doctor per 20,000 people is common in many under-developed countries, the figures for some parts of Africa are even lower. For example, in Chad, one medical doctor is shared among 48,000 people, Equatorial Guinea, one to 65,000 people and Ethiopia one medical doctor is shared among 78, 000 people. In comparison, the ratio of medical doctors in developed countries is one to two hundred to five hundred inhabitants (*World Development*, 1992:233).

To add more on the catalogue of African poverty—out of every hundred Africans about seventy are either destitute or on the verge of absolute poverty, and three out of four Africans have no access to clean drinking water. While the African population is increasing at a rate of about three percent; per annum, the availability of food increases by half. Even this has become unattainable in many countries and as a result millions of people perish from famine. The population of Africa is increasing at a rate of ten times of that of Europe and three times more than USA, and this adds more problems and more burdens to the environment which again deepens poverty (World Resource, 1986).[1] In this manner poverty hinders development and development becomes unattainable because of poverty.

Explanations for Post-colonial African Poverty

Post-independence modernization of Africa brought about new tastes, new ways of living and new expectations. These in turn fragmented the traditional societies of Africa into many parts. The major difference being between those who were inspired by the new ideas and supported Westernization and those who were uncertain as to what the benefits of such modernization might be. The generation brought up during the post-colonial period accepted the new life style without questioning the nature of the society in which this new system was to be fostered. As a consequence, Africa found itself at a cross-roads and was undecided as to which route to take.[2]

This confusion and uncertainty left the door open for many social, political and economic experiments by foreign agencies in collaboration with local elites. As a result, most of the recent experiments in social, economic and political transformation that took place on African soil became not only foreign in their nature but also proved to be incapable of curing the people of Africa of their chronic poverty. The seriousness of the matter becomes alarming when one is aware of how Africa is forced to depart from its origins and how many new concepts, new strategies and new practices for eradicating its poverty (without significant impact) have been introduced over the past several decades by both outsiders and governments.

The argument here is that the application of economic theories and practices that originated from Western experiences or the transmission of the industrial nations experiences to the non-industrial societies of Africa as a means of eliminating material poverty has precipitated tragic crises. Unlike the West, African economies are largely run by the informal sector where family, clan and ethnic ties play major roles (Hyden, 1983; Nedegwa, 1985). Nearly all types of work done in and around the home are executed by women and children and such performance is difficult to quantify in terms of GNP or other standardized measurements. The whole irony is that it is the absence of these basic economic factors that development planners draw models and desire Africa to develop in a fashion similar to that of industrial nations.

Moreover, as UNDP's report (1994:15) states, "Many countries have a high GNP per capita, but low human development indicators—and vice versa." The report substantiates its argument by giving some underdeveloped countries that have between USD 400 and 500 GNP *per capita* but have better performances in their life expectancy, adult literacy, infant mortality rates etc.[3]

The fundamental question then is—can economic theories and practices, which have served the Western (capitalist) system, be replicated, as it is, in altogether different socio-economic systems? Can they simply be transplanted into any society? The answer perhaps is, with regard to problems of development dealing as they do with different societies, which exhibit distinct cultural identities, ethos and behaviors that it would simply be difficult to generalize and suggest the same formula for all. Let me illustrate this further.

As distinct from the West, the major form of capital in Africa is principally land, followed by livestock. As Nyerere (1967) puts it, the basic goods of life in Africa are "land, food and cattle." Savings depend on the life span of these animals and if certain peasant families possess a little more than their daily consumption they buy some goods, which may then be sold in the event of future difficulties. Investments are fixed in expanded land holdings and purchase of the tools of production—at best oxen. Additionally, the majority of the peasantry is active during harvest season and then remains without much income for the rest of the year. Since their income is limited, their consumption of manufactured products is also low.

Thus, the path of transformation, which many African countries follow today, could not address Africa's basic problems. For example, education, which is fundamental for African development, is not geared to the enrichment of indigenous know-how that will result, for instance, in producing better farming techniques to provide enough food or to protect the continent from natural degradation. African education not only refrains from addressing African problems, but is also far from local realities, i.e. educational syllabi are not designed to develop new techniques to enrich local handicrafts, local manufacturing, food processing etc., but instead invite the inhabitants to depend on imports from developed countries. What are, then, the theories employed, the paths indicated, and the methods adopted, to save Africa from its chronic poverty?

PRESCRIPTIONS FOR AFRICAN POVERTY

Theoretical Discourses and Their Applications

In examining post-colonial development efforts in Africa, the following paths appear to be dominant: (a) Western (capitalist) oriented, (b) socialist oriented and (c) alternative paths.

Prior to independence the major debates in Africa were concerned primarily with colonialism, and thus all African efforts were focused on breaking free from the sufferings that had been perpetuated on the people for centuries. To this end, some countries started armed struggles while others preferred diplomatic methods. After many years of struggle the long awaited independence came to many countries at the end of the 1950s and through the 1960s. With independence also came discussions on how to achieve economic development in order to maintain and strengthen the political freedom achieved.

In these discussions, there were initially two main lines. One was a radical group (socialist oriented) boldly opposing the idea that old colonial powers should regain control of Africa—this was known as the Casablanca Group, (named after the capital city of Morocco, where the agreement was reached). Opposed to this was a moderate group (capitalist oriented) which preferred to stay in a strong alliance with their former colonial powers, called the Monrovia Group, which was named after the capital of Liberia (Onimode, 1988). Among the radicals, first Ghana (on her independence in 1957) then followed by Guinea (1958) and Mali (1960) introduced socialist oriented system of government in Africa.

The moderate group, on the contrary, not only advocated a continuation of their ties with former colonial powers openly, but also even strengthened their alliances with them. Such a difference in the choice of paths of development created an unpleasant situation, which worked against African unity, an issue high on the agenda just then. Nevertheless, in order to create the Organization of African Unity (OAU) in 1963 in Addis Ababa, after tough debating, these two models were made to compromise and OAU was established. It must be stressed here; however, the difference between socialist or capitalist development models remained unresolved in OAU. What happened then was that each country was left to exercise whatever was considered right in its (leader) eyes. According to Nedegwa (1985), this was so because at that time OAU was focusing on *panafricanism*—a movement geared to unify Africa—and thus, could not afford to enter into such debates.[4]

Therefore, starting from the birth of the new Africa, these two schools dominated ideological debates. The socialist oriented school could be characterized as seekers of new power relations while the capitalists advocated the old guard, former colonial powers. In between, a few countries searched for alternative systems and attempted to promote neutralistic policies but these did not materialize to become a new social, political and economic system different to the other two blocks. It, therefore, becomes evident that from the days of independence, many African states were born with a socialist or a capitalist birthmark. It is to the roots of these paths chosen in relationship to poverty alleviation efforts that I turn now.

Capitalist Oriented Development Theories and Applications

In the late 1950s, neo-classical economists such as Harrod and Domar introduced an economic model of savings and investments—known as a Harrod-Domar model[5]—which was considered to suit underdeveloped nations (Todaro, 1983). The Harrod-Domar model, in short, was built on the idea that underdevelopment or poverty resulted merely from a lack of capital and once this bottleneck was removed, say, through savings, investments and additional capital stock, development was bound to follow. In the 1950s and early 1960's this theory was the central idea behind the neo-classical version of economic development in developing countries. The reality however, proved to be far more complex than this model proposed and thus the theory failed to assume a position as an appropriate solution to minimize poverty.

In the period of post-independence the neo-Keynesian school of thought played an important role in the debates on development theories and in practices as applied in many less developed countries including those of Africa.[6] To address my point, let me briefly cite one of the representatives of neo-Keynesian school, namely Rostow. Rostow (1960) in his essay named certain specific stages of economic growth that societies pass through. These stages are traditional, *pre-conditions for take-off, the drive to maturity and finally the stage of mass consumption.* According to Rostow then, for each society to develop from one stage to the next the key element is to mobilize savings in order to generate sufficient investments that in turn accelerate economic growth. Finally, this theory became the basis of many of the development assistance programs applied in underdeveloped countries. This again, as we can all bear witness, could not become a grand theory to minimize poverty.

However, we have to bear in mind that the 1950s and 1960s development theories have some positive and negative aspects. Positive because, although they did not help to bring forth development as anticipated, they had helped to abandon the earlier colonial explanations of poverty associated with laziness, less motivation for work, unsuitable climate, etc. At this stage development theories' major concerns had shifted to more emphasis on lack of economic factors such as capital and savings to generate the necessary investments. Such an effort, by and large, had negative influence because, the theory starkly focused on lack of capital followed by lack of know-how to use the capital invested in a rational manner as the main cause for the poverty prevailing in the underdeveloped countries. This again, led to the erroneous conclusion that industrial countries should concentrate on transfer of capital and assistance in the form of Western technical expertise to these poor countries, which in its turn, suffocated the revival and development of African indigenous knowledge and traditional practices.

The Application of Capitalist Oriented Development in Africa: Selected Examples

Western development theories were the mainstay of the socio-economic transformation of post-independence Africa sponsored by the advanced countries and applied in for example Ivory Coast, Senegal, Nigeria, Malawi, Kenya, etc. Western Development theories are also the backbone of the programs and projects carried out by many international aid agencies, financial institutions and multinational corporations. To illustrate my arguments, below are described two African countries namely Ivory Coast and Kenya, which followed the capitalist path of development and yet manifest various types of poverty.

Ivory Coast, one of the smallest countries in West Africa, has a population of less than nine million. When industrialization began in the 1950s there were not more than fifty small manufacturing industries in existence there, however to date the country has increased its enterprises with positive annual turnover. The agricultural sector plays the major role and supplies over half the raw materials to the manufacturing. It is also worth noting here that workers from the neighboring countries of Burkina Faso and Mali account for a substantial portion of the labor force (more than 30 percent) and thereby help the economy to blossom (Sandbrook, 1985).

The success of the Ivorian economy mentioned above is only one half of the story. For example, the process of Africanization which had been warmly advocated since independence has only succeeded in putting about 13 percent of the qualified positions in the hands of local staff, whilst the rest are still in the hands of French personnel. Privately owned Ivorian enterprises in the 1980s accounted for 11 percent, while foreign firms accounted for 36 percent and the rest, i.e. 53 percent, was owned by the state.

Ivory Coast is characterized as the breeding center for what Sandbrook (1985) called *neopatrimonialism*, i.e. patrimonialism in its new form, where the rulers are the unchallenged authority enjoying the full support of the French army. One may here argue that, though the economy in comparison to many other African countries is in better condition, it has failed to foster democracy in the country. A country without fundamental democratic pillars, in my opinion, is vulnerable to unrest.

Kenya is another relatively African success story, which has followed a capitalist path of development since independence. The reasons behind the Kenyan success are several. Firstly, Kenya was one of the African countries in which colonial settlers developed relatively advanced commercial agriculture. The development of colonial agriculture, as in many settler colonies, brought certain capitalist elements such as hired labor, a cash economy and basic infrastructures. With these in place, developed credit and banking systems followed, institutions, which are essential for further economic development (Hyden, 1983; Sandbrook, 1985). Secondly, post-colonial Kenya has adopted policies in favor of the growth of capitalism. This was also based on the fact that the earlier, settler economy helped the Kikuyu ethnic group to accumulate capital and know-how. The white settlers' form of commercial agriculture was nationalized with considerable success, which in turn provided a good entry point for the development of capitalism in Kenya. In addition, on its independence, Kenya possessed a dominant local entrepreneur core (having some elements of a national bourgeoisie) capable enough of steering the economy.

Apart from these economic factors, the anti-colonial *mau mau* movement's political training in Kenya was helpful in fostering nationalism under a common symbol (Nedegwa, 1985). This nationalist agitation pulled the people of Kenya together and made the peasants conscious of their property and individual rights. Later, with independence, the elite obtained the political power and all the benefits that go with it, and the peasants received their land.

On the plus side of Kenyan pragmatism, I may add, their indigenous involvement in commerce and manufacturing was relatively better than most East African countries. The Asian communities for example, were not destabilized in the name of Africanization but were made to co-exist. This was a pragmatic decision on the Kenyan part especially when compared to Idi Amin`s government (1972-79) policy of sudden expulsion of Indian business communities from Uganda, which negatively effected the overall economic development of the country. Instead in Kenya, local entrepreneurs were encouraged to venture into business through favorable provision of credit and training facilities. Most importantly, a healthy partnership between the public and the private sectors has helped Kenyan capitalism to survive.

Despite the catalogue of positive policies named above, development in Kenya is marked by a greater inequity of distribution of incomes than in most sub-Saharan African countries. Additionally, like any affluent African elite, the Kenyan upper middle class was unable to play the role of European bourgeoisie in the transformation of its society. On the contrary, the Kenyan bourgeoisie indulged in conspicuous consumption and appeared to embrace a pre-capitalist mentality similar to that of the landed aristocracy of Ethiopia.

As Sandbrook (1985) observed, post-independence Kenya failed to properly manage the country's most precious economic sector, agriculture. Parastatal intervention is strong and corruption is rife in the political sphere, like many countries in Africa its democratization process is vague. Kenya is not free from problems of ethnicity. Though much effort has been put into the fostering of Kenyan nationalism, these problems still remain on the agenda.

Pros and Cons of a Capitalist Oriented Path

What may be boldly stated here is that in both countries capitalist oriented development survived as a result of political stability and the continuity of the development path chosen. These two factors are essential for economic development and eventually an attack on poverty. Political instability and discontinuity of path of development have hampered socio-economic development in many countries of African and are factors that deepen poverty. Development to a greater extent, needs stability just to create confidence in economic actors.

Beyond these successes however, it is essential to stress here that in both cases external forces have influenced and steered the development of these country. As a result both economies are geared to industrialization based on import of capital from France and Britain respectively. Less participation of the weaker sections of the population is observed and both countries have failed to show significant efforts to use and develop African indigenous knowledge and traditional practices that would liberate their people from external pressures and thereby reduce their poverty to a considerable degree.

Socialist Oriented Development Theories

The socialist orientation, which emerged in post-independence Africa appeared to be motivated by a need to fill the vacuum after the departure of the colonial powers. The models of socialist paths of development advanced in Africa came from at least three directions, i.e. from the USSR (non-capitalist model), China (New Democracy)[7] and finally from the neo-Marxists school of dependency. In this text I only focus on the first model which was advanced by the USSR. This was USSR's alternative theory and was especially tailored to suit developing countries in general and Africa in particular. It is known as *a non-capitalist way of development* (Solodovnikov, 1975).

Non-capitalist Theory[8]

The non-capitalist path of development advocated by the Soviet Union's leadership (especially from 1960s to the end of 1980s) has affected the lives of many millions of people in post-colonial Africa. According to the proponents of this theory, non-capitalism is a transition state between capitalism and socialism. Palmberg (1978) states that the non-capitalist path is initiated by national liberation movements who are revolutionary democrats that took arms against colonialism and international capitalism, and thus it is a *national democratic* path.

In the minds of its opponents, however, non-capitalism was designed to incorporate the newly independent countries of Africa (and the developing states of Asia and Latin American) into the socialist (USSR) sphere of influence. Its primary aim was to break the newly liberated African countries' ties with the old colonial powers and win them over to the socialist camp. It propagated for social change or revolution in these countries. This becomes clear when we closely examine the arguments put forward by one of the leading institutions on foreign relations, namely the School of Oriental Studies in Moscow.

According to this school, the non-capitalist approach in the economic sphere, for instance, is simply an attack on the positions of large and medium sized foreign and local capital through the nationalization of basic means of production. The nationalized instruments of production and other small properties will be owned by the state and run through co-operatives. In the political sphere, non-capitalist development helps to create conditions by which the working class can directly seize power (through one party i.e. the party of the proletariat). This transition of power according to the theory could successfully be carried out by military officers. Thus, non-capitalist development encourages newly independent countries to accept socialist (ex-Soviet) doctrine and then these newly independent countries could seek assistance from sister socialist countries spearheaded by the USSR (Solodovinikov, 1975:246-252). Non-capitalist theory was practiced in different ways in Egypt, especially under Nasser, Guinea, Congo Brazzaville, Algeria, Ghana, Mali, Tanzania, Sudan, Somalia, Mozambique, Angola and Ethiopia.

What is wrong with this non-capitalist path of development? One of its major shortcomings is that it presupposed working class revolutions in predominantly peasant societies (where there are insignificant numbers of organized workers). In so doing, the theory led to the faulty practice of building socialism in societies where pre-conditions for socialist constructions were not fulfilled. Moreover, the non-capitalist path simply means bypassing capitalist development and "walking directly to socialist orientation." However, socialism according to the theory of Marx, is a more advanced social and economic system than capitalism, and the development of the latter is the prerequisite of the first (Marx and Engles, 1969). Thus, the very term, "non-capitalist" negates this foundation of socialism. This may be what Hyden (1983:5) had in mind when he states, African countries completely disregarded that "the Marxist-Leninist approach they advocate is only a more complex version of capitalism."

Moreover, the assumption that (a) the African struggle against colonial powers would "automatically and directly lead to socialist orientation," (b) national liberation movements and their leaders are revolutionary and progressive and (c) national liberation movements' leaders are well supported by the peasants and workers (Palmberg, 1987) all proved to be wrong. Such lopsided support later on was also extended to ethnically-based movements rebelling against their national states on the pretext of establishing a "socialist" society seceded from a sovereign state, and in so doing, it contributed to the instability of some African countries.

More importantly, the legitimacy awarded to the military officers as the vanguard, which is destined to lead their people into "socialism" encouraged many young African military officers to seize state power without the consent of their people. This theory simply fits the dreams of African political elites (be it civilian or military) to self-style themselves as the sole representative of the people.[9] Most importantly, because the theory calls for socialist or foreign assistance first and self reliance second, it left no room for indigenous practices to develop and reproduce.

As a result, what happened in many parts of Africa is that under the cover of non-capitalism the military assumed the role of a socialist revolutionary body. In some countries, simply bearing the name of a workers' party military alliances would result in nationalizing the people's property without any control of the leadership by the workers. Because of the benefit it gave, civilian political elites allied themselves with the military forces and both amassed public properties under the cover of building socialism through indiscriminate nationalization.

Therefore, as (a) the poor African countries lack the material base to build socialism and (b) as both the military and the civilian elites could not be free from the capitalist system in all its aspects (especially being dependent on the capitalist mode of production), Africa's socialism appeared only in rhetoric. The African political elites, be they civil or military, socialist or capitalist, their interests, as Ake (1990:35-36) said, "...coincide on the fundamental issue of maintaining capitalist relations of production. The African ruling elite survives in so far as capitalist relations of production are maintained". Thus, since the very foundation of the present African elite rests on world capitalist systems it is doubtful, under the present circumstances, if it could evolve a sustainable socialist system.

Before concluding this discussion, I would like to emphasize on two points. One is the damage done to many African countries through the process of nationalization blessed by the non-capitalist approach and the other is the freedom for which the African people bitterly struggled for many years and which was finally sabotaged by the non-capitalist path of development as applied in many countries of Africa especially in Ethiopia.[10] When all these points are put together non-capitalist path proved to be more political than a mechanism to minimize poverty.

Nationalization, which took place in the name of socialism in many countries of Africa for instance, has served the political elites as access to power. Nationalization has tipped the balance towards state ownership of public property and clears the way not in the direction of socialism (equity) but to what is called state capitalism—geared for the betterment of the political elites and to the creation of African bureaucratic bourgeoisie who, instead of reducing poverty, have succeeded in increasing it.

Non-capitalism in relationship to freedom and democracy as applied in many parts of Africa appears to lose its socialist basis. Freedom and democracy are products gained through the bitter struggles of the disadvantaged sectors of societies. Classical socialists such as Rosa Luxembourg referred to freedom as the achievement of the toiling masses. Freedom, according to Rosa Luxembourg, for example, "is always and exclusively for the one who thinks differently" (quoted in Palmberg, 1978:32). However, the non-capitalist leaders of Africa denied the masses this right, which are not only basic for building socialism, but also a human right. The African people struggled against slave traders, direct and indirect colonial powers and were just about to gain their full freedom. Those who curtail these rights, be they local or foreign, always remain to be opponent to the people's need and aspirations.

The Application of Socialist Oriented Theories in Africa: Selected Examples

Generally speaking, in the post-independence period, the debate on transformation in Africa predominantly focused on socialist orientation. This is not accidental. Firstly, because of the fact that the newly independent countries of Africa were colonized by Western powers for so long and had suffered to gain freedom from them, they naturally developed negative attitudes towards those colonial powers. When some African countries decided to disassociate themselves from their former colonial links, they also knew that they could not stand by themselves. To some countries the available alternative at that time was to accept "socialism" and ally with socialist states, then led by the USSR. Secondly, there were many political leaders and groups of influential intellectuals who seriously believed that "socialism" as a political, economic and social system that could be an alternative to the capitalist path of development.

It is stated that at the independence of Ghana in 1957, its leader Nkrumah declared for socialism. Thus, Ghana became the first African country to have a socialist oriented government. However, Nkrumah's socialism at that stage according to Onimode, (1988), was a mixture of Christian ethics and Islamic culture presented as an ideology for African development. It was only after he was toppled from political power and lived in Guinea, according to the same author that he had developed a settled socialist ideology based on class struggle free from religious influences. All the same, in the 1970s and 1980s Ghana carried out social revolutions in the name of National (or New) Democratic Revolution (NDR) entering into the new era of what it called "scientific socialism."[11] But the question remains, what are the results of the socialist path followed in Ghana? Sandbrook (1985:2-3) has answers to that:

The Paradox of African Poverty

The first colony to be independent, Ghana emerged as a sovereign nation in 1957 with living standards, infrastructure and administrative competence unequalled in Black Africa...[but now] annual price inflation averaged 50-100 percent...while the modern economy collapsed...black market or parallel economy—flourished...two days of labor for a loaf of bread....

After all the hardships the people of Ghana had undergone, the achievements are not so progressive. For example, outputs of primarily agricultural products such as cocoa and timber including mining and other essential products have been minimized. Roads and other means of transport have deteriorated, ethnic conflicts and corruption became the norm and finally, many people left for neighboring countries (e.g. Nigeria and Ivory Coast) in search of better opportunities of securing income. In short, the revolution failed to attack poverty.

Another socialist experiment took place in Tanzania. The country's independence came in 1960, and seven years later Nyerere proclaimed a socialist government. From then onwards, as Blomström and Hettne (1984) pointed out, Tanzania became a laboratory of socialist experiments. A close look at Tanzania can illustrate another pattern of African socialism slightly different from that of Ghana discussed above, and Ethiopia, presented later.

Tanzania's socialism in the initial period was mainly expressed in Nyerere's vision of a social revolution put together as the *Arusha Declaration* (1967). The points focused on in the Arusha declaration among others were, profession of faith in man, rejection of exploitation of man by man, control of major means of production and distribution by workers and peasants, popular democratic government of workers and peasants, faith and dedication to socialism, policy of self-reliance, etc.

In the second phase of Tanzania's socialism (1970s) Nyerere's African traditional socialism vision was blended with the ideas of dependency school (Blomström, Hettne, 1984). According to the same source, the influence of dependency theory in Tanzania was much more than any country outside of Latin America and the Caribbean.

The outcome of the Tanzanian socialist experiment was assessed by many such as Shivji, (1975), Hyden, (1968), Onimode (1980) and Nyerere (1967b) and reflections from all suggest that the socialist path of development as applied in Tanzania failed to bring about the anticipated economic lift. Economically, according to FAO (1992) twenty-five years ago 88 percent of Tanzanian export income was generated from agriculture, today the country is a net importer of agricultural products. Politically, the Tanzanian socialism model or the philosophy of Ujamaa (Ujamaa means African socialism based on villagization) is criticized from both socialist and capitalist sides. The capitalist criticism is simple—they never see socialist economy as any real alternative to capitalism. The main argument from the socialist camp focuses on Tanzanias compromising stand on class and class struggle. This argument may be well summarized by Shivji (1975:7-8):

> Since the power of the ruling class is always concentrated in the organization of the state, the opposed class must aim directly against the mechanism of the state. Every class struggle is thus a political struggle, which in its objectives aims at the abolition of the existing social order and at the establishment of a new social system. To separate a question of state power from that of class struggle is most misleading.

A similar criticism is also directed from another angle. For example, Onimode (1980:250) states that Ujamaa was a halfway socialism and Nyerere is looking for,

> ... a new synthesis of man and society, a search for the ideal polity. Nyerere defined socialism as an attitude of mind, like democracy, so that the possession and non-possession of wealth are irrelevant. Ujaama is thus said to be opposed to both capitalism and "doctrinaire" socialism. It maintains that African life was traditionally socialistic, that the basis of African socialism is not class struggle, but the extended family, since Africa is regarded as classless.

Though it is true that the socialist oriented path of development in Tanzania may have not born fruit as expected, but many times the criticisms of the Tanzanian effort seem to lack balance. Tanzania has made genuine efforts to improve the living conditions of the poor and many of the people who participated in the struggle against poverty paid a heavy price for their efforts to change the situation.

Lessons from African Socialist Experiments

Firstly, there seems to be a lack of thoroughness in the examination of indigenous knowledge and traditional practices prevalent in a country and with a view to making use of them for further development. The socialist path of development, like capitalism is also based on industrial countries experience, realities, culture and institutions, which are different from Africa in many respects. To overcome this reality some African countries adopted half-way guidelines or ideologies such as *African Socialism or Ujamaa* in Tanzania; *Arab Socialism* mixed with the teaching of Koran in Libya and Egypt; *Humanism* in Zambia; *Negritude* in Senegal; *Authenticity* in Zaire; *Hibersebawinet* in Ethiopia etc. These are theories, which have one foot in African traditions and the other in Western realities.

At this juncture, one may ask what is wrong with Africanizing this ideology and is that not what this study advocates? This question may be answered from two points of departure. Firstly, reading socialist literature and studying, for instance, the Russian or Chinese Communist Parties or the development of social democracy in Germany could not help Africa to become socialist, unless these experiences were closely allied to the African experience, reality and cultural heritage. This kind of thorough study on African heritage and cultural milieu in relation to the adaptation of socialism did not take place in many of the countries that claimed they had adopted socialism. Secondly, when socialism was employed in some countries of Africa, its advocates merely renamed it in an African language or blended it with some leaders' teachings without thoroughly examining the available indigenous knowledge, traditional practices and above all failing to utilize the capacity of local institutions, which were the bearers of these "new social structures" (see the Ethiopian case for details). In short, local indigenous knowledge and traditional experience were not fully examined, consulted, and properly blended with the new ideas.

The other problem area in the socialist oriented path of development is its leadership. Cabral (1969) for example, boldly stated that in the African context (where there are largely unorganized peasants and a tiny industrial working class) the leadership of a socialist revolution essentially lay in the hands of the owners of small enterprises, small merchants, the intelligentsia, the bureaucracy, and the armed forces—what usually referred to as petty bourgeoisie. His main argument was that in most of the countries of Africa the petty bourgeoisie are frustrated, because their opportunities to be transformed into a higher class have been hampered by Western oriented socio-economic development. Thus, they would be willing to sacrifice their time and energy to see change. However, this kind of African revolutionary change lead by the petty bourgeoisie, may not lead to a socialist state as long as the countries' predominant production relationships remain capitalistic.

Two basic problems can be mentioned here. One is, time and time again Africa has found itself in difficulties with the feeding of its population, let alone being able to meet basic material, organizational and institutional requirements necessary for building European type socialism. The other is, even to those who are bold enough to accept socialism as a remedy, the very backbone of socialism—class struggle—was omitted from their schemes, because of its possible backfire into ethnic problems. That is to say, the ethnic group in power often accused opposition based on an ethnic point of view rather than a legitimate political, social or economic question. In this case, the opposition may also use this opportunity to its advantage and start, a single or a united front, ethnically based mobilization (see Chapter Three). Because of such complex issues inherent in the application of socialist theories and practices the major aim, attacking poverty, became unattainable.

CONCLUSION

The development theories and strategies so far applied, seem to indicate false start for Africa. False because, (a) they equate industrialization with modernization, which is again assumed to be equal to development, (b) the strategies or practices advocate for industrialization in predominantly non-industrial societies without taking into account the socio-economic, cultural and behavioral differences, and (c) they give less emphasis to meet basic human needs, as accounted earlier.

In short, conventional theories of development, whether capitalist or socialist, fail to address African poverty. The major problem in both theories, as applied in many countries of Africa, is that they are based on the assumption that there are formal economic sectors, formal institutions and democratic states (Western types) to carry out and implement policy decisions and radical declarations tailored to suit. However, societies in many parts of Africa, on the contrary, are mainly informal.

Commonly, the difference between the capitalist and socialist paths, as manifested in many countries of Africa, is more of rhetoric than real differences. For instance, in socialist oriented countries, incentives are applied and management is the miracle word. In capitalist oriented economies state intervention, through central planning and various centralization are common. And yet, many damages have been done as the results of the rhetoric since they are used as instruments of gaining power.

Be that as it may, the African paths of development, so far, have swung between capitalist (market economy) and socialist (planned economy), but the present status is that the latter seem to have surrendered in order to provide more space for the former. Thus, current issues have forced the pendulum to swing towards market economies as prescribed by the strong financial institutions like The World Bank and International Monetary Fund as described in the next chapter.

NOTES

1. According to *World Resource*, 1986, African female fertility rate is between six to eight children per woman. Comparatively, Latin America has about three and European countries have one to two children per woman.

2. For further discussion on modernization in relationship to development, see Long, N. (1977:9-40).

3. Libya, according to the World Bank (1991) belongs to the upper middle-income countries having GNP *per capita* over USD 6000; and Libyans' life expectancy at birth in 1988 was 61 years. In contrast, Cameroon belongs to lower middle-income countries (i.e., lower than Libya) with GNP *per capita* of nearly USD 1000; but the people of Cameroon have better life expectancy, 73 years, which is almost equal to Belgium (which belongs to the high-income economies group). Zimbabwe also belongs to the middle-income economies but the infant mortality rate in 1988 was 49 per 1000 live births. By contrast, Algeria, which has a higher GNP *per capita*, out of the country's 1000 born infants 72 of them died. The GNP *per capita* of Ethiopia is USD 12; i.e. 10 dollars per month, which cannot sustain life even for the poorest family's consumption. However, this should not be confused with other useful measurements adopted to give some indication and comparative pictures of different realities like, what is called The

Human Development Index, as presented herein. (See *World Development Report*, 1990, Statistics Tables pp. 178-241; *Human Development Reports of UNDP*, 1993 and 1994).

4. Houphonet Boigny of Ivory-Coast did not hide his fear how "the moral bond," which unites Africa with France could be cut. Another advocate of the moderate group, Sengor of Senegal also openly defended the "marriage" between France and Africa (Nkrumah, 1965). All these show how difficult it was for many African countries to abandon their long ties. The question unanswered on the agenda, however, was—how could this unity be possible without finding a model to minimize the gaps between these opposite forces.

5. Harrod-Domar economic growth model's main concern is to increase the total capital stock, which will generate more GNP through which more investments and savings can take place and in return further economic expansion can be attained. In simplified language—if we assume that USD 3 of newly injected capital or investment can produce an additional USD 1 to the sum of the GNP—then it means that any net addition to the capital stock in the form of new investment will bring about corresponding increases in the flow of national output (see Todaro 1983:56-79).

6. The Keynesian model was developed by Lord John Maynard Keynes in the early 1920s to explain and alleviate the causes of economic depression in the western industrial countries by increasing what is called Aggregate Demands (AD) and the term neo-Keynsian denotes the followers of Keynes ideas.

7. China's slightly different socialist path of development sought to be suitable for herself and other underdeveloped countries is referred to as *new democracy or national democratic path of development*. There are slight differences between the Soviet driven non-capitalist theory and the Chinese model of new democracy. Though the national democratic revolution model of China advocates the nationalization of the major instruments of production, opposes the non-capitalist theory, it accepts the necessity of the coalition of the peasants, the workers and intelligentsia and a section of the petty bourgeoisie's leadership (no special importance was given to the military as in the non-capitalist path). In one of Mao Tse-Tung's works the difference between the three forms of republics and their leaderships are stated as: (a) republic under bourgeois leadership (Western countries), (b) a republic under the

The Paradox of African Poverty

dictatorship of the proletarian (former USSR), and (c) a republic under joint leadership of several classes (developing countries
including China—Mao, 1975;339-380). The major difference,
which should come to light, is that while the non-capitalist advocates assistance from outside (socialist block) the new democracy
strongly advocates self-reliance.

8. In referring to the historical appearance of non-capitalist theory,
Thomas (1978 in Palmberg) argues that it was first used in the
Second Congress of the Communist International (Comintern)
in 1920 and was also discussed in the Sixth Congress of
Comintern, in 1928—thereafter the concept was widely intro-
duced.

9. There are many who argue that this Soviet model helped a handful of political elites to transform themselves into pure bureaucratic bourgeoisie running a bureaucratic capitalist state where all
important means of production served the vested interests of
these political elites.

10. Under non-capitalist path of development as applied in Ethiopia
not only were many lives lost in civil wars but the people were
also forbidden from moving from place to place within their own
country.

11. A term popularized especially after the Chinese revolution, which
means a revolution carried out by the small working class found
in developing countries with strong alliances with the peasantry.
In this revolution the petty and the national bourgeoisie take the
political leadership. In the Chinese revolution, the advocate of
the theory Mao, for example, regarded China's new democratic
revolution as preliminary to a socialist revolution rather than a
socialist revolution itself. For further information, see Mao Tse-
Tung's *On New Democracy*, (1975, Vol. II, pp. 339-380).

Chapter Three

DEEPENING
AFRICAN POVERTY

The purpose of this chapter is to illustrate how some of the development practices so far employed have increased African poverty. The postulation in this chapter is approached from two angles. First external efforts are presented, i.e. foreign development assistance (or aid programs), financial institutions (especially World Bank and International Monetary Fund), multinational corporations (MNCs) and international trade agreements. The intentions are not to cover such wide areas completely but to critically assess some of their counter-effects on the reduction of African poverty.

In the case of aid programs, for example, the attempt made here is to indicate how certain African countries became heavily dependent on donor countries, which finally limited their attainment of self-reliant development to reduce their poverty. In discussing the World Bank (WB) and International Monetary Fund (IMF) the issues critically reviewed are how their "adjustment and recovery" programs incur debt and thereby aggravate poverty. In the case of MNCs the aim is to show how their "transfer of appropriate (Western) technology" discourages indigenous efforts. The international trade arrangements—General Agreements on Trade and Tariff (GATT) through under-priced terms of trade exacerbated African poverty.

The second part of this chapter describes the efforts of internal (domestic) forces, i.e. African governments' initiatives and priorities.

Here again, the attempt is not to review each and every African government activity, but to identify certain common features and point out deflected priorities.

THE EFFORTS OF EXTERNAL AGENTS

Development Assistance and Dependence

It is pleasant to feel that you are helping your neighbors, and at the same time increasing your own profit...Before the decline of colonialism what is to day known as "aid" was simply foreign investment (Nkrumah, 1965:51).

Development assistance in Africa accelerated in the 1960s. The newly independent African countries, were (and still are) economically poor and for most of them, independence came to mean new flags and new names but not much difference in social conditions compared to colonial times (Arnold 1985). In the period of post-independence the gap between expectations and reality expanded drastically and the governments of many of these newly independent African states were forced to seek external assistance. The search for assistance was mainly directed to former colonial powers, other friendly countries, international development organizations (different agencies of the United Nations) and international finance institutions. From then onwards development assistance became the sine qua non for African transformation.

What, is development assistance? Arnold (1985:100) describes it in the following manner:

> By its nature aid is highly political. Some people mistakenly regarded it as a charity. This is not the case. Aid is part of a bargain between donor and recipient. The donors have a surplus of capital and know-how and are willing to make it available to developing countries at a price. The price varies. It may be a question of influence or military base facilities, it may result in protection of trading, investment or other interest; it is not done for nothing.

If we start from the statement made above it becomes clear that the main steering force of development assistance is not the poverty of recipient countries but their political and socio-economic commitments to the donor countries. However, for many years people in the developing countries regarded aid as help for them to be able to tackle their poverty but, assistance given to governments and non-governmental organizations is not free from conditions. The process of fulfilling these conditions is carried out by the utilization of different methods. One method may be that recipient countries are asked to submit project proposals specifying the use of the support. The proposals are then evaluated by Western experts. Therefore, in order to secure this aid, recipient countries, most of the time, bend project proposals to suit donor yardsticks rather than their own immediate needs. In this manner African countries are forced to follow the standards once set by the donors, which again reflects the richer countries' vested interests.

Aid often includes features other than simply assistance, i.e. it also strives to sustain and control raw materials and markets, and in this respect it always remains within the interest of foreign policy of donor countries (Hyden, 1983). Additionally, foreign aid is instrumental for control rather than, as many assume, leverage of economic development and social change. As a matter of fact, foreign aid is an enterprise calculated in terms of short and long-term investments and anticipated to bring forth attractive returns. In short, aid is not only assistance and gifts, as many people assume, but also a well-calculated enterprise (Arnold,1985).[1]

In commenting on aid in Africa, Hyden (1983) argues that development aid has enabled developing countries to deny their historical past. This statement is true when one looks, for example, at the neglect of utilizing African cultural heritage and indigenous practices for development. What is witnessed here is that instead of helping local handicrafts to develop devices for local needs, aid programs often advise the import of modern machines, which not only lack spare-parts, but also enough
trained people to maintain and repair them. Though development assistance sometimes comprises grants to a certain degree, the paradoxical results of aid programs is that they have driven many African countries into debt, enforced dependency and in so doing, deepened poverty.

The indebtedness starts, for instance, with low world market prices set for African primary products. The fall in prices of raw materials together with the increase in prices of manufactured goods from industrial countries finally forced many African countries to secure finance from other sources. The problems do not stop here. For example, if a given poor country, succeeds in securing more financial provision, part of this foreign aid will be paid back to the donor countries and/or to MNCs as interest plus amortization of standing debts and/or purchase of spare parts for the tractors or harvesters which have been brought into the country in the name of aid. Trapped in such process the poverty stricken African countries do not accumulate their surpluses for their own development purposes.

TABLE 3:1
AID DISPENSE AS PERCENTAGE OF GNP IN SOME SELECTED AFRICAN COUNTRIES, 1990

Recipient Country	Dispense Percentage	Per Capita (USD)
Mozambique	83.2	80
Somalia	41.8	170
Tanzania	37.6	120
Madagascar	15.8	230
Ethiopia	27.0	120
Kenya	13.7	370

Source: Computed from *OECD Report*, (1991:189), *World Development* (1990:178).

Thus, through such transactions a number of African countries are caught in the vicious circle of what is termed aid dependency, which is nothing but chronic poverty. For example, as it is shown in Table 3:1 aid dependency for Tanzania, Somalia, and Mozambique has reached 37, 40, and 80 percent, of their respective GNPs (*OECD Report*, 1990:178, Table 3:1).[2]

Aid and Poverty
Generally speaking, aid has nothing to do with poverty and the World Bank Report (1990) confirms this bitter truth. The report explains how donor countries give aid to middle and high-income countries based on commercial and strategic interests rather than to assist the poor. Further, the report reveals that for example, in 1986, out of the total US aid only 8 percent went to low income countries (1990:12) and the same is true for many other donor countries.

Even the countries that attract considerable levels of development assistance did not succeeded in ameliorating their poverty and are instead trapped in dependency. This is clearly illustrated in the case of Tanzania. Tanzania which had a positive GDP growth just after independence has now successively decreased her GDP growth whilst substantial sums of aid have been injected into the country. For example, in the years 1961-1967 Tanzania experienced a 6 percent growth in GDP; between 1967-1973 it decreased to 4.3 percent; 1973-1979 down to 2.5 percent and in 1979-85 a further decline to 1.4 percent (World Bank 1990:130). As stated above, in these years Tanzania's international aid allocations increased. And, it is paradoxical to see here that aid and development are inversely related.

In addition to these, the 1991 *OECD Report* expressed its concern on how development assistance has shifted heavily into programs of "structural adjustment" headed by the World Bank and International Monetary Fund, and how thereafter, many poor countries diverted their attention from poverty reduction priorities and concentrated mainly on servicing their debts (OECD, 1991:18).

International Financial Institutions

Aid dependency has become apparent in recent years when the lion's share of development assistance resources from donor countries have been obtained through The World Bank (WB) and the International Monetary Fund (IMF). With the introduction of these two institutions the nature of development assistance changed. The role of the WB/IMF has also been changing since their inception in Bretton Woods in 1944.

Initially the tasks of these two organizations were different and distinct. The IMF, provided loans to member countries with balance of payment deficits, while the WB offered loans for anti-poverty projects and remained strictly a supporter of rural development programs (South Commission, 1991). Since the mid 1970's and early 1980's, when the newly independent African countries faced shortages in foreign exchange to finance their development programs, the two institutions coordinated their activities and begun to prescribe their austere polices known as Structural Adjustment (SAP) and Economic Recovery Programs (ERP).

The standard solutions usually prescribed by these two institutions for the problems of poor countries are among others: re-financing of foreign debts (effective control of debt servicing), devaluation of national currency, exchange control, trade liberalization, reduction of spending on social services, privatization of public enterprises etc. In accordance with arguments so far discussed, however, these seem to have little to do with the structural problems of many poor African countries.

The SAP/ERP programs were intensified in the 1980s and in these years about 70-80 percent of African countries, against their will, implemented one type of program or another designed by the WB/IMF. As Gibbon (1992:127) notes:

> ...between 1982 to 1987 at least two thirds of sub-Saharan African countries implemented varieties of structural adjustment programs...Of the IMF supported reforms, 21 sub-Saharan African countries raised agricultural producers' prices, 16 devaluated exchange rates, 14 eliminated or reduced subsidies for agricultural inputs, 8 reduced or eliminated food subsidies.

The above statements are supported by many similar studies undertaken in different African countries where SAP/ERPs were implemented, and in many of these countries WB/IMF have showed negative response towards poverty reducing public policies. Some examples are given below.

Debt and Poverty: Results of Structural Adjustment and Economic Recovery Programs

In Zambia, WB/IMF were active in the economic sphere of the country for more than a decade (1977-1987/88). Within this decade, employment fell by more than 10 percent (in the name of rationalization or budgetary restrictions), real wages were cut by 50-60 percent and inflation reached over 60 percent. The whole exercise of the WB/IMF packages finally led to shortage of staple food (corn meal) which in its turn brought political unrest in the country (Gibbon, 1992).

In Tanzania for example, WB/IMF (1987-1989) reported one percent increase in GDP and over 10 percent export increase per annum after the implementation of their programs. However, the WB/IMF fails to report the decrease of major manufactured goods and production of food grains. The WB/IMF also fails to mention how their remedy for Tanzania brought over 30 percent inflation and a decline of earnings to about half of that of the 1970s (Gibbon, 1992; Fantu Cheru, 1992; Onimode, 1992).

The WB/IMF contributions to Nigeria were no better than those to Tanzania and Zambia. After carefully studying the living conditions of workers, professionals and youths of Nigeria under structural adjustment programs by the banks Mustapha (1992:188) concluded:

SAP has had fundamental consequences for Nigerian society, politics and economy. Nowhere are these consequences as profound as in the drastic fall in the living standards of those sections of the population dependent on fixed salaries. Equally effected are some sections of the rural population and urban artisan groups. This erosion of living standards has spurred many households to seek additional income by engaging in multiple jobs.

Mustapha confirmed that had there not been African informal sector undertakings and solidarity, SAP would have resulted in still more negative consequences (for informal sector see Chapter Seven).

Under the guidance of WB/IMF between 1984-86, food production in Ghana, for instance, fell by 20 percent (Gibbon, 1992). The fall of food production is a direct result of the misguided programs of export-led agricultural development of SAP. This food shortage in many countries of Africa has forced the continent to import grains for a sum of about MUSD 18,000 (exclusive food aid). WB/IMF know very well that food import brings at least two potential dangers. One is, it develops food habits not based on locally available grains (e.g. wheat, rice, etc) which will finally lead to severe dependency. The other is that the accumulation of debt arising from the purchase of food grains from abroad has dramatically increased.

Inferred from the points made above, SAP/ERPs have not so far produce tangible results as far as improving poverty in the countries they have been operating in for a decade or two. Studies so far conducted in many African countries (Fantu Cheru, 1989; Gibbon, 1992; Onimode, 1992; Mustapha, 1992) suggest that living standards in the countries where these programs were imposed fell 20-30 percent lower than a decade earlier.

Budget restrictions and monetary policy imposed by SAP/ERPs left government employees in many African countries unemployed. For example, in 1988 in Ghana over 81,000 civil servants were sacked from their offices in the name of cutbacks in order to carry out productive investments, which have never materialized. The same procedure is now taking place in Ethiopia. Such measures carry severe consequences for Africa's development for a long time to come.

The sacked civil servants were trained for many years and had accumulated experience in planning, policymaking, teaching, and often are senior technocrats used to working in different public sectors. These people studied for many years, both at home and abroad, using the tax payers' (the peasants') money and sacking these people just as they are to pay back their debt to the nation in service is a loss of invested capital which the poor people of Africa cannot afford. Today, the only civil servants left in office are the political elites, who hardly possess any of these capacities and in this respect, SAP and ERPs are counterproductive.

Moreover, in today's Africa, many of the states are much stronger and have for many years suffocated the "private sector" and become the largest employer of the educated labor force. Apart from the states, what might be called the private sector is, by and large, the informal sector. However, the available economic capacity of this private sector (mostly of informal type) is unable to absorb the educated labor force. In light of this background, it is amazing that WB/IMF advise and accelerate the extensive sacking of African civil servants without preparing any alternative to embrace them. Moreover, the budgetary restriction programs of WB/IMF through the decrease of government subsidies have severely deteriorated services to the weaker sections of African societies. As a result, students, the sick and weak, children and women have all been made to suffer more.

One of the items on the agenda of WB/IMF programs seems to integrate the peripherals into a world economy in the name of "freeing the market" (Mamdani 1989). Another, equally important mission of the WB/IMF programs perhaps, is that the donor (industrial) countries retain their secure position as the leading nations of the world. The latter, for instance, was clearly demonstrated during the 1990s Gulf War. In the 1970s and 1980s, Sudan established a strategically important alliance with the West in general and the USA in particular. During these years the WB/IMF were major financial sources for the government. When the Gulf crisis came into the picture and the government of Sudan denied its support for the USA-led Gulf War, the WB/IMF suddenly closed the financial tap. Today, Sudan is suffering from this economic boycott and is also forced to look into other desperate solutions.

The WB/IMF agenda of integrating the peripherals into a world economy is well summarized by Mamdani (1989), when he analyzed the impact of these financial institutions in Uganda. Mamdani first notes how WB/IMF describes the African crisis based on (a) budgetary crisis, for which WB/IMF put forward remedies—sharp cuts in income through freeze on wages, drastic cuts in social welfare programs, reductions of subsidies, etc. all together known as the shock, (b) crisis of supply and the remedies include a transfer of resources from those who consume (workers, peasants, civil servants) to those who can invest like, rich merchants, export and importers—referred to as entrepreneurs. This, I think is nothing but a shift of available resources from poor to rich serving as links between the center and the periphery.

Mamdani also described WB/IMF's outstripped policies called conditionalities or "devaluation," the transfer of bank credits from the state sector to private sectors and liberalization of trade, or what the IMF calls "freeing the market." However, the African problem is not to free the nonexistent market. On the contrary, it is to create wider markets, lots of consumers and mobilize the available human and natural resources to the benefit of all.

The question that may be raised at this juncture is, how do WB/IMF programs incur debt and deepen poverty? According to the 1991 OECD report, real interest rates were exceptionally low during 1979/1980 and it was also during this period that many poor countries of Africa were generously invited to borrow the excess funds in circulation, which had been generated by the oil producing countries. However, the present interest rates of these borrowed money are very high—on average more than twice the level of 1979 (OECD, 1991). Today, one of the preoccupations of IMF/WB is to ensure that poor countries service their debts, which in itself has become a lucrative business.

The 1990's *World Bank Report* notes that out of twenty-six heavily indebted countries only two are outside sub-Saharan Africa. In some of these countries the ratio of debt to GNP has reached 111 percent. Understanding the severity of the problem today, some donor countries have transformed these debts into grants and/or written them off. Though it is a nice gesture, this action alone has not been much help. This is because, (a) the cancelled debts were insignificant (i.e. only 3 percent of the total standing debt) and (b) the loans obtained (by the poor countries) were not invested in productive activities that could generate more income to reduce the debts. The loans have already been used on imports of spare parts and/or have ended up in the pockets of political elites whose primary task was conspicuous consumption. (c) Even if we assume these poor countries increase the export of primary goods, the profit from this would not help to reduce their debts by much for the simple reason that the prices of these products are set by the buyers, i.e. industrialize countries. As a result these states are often unable to run, maintain and invest in day-to-day economic undertakings. The above statements are supported by the *World Bank Annual Report* (1993:106). It states that, "Despite incidences of debt forgiveness and rescheduling, the region's debt stock changed to 111 percent of GNP and 345 percent of exports. The annual debt-service ratio also remained high and unchanged."

The crux is, if these poor countries wish to obtain further loans to purchase food grains or material supplies essential for their primary industries, for example, they still have to pay the standing debts, and for that they have to secure loans from somewhere, and this leaves them in a circle of indebtedness, the greenhouse in which, poverty grows.

Multinational Corporations (MNCs)

Many people misunderstand MNCs' interest in Africa. For instance, whenever there are discussions of the MNCs role in Africa, people tend not to be anxious as they think either Africa is so poor that MNCs do not have any interest in the continent in general, or if MNCs are present there at all, they are just there to help. However, both assumptions are false.

One of the major advocates of the use of MNCs as agents of African socio-economic transformation is The Independent Commission on International Development Issues (also referred to as North/South Commission). The first report of the commission appeared in the early 1980's recommending a massive transfer of capital and know-how from the North (the industrial societies), to the South (the developing nations). A central recommendation of the commission, among others, was an increased flow of development assistance, and more and attractive roles for the MNCs in transferring financial resources and appropriate technology to the developing countries (North/South Commission, 1980).

Though the rationale put forward by the commission has no doubt contributed significantly towards bringing African and other developing countries' problems to the attention of the world, such recommendations left many questions unanswered. For example, how could advanced technology from the north be successfully transferred to Africa where the necessary basic qualifications and institutional set up are generally lacking? Do MNCs have the desire to help these poor countries—a commitment that would entail sacrificing some profits?

Development assistance agents, international financial institutions and MNCs work hand-in-hand and the special goal of the MNCs is to gain control of resources essential for the manufacturing and marketing of their products and to secure strategic, primary product exports.[3]

The industrial countries particularly the USA, the UK, France and West Germany control nearly 80 percent of MNCs. Of the top ten MNCs that dominate the world economy, eight are USA based. Their investments mainly involve huge economic potential in industry, mining, plantations, hydroelectric plants, etc. (Todaro, 1983).[4]

As illustrated in Table 3:2, the leading MNCs control African mining, such as South African gold and asbestos; Zimbabwe's copper, asbestos, chrome, nickel and vanadium; Namibia's tin and wolfram; Sierra Leone's rutile and diamonds. The amazing point is that the MNCs control of these mineral outputs in many of the African countries is total, i.e. up to a 100 percent.

TABLE 3:2
PERCENTAGE SHARE OF MNCs IN AFRICA'S MINERAL PRODUCTION, SELECTED COUNTRIES

Home Country	Host Country	Mineral Share	Percentage
Britain	S Africa	Gold, Asbestos	100
	Zimbabwe	Copper, Asbestos	100
	Nigeria	Tin	83
	Sierra Leone	Iron Ore	95
USA	Nigeria	Aluminum	73
	Ghana	Aluminum, Bauxite	90
	Zimbabwe	Chrome, Vanadium	100
	S Africa	Chrome	100
	Namibia	Copper, Silver	75
	Namibia	Tin, Wolfram	100
France	Madagascar	Chrome	70
	Niger	Uranium	69
	Gabon	Uranium	75

Source: Onimode, 1988.

The sectoral distribution of MNC investments in Africa, as is shown in Table 3:2, is mainly concentrated around mineral extraction and related activities. A rough breakdown of MNC investments in Africa is about 30 percent in oil; 20 percent in mining; 25 percent in the processing sectors of manufacturing and petroleum refining; 5 percent in textile and assembly; and about 20 percent in export-import, which is again servicing these products. One of the places where MNCs congregate in Africa is Nigeria. Nigeria supplies about 40 percent of US oil imports, and it is also the single leading export market for

Britain outside the OECD countries (Sandbrook, 1985; Onimode, 1988).

Other sectors of concentration of MNCs in Africa include textiles and some assembly or processing activities. These require more physical labor than transfer of technology, contrary to what its advocates usually maintain. In MNCs African workers earn much less than their counterpart in Europe or North America (Table 3:3). The number of working hours, social security, conditions at the work place and in general, the care expressed for the lives of the workers by MNCs operating in African countries are far less than the norm in Europe and North America. As is indicated in Table 3:3, for example, if we take the wage paid in USA as a 100 percent, the African workers earn 87 percent less than their American counterparts and 59 percent less than their counterparts in Portugal, Spain or Greece.

TABLE 3:3
AVERAGE HOURLY WAGE FOR MANUAL WORKERS
PAID BY MNCs IN DIFFERENT REGIONS

Region of Operation	Wage in USD	Difference (%)
USA	8.76	100
Portugal, Spain, Greece	6.34	72
Other Affiliates*	4.92	56
Indian Sub Continent	1.27	15
Africa	1.16	13
Philippines	0.57	6.7

Source: Onimode, 1988:48.   *regions other than Africa and Asia

Additionally, MNCs often create environmental disasters. Environmentally hazardous materials (most of which contain toxins) have devastating effects on both nature and people. It has recently been revealed that European and North American MNCs attempted to use some poor Africa countries to dispose of their nuclear waste.5

It is not always necessary that MNCs bring capital with them to the developing countries as many people would assume. They may borrow capital from the local money market and then after control resources. MNCs normally possess capable management, advanced technology, highly developed marketing skills and above all, better product selection with which to control local enterprises in an effective way and remit the lions-share of profits to the parent company situated in one of the metropolises of Europe and/or North America.

Results of MNCs Undertakings

The points that should be addressed with regard to MNCs are that African entrepreneurs' ability to grow and compete with the MNCs in making use of their natural resources, in obtaining market shares and then accumulating capital for further investments is almost impossible. Also, MNCs extract and transfer local capital, displacing priorities and creating artificial needs and (c) the few technologies brought by MNCs into Africa are inappropriate for local conditions. In emphasizing the transfer of technology, local talent and traditions for solving domestic needs with indigenous methods are pushed aside. And the argument that MNCs offer employment and higher wages is far from the truth. MNCs, to repeat, concentrate their investments in certain lucrative sectors such as mining and oil production. When they invest in agriculture, MNCs encourage the production of cash-crops, which causes the stagnation in production of local crops (Onimode, 1980; South Commission, 1991).

Hulme and Turner (1990) summarize this discussion in a comprehensive manner. They state that MNCs are motivated to maximize their profits, whereas poor (host) countries strive to obtain higher earnings levels; host countries need more job creation while MNCs rely on capital intensive technology with less labor costs and more profit; developing countries are eager to obtain some kind of transfer of technology, but MNCs have no interest in domestic industrialization; poor countries need to increase the use of their indigenous knowledge and practices to be integrated into the modern sector, whereas MNCs have no interest in their national development.

International Trade and African Poverty

In the eighteenth century, laissez-faire trade was seen as a short cut to prosperity and practiced for many centuries by the Europeans and North Americans. In the modern world, especially after the 1940s, the industrial nations wanted the world to be organized under what is known as the General Agreement in Tariff and Trade (GATT).

The origin of GATT, according to Gupta (1976) may be traced back to the Atlantic Charter of August, 1941, in which the United Kingdom and the United States of America anticipated the creation of an international trade agreement by which trading nations of the world could work together. After many years of conferences (referred to as "rounds" in GATT and other International documents) the present GATT agreement was reached.

The main points in GATT relevant to this study are multilateral (international) contractual agreements the fundamental objective of non-discriminatory agreements, and what is called "preferential treatment" (which ought to be advantageous to the poorer countries). Let me review them in brief and see if they really serve to reduce poverty in the developing countries as the proponents of GATT argue.

The basic characteristic of GATT lies in international, or multilateral agreements. GATT does not encourage bilateral agreements because, according to GATT, bilateral agreements (a) provide no better alternatives (b) restrict the distribution of traded surplus by limiting trade to between two countries, and (c) increase the dependency of partners on each other. The last point is relevant here.

Many donor countries, which are also signatories of GATT today run international trade outside of the agreements reached among themselves. To understand this situation in clear terms, let us assume that there is a donor country—first, it "donates," e.g. agricultural machinery such as tractors. Firstly, these tractors need spare parts. Secondly, the recipient country, also will be advised to buy accessories such as combine harvesters etc. from the same manufacturer— at a price set by the donor, which too often is higher than international market prices. This is termed the "backdoor" of the arrangements reached in GATT. Above all, this could not help to reduce poverty in the recipient country, as long as the accessories and spare parts are sold at above market (i.e. competitive) prices, and such arrangements continue the dependency of the recipient country.

The fundamental objective of GATT is promotion of free and non-discriminatory trade as described in most favored nations treatment—a treatment that stands for every member nation's participation without any discriminatory features. The clause seems to address the inequalities arising from bilateral agreements, but in reality this is problematic when put into practice. The clause misses a fundamental principle as correctly noted in Gupta (1976:55), "equality of treatment is equitable only between equals." It is difficult to perceive equality between unequals, e.g. industrial nations and Africa in general.

Thus, today many of the industrial nations increasingly ignore the GATT trading rules and conclude bilateral, discriminatory and restrictive agreements from which many African exports of primary products suffer most. To combat such inequalities, GATT adopted a policy to benefit poor countries from international trade through an agreement called "preferential treatment," which again indirectly helped the lion's share of benefit to return to industrial nations. How? Gupta (1976) identifies two types of preferential systems: preferences by developed countries in favor of poor countries and preferential agreements between poor countries. The advantages in both cases are that underdeveloped countries would open broader markets for exports and thereby provide an additional stimulus to industrial growth from rich countries to the less fortunate ones.

From the statement made above it would be very easy to conclude who benefits from such arrangements. In fact, this is one way of making use of low-cost labor available to MNCs. Under such a cover MNCs entered into agreements with many developing countries, used the "cheap labor," entered the world market in the name of "exports from developing countries" and as earlier reported, the MNCs then remitted the lion's share to "the parent firm" in Europe or N. America. This has nothing to do with reducing poverty. The point perhaps is that low-wage developing countries could not even use the comparative advantage of their "cheap labor," i.e. they could not introduce their low-wage labor products into a competitive world market and utilize the surplus for their own benefit.

In whatever manner it is described, developing countries especially in Africa are not benefited by current forms of international trade. As one report of GATT states,

> Those countries producing mainly agricultural and primary products have found themselves worst placed [in international trade]. Africa has fared disastrously, with a lower rate of growth than any other part of the world ... because anticipated export earnings never materialized owing to recession, deteriorating terms of trade... (*Trade Policies*, 1985:16-17).

What were these anticipated export earnings? First let us look at the comparative advantages that many African countries have. These are, by and large, the possession of agricultural products and raw materials, such as minerals.

Protection for agriculture in developed countries has direct impact on developing countries. Agricultural activities in many of the industrial countries are developed businesses protected and subsidized by their governments. They have modern farm facilities, access to markets, well-developed research that in turn enables the sector to produce and sell relatively cheaply. The other most visible inequality of international trade is with regard to the fall in prices of tropical products such as coffee, cocoa, tea, vegetable oils, etc. For example, Brundi's coffee export earnings dropped by 30 percent in 1992, despite its unchanged volume of production. The drop in world cotton prices hurt producing countries, especially Sudan (World Bank, 1993). The hard economic situations in these countries seem to clear the path for political unrests.

Theoretically, African countries have a clear advantage over industrial countries where such cash-crops do not grow, Because of the nature of the international trade system through which industrial nations' interests are protected, the producing countries do not gain any advantage from the products they have at their disposal.

The major paradox of international trade agreements, therefore, is that the industrial countries of the north, by creating buyer monopolies (oligopsony) depress the prices of these products. Their market is called the "international market" and it is there that prices of African primary products are determined.

Double Standard in "Comparative Advantage"

The inequalities of such a system are demonstrated by discriminatory tariffs set by richer countries over poorer ones. For example, if an African cocoa or coffee producing country semi-processed its products (e.g. making coffee or cocoa powder) it is difficult to sell on the world market because the tariff set on these products often more than doubles their price. If they sell as a finished product the tariff will be as high as 100 percent (this process is called tariff escalation). In the international order, underdeveloped countries are forced to sell raw metal, crude oil and unprocessed agricultural products rather than refined commodities (*Trade Policies* 1985:44).

This "tariff escalation" seems to be well designed to discourage poor countries from processing their own products and selling them at competitive prices on the world market and thereby helping to ameliorate their poverty. Since this is not possible because of the tariff barriers imposed, more than 70 percent of African products (cocoa, coffee, vegetables, etc.) are sold as primary products at low prices. In so doing, industrial countries benefit at least twice. First, they buy cheap, at times even under production price and in this case the industrial countries indirectly take advantage of the cheap labor force of poor countries. Second, by manufacturing or refining the primary products, the rich countries provide employment at home. In the end, the finished product is re-exported to the poor countries and sold at a much better price.

The recent (1994) international trade agreements are not favorable for Africa. As one report of Development Assistance Co-operation (DAC) estimates, while developing countries as a group could increase their earnings from export by about 20 percent, (mostly Asia and Latin American countries), the cocoa and coffee producing countries of Africa cannot expect increases in income as GATT will not provide new markets for them (DAC Report, 1994:42-45).

The 1991 OECD Report notes that the removal of industrial countries' barriers against poor countries would increase the latter's income by about twice the value of the development aid allocated to them. Because of trade barriers, poor countries loose an estimated USD 10,000 per year. This means that poor countries must demand fair trade and less aid. However, this is against the vested interest of the rich nations, as illustrated above.

The industrial nations, will continue these practices and the long history of Africa is witness to this (Chapter One). As Hyden (1983:3) also states, the industrial nations, the international financial giants and MNCs "will continue to dictate their demands since African economies show no sign of strength and self-reliance." Therefore, to force these powers to change their agenda, Africa countries must mobilize their forces, better yet, work in regional co-operation. This task may be opposed and hindered by interest groups as it runs counter to the interests of the richer nations that advocate globalize as opposed to regionalism (this discussion will be further developed in Chapter Eight).

DEEPENING AFRICAN POVERTY: INTERNAL EFFORTS

The previous part of this book dealt with external influences. This half attempts to identify the causes of the failure of local government initiatives and priorities. The presentation below concentrates on (a) political crises, which again are defined as (i) crises in ideology and vision, (ii) crisis of accountability and transparency, (iii) ethnic problems and (iv) lack of fundamental human rights; (b) lop-sided economic priorities, which in turn are based on (i) misallocation of resources and (ii) dependency on foreign experts, lack of local entrepreneurs, and neglect of traditional knowledge and practices.

Most importantly, this section tries to demonstrate the newly independent African states' fixation on Westernization and "socialism" before they consider the mobilization of locally available resources. The fixation on Westernization, for example, increases the appetite of the political elites for Western material consumption. This damages African societies, at least, in two ways: First, it remits capital extracted from natural resources and poor peasants to the industrial countries. Secondly, and most importantly, it discourages the development of indigenous knowledge, traditional practices and local institutions. This neglect in turn has affected African self-confidence and deepened a feeling of inferiority, which has resulted in the inability to solve their own problems. And finally, had led to crises of accountability and transparency.

In what ways are these—what are referred to here as crises in ideology, accountability, transparency and ethnic problems—related to indigenous activities and poverty? There is a direct relationship between these political manifestations and the neglect of indigenous knowledge, traditional practices and local institutions. Traditional activities used to protect African societies from ill manners, used to help, embrace and foster common identity and symbols within a given society and in this manner build self-confidence. The neglect of traditional norms and the lack of the local institutional control over the members of a given community, allow political elites to misbehave and become aggressively corrupt.

Political Crises
A critical review of post-colonial African political crises is beyond the capacity of this study, however, below are given some political factors, which have strongly and directly influenced the deepening of African poverty.
(i) Crises in ideology and vision
In addition to the many reasons illustrated so far the bottom line of post-colonial African poverty appears to be the crisis in ideology, a lack of vision and prospects for the future. Ideology here is taken to mean ideas employed to make life relevant or as Bierstedt (1963:171) notes, "an idea supported by a norm," which is useful to mobilize and liberate available internal resources.

As is presented earlier, such ideological positions were stronger just after African independence as exhibited, for example, by Nkrumah's vision of panafricanism—a vision of a united Africa. There was also a clear blueprint drawn by Cabral who placed African society in the center of a grass-roots development movement based on equity and justice. Deaf ears were turned to these ideas and visions of equity and justice seem to fade away. Leaders were toppled from power by coups and counter coups and/or assassinated. African leaders were thrown out of their offices by military coups. African ideologues, such as Amilcal Cabral of Guinea, Patrice Lummumba of Congo, were murdered by their political opponents. What Africa got instead were slaughterers, self-centered and humiliating leaders.[6] What I wish to establish here is that a crisis of ideology breeds a crisis of leadership and together they can deepen the crisis of accountability and transparency and thereby pave the way for further poverty.

(ii) Crisis of accountability and transparency

Accountability means being responsible for the well being of the people. That is different from the misuse of public properties and living up to the expectations of the people. Transparency is used here generally to mean openness in government, political and budget decisions. These two factors are essential guarantees for the well being of a nation. Absence of accountability could lead to mystification and discriminatory processes and then, pave the way for misuse of public support and create power arrogance. The lack of transparency could allow corruption and nepotism. Lack of transparency and accountability are directly related to a lack of democratic tradition and are fertile ground for autocracy, dictatorship, nepotism and ultimately, hinder the people from fighting against poverty. Why are crises of accountability and transparency the norm in Africa?

The Post-colonial African political leadership emerged from armed struggles against colonial powers. This is especially true for the first generation of African leaders. In other cases, where colonial powers left their colonies without much armed struggle, they often left power to specific ethnic groups which had assisted them during the colonial era. In both cases, some of these leaders understood power to be permanent for them and for their successors. Thus popular participation in the political and economic spheres was curtailed by these privileged groups. As a result, the mass of the population has been deprived of exercising political and economic democracy. Attempts at broad mobilization and the building of a mass consciousness for democratic rule, which could have taken place after independence, were cut short. Thus, accountability to the public was pushed aside.

Without belittling the struggle waged by these people against colonialism or their striving to learn colonial administration—the point I would like to address here is how undemocratic traditions developed in Africa, how later on such practices suppressed open and healthy dialogue between different groups of people; and how it forced opposition groups to resort to arms in order to be heard.

It is widely known today that the African political elite control their societies through more or less undemocratic procedures, without rule of law and popular legitimacy. The preoccupation of post-independence political elite is mainly to enrich themselves, through the control of access to power, which in turn operates through nationalization, nepotism and corruption (Hyden, 1983; Sandbrook, 1985).[7]

Ghartey (1987) argues that the main root of African underdevelopment lies in the lack of accountability of the political elite. This is clearly observable in many African countries' maladministration. The self-centered political elites are neither willing to leave their positions freely (democratically) nor share (decentralize) power. Today, it is clear many African governments, parastatals, judicial institutions etc. are serving their own vested interests and studies have revealed that the ordinary African people have lost faith in their leaders and institutions. The lack of accountability and transparency in African states and parastatals have forced the people to turn inwards their ethnic groups.

(iii) Ethnic problems

A number of social scientists have devoted their time to the analysis of class alliances, class formation and relationships as important factors in understanding poverty, but in the African context, ethnic conflicts have become one of the main factors which aggravate poverty. Below, African ethnic problems are approached from two sides; one is the legacy of colonialism, the other is home brewed.

We have seen how colonialism disrupted socio-political development in Africa, which today manifests itself as one of the fundamental problems on the continent (Chapter One). It is helpful to consider Mazrui's (1986) argument that the colonial period dismantled African indigenous and authentic states.[8] Pre-colonial African kingdoms were strong and centralized. All were demilitarized by colonial powers and colonialism portioned these authentic and centralized states into small pockets that were easily controlled.

The arbitrary division of Africa's ethnic groups by colonialism arrested the process of nation formation in Africa for centuries. As a result, the present African states are not strong and consolidated "nation states" in its strict Western meaning. The process of state formation in many African countries appears to be volatile to the present day. As Hyden (1983:19) says, "the existence of a state [in Africa] with no structural roots in society which, as a balloon suspended in mid-air" is a reality common in many parts of Africa.

Ethnic problems are not always the product of colonialism. Ethiopia for example, was not colonized by European powers and yet continues to experience ethnic problems and many ethnically based armed fronts. The longest African war (30 years) was fought between secessionist Eritrea and Ethiopia and the dominating debate within the Ethiopian intelligentsia concerns national and ethnic issues.[9]

Whether colonially initiated or locally impeded, the causes of ethnically-based conflicts are mainly the discriminatory policies of the ruling political elite (Hulme and Turner, 1990). Ethnic problems are aggravated, as stated earlier, when power is always in the hands of one or two ethnic groups and excludes others. Those who feel that they are pushed away from the center of power often resort to obtaining it by violent means. Since there are no outlets to vent differences through dialogue or other democratic institutions, violence is considered the legitimate method of transferring power from one group to another.

Discriminatory policies that exclude ethnic groups from participation, force these groups to search for self-identification, self-awareness and new symbols of their own. Such measures disassociate these groups from common goals and the sharing of common symbols, and finally erode the feeling of belonging to one "nation-state."

The issues raised by ethnic groups also depend on the level of their integration in a given country. For example, in a situation where there is limited integration, ethnic groups may demand greater participation, greater freedom and more autonomy. In another situation, say, where there is less integration, demands may range from self-determination to secession or a declaration of independence. Both situations, for example, have taken place in Ethiopia. In the former case, The Tigray Liberation Movement fought for more than seven years for self-determination and finally succeeded in toppling the military government of Ethiopia, in May 1991. The latter situation may be explained with the help of the Eritrean Liberation Front that struggled for thirty years to disassociate itself from Ethiopia and assumed its independence in the same year.

The lessons we draw from the examples given above are that however weak ethnic groups may be, if the situation remains unfavorable, they could grow and become factors to be reckoned with.

Thus, in the present political context, paying attention to ethnic problems may be one step nearer to understanding the nature of African reality. Unless Africa tackles these problems boldly and properly it will be difficult to discuss democracy. It may probably be absurd to talk of national-identity, national-cohesion and nation-building where there is no nation but a state and different ethnic groups. It is also equally frustrating to discuss national development in a situation where the boundary between the nation and ethnic groups is not yet clear. Unless ethnic problems are solved in a democratic manner, they could easily become cause for conflicts at any time, which will, without exception, aggravate poverty. Good examples of this are the ethnic crises in Somalia , Rwanda, Burundi, etc.

(iv) Lack of fundamental human rights

The political crisis of Africa has not only resulted in the amassing of wealth, a continuing struggle for power or any of the specific ethnically-based divisions, but are also responsible for many Africans lives lost and for the number of people who are forced to leave their homes.

Amnesty International (Swedish Section) in its 1993 report, states that of fifty-two African countries, forty-eight are criticized for their high numbers of political prisoners, torture, and having turned their citizens into refugees. In the decade before independence there were less than 200,000 African refugees living in exile. Today, the number stands at between five and six million (UNHCR 1986). With regard to internal displacement a recent document from UNHCR (1994), reveals that of twenty-five million people displaced in their own countries the majority are from Africa.[10] The bulk of Africans take refuge in neighboring countries and since one country is no better than the next it has become a burden for all (Mekuria Bulcha, 1988). If the problem continues as at present, conservatively estimated, the number of refugees will rise to somewhere between fifteen and twenty million before the end of this century.[11]

Lopsided Economic Priorities

(i) Allocation of resources to industry in predominantly agricultural societies

In the discussions, held to date, it is repeatedly stated that negative social and economic development in Africa mainly stems from inappropriate priorities and an erroneous path of development. As a result many African countries became victims of a series of civil wars, famines and other man-made suffering. The recurring famine and the decline of the general standard of living in many African has countries forced many people to question the basic priorities made on the continent as a whole.

Since independence (1960s) of most African governments have exhibited their commitment to the development of their countries through different priorities. However, many of these efforts seem to be fundamentally flawed. Major shortcomings are, as repeatedly noted, priority in allocation of resources to industry in predominantly agricultural societies and lack in originality to address African poverty.

In many African countries, growth oriented strategies of development with major emphasis on industrialization have often been pursued at the expense of agriculture (Table 3:4). Even in countries where there is some focus on agriculture, capital intensive farming is promoted, which mainly encourages cash-crops instead of food grains. Such planning has tended to benefit the states and inhabitants of the larger cities, but the living conditions of the rural poor have shown neither improved food supplies nor increased real income (*UN Ad Hoc Group Report*, 1981).

TABLE 3:4
DEVELOPING COUNTRIES' DISTRIBUTION OF ECONOMIC OUTPUT BY SECTOR, PERCENTAGE OF GDP, 1960 AND 1980.

SECTOR	1960	1980
Agriculture	32%	16%
Industry	21%	34%
Construction & Service	47%	50%

Source: *The Report of the South Commission*, (1990:34).

(ii) Dependency on foreign experts, lack of local entrepreneurs and neglect of traditional knowledge and practices

In connection to the statements made above, upon independence, African countries lacked the funds and the technical know-how to realize their plans or their development priorities and therefore, had to rely on the developed countries not only for funds but also for planning expertise as well. Thus, the foreign planning experts utilized the priorities they considered to be the right ones. However, today, when Africa has begun to question the priorities so far established —there is no relationship between what is planned and what is needed locally. Generally stated, what is produced is not locally consumed, and what is consumed at home is given less priority.

The question is, what are the fundamental origins of these problems? The explanations provided date back to the early days of the post-colonial period, when African countries had difficulties producing indigenous entrepreneurs and national bourgeoisie. In relation to this, Fanon's (1963) observation from over thirty years ago—that the authentic national bourgeoisie and national capitalism on the continent was irreversibly arrested by the former colonialists—is still relevant.

What is often referred to as "bourgeois" in most parts of Africa is the upper middle class, and this strata comprises the civilian bureaucrats and high ranking military officers.[12] In this upper middle class there is an intermediate social strata. Rudebeck (1990:11-12), based on his study of Guinea Bissau, discusses this intermediate strata in Africa,

> ...is made up of, on the one hand, the owners of medium and small enterprises, merchants, and artisans, and on the other hand administrative officials military people, teachers other intellectuals and salaried employees at various levels.

Apart from these the vast majority of African society belongs to the peasantry. Sandbrook (1985) also confirms that what evolved from colonial rule in Africa was a peasant class not a capitalist one. Colonial rule only helped parts of Africa, especially where Europeans settled, to transform from communal farmers (or simple cultivators) to peasants. What is often termed the African bourgeoisie and proletariat are only in their embryonic stages. The continent of Africa, therefore, is largely made up of peasant settlements, which to a considerable degree are still in subsistence economies. The lag in economic development did not allow local entrepreneurs to develop. Or it may equally be said that the underdevelopment of local entrepreneurs hinders economic growth, which in turn, aggravates poverty.

CONCLUSION

Inferred from the discussion above, many development assistance programs have directly or indirectly fostered Western type modernization (industrialization) at the expense of indigenous efforts. Steered mainly by Western experts, foreign ideas have attempted to re-shape the traditional societies of Africa into limitations of the industrialized societies.

Foreign aid in general, cannot serve as a remedy, at best it they could play a catalytic role in efforts undertaken locally. The emphasis here again is that development assistance is very much welcome as long as it is productive. It is welcomed as long as its efforts is to achieve necessary transformation, which could be demonstrated in such ways as encouraging traditional practices, indigenous knowledge and local institutions.

The motives for MNCs' investments in developing countries generally, are not for the purpose of transfer of technology per se, as its proponents advocate, but motivated by: (a) the search for profits in new markets, (b) the desire for control of economically important resources such as essential minerals, (c) the search for low-paid labor and (d) to avoid environmental controls and taxation on investment activities.

NOTES

1. The nature of the returns differs from country to country and from period to period. Some donors seek immediate returns and others invest with longer-term returns in mind.

2. Two and half decades ago, Magdoff (1969) reveals that, "What we find is that 73 percent [even higher to 87%] of the aid that was given over the years to the advanced industrial partners of the United States was in the form of grants. But when we come to the bulk of the underdeveloped world, only 42 percent was in the form of grants" (Magdoff 1969:151 Emphasis added). Today, this grant portion of development assistance to developing countries is much less than Magdoff observed in the mid 1960s. At present, the grants given to former East European countries are much greater than the grants given to African countries (OECD Report, 1991).

3. Considering their approach and methods of operation the work of MNCs is reminiscent of the colonial period. During that era, for example, material resources and markets were directly controlled by the colonial powers. In the period of neo-colonialism, this is done, though discretely by the MNCs.

4. In 1971, the UN estimated the overall value of MNCs at US $500 billion. A decade later, 1981 MNCs investments had risen to US $830 billion (Todaro, 1983). This accumulated wealth is controlled mainly by a few MNCs, which are owned by Americans, British, French and the Netherlands. For example,

Exxon, ITT, Shell and BP have over 200 subsidiaries in more than 100 countries (Onimode, 1988). This handful of MNCs account for over 90% of the total flow of capital to underdeveloped countries and thereby control the strategical economic resources. Not surprisingly, the total turnover of many of the USA and UK based multinational firms easily exceeds the total GNP of a typical middle income nation. Indeed, the total sales of MNCs foreign affiliates in the end of 1970s were estimated at US $830 billion, which is almost equal to the combined GNPs of all developing countries, excluding OPEC member states. The three largest MNCs alone, namely Exxon, General Motors (GM) and Royal Dutch Shell has gross sales [seems like something is missing here]

5. Recent environmental catastrophes in Mexico and some countries in Africa, where MNCs mushroomed in the 1980s had left huge environmental problems evidence of mismanagement or destruction of the environment.

6. Like Amin of Uganda, Bagkassa of Central Africa, Mengistu of Ethiopia, Mobutu of Zaire, etc.

7. In the African context, the political elite represent a small portion of society, belonging to the upper middle class mainly engaged in some sort of bureaucratic work. Some refer to these political elites as bureaucratic bourgeoisie. There are some who argue that many African states entertain capitalist modes of production run by the bureaucratic bourgeoisie and reference to these states as bureaucratic capitalist states. The overall character of the socio-economic and political development in Africa is pre-capitalistic or semi-capitalistic in character. Regardless, whether a state calls itself socialist, capitalist or mixed, their nature remains the same—bureaucratic state capitalist.

8. The colonial powers crushed the well established kingdom of Dahomey in Madagascar, the kingdom of Egypt, the kingdom and the civilization of Mahdist in Sudan, the civilization of the Asante Benin, and the Yorube in Nigeria (Davidson, 1989; Onimode, 1988).

9. National question, see the Ethiopian student journals, Tatek, September/October 1973, Challenge, Vol. XI, No. 2, July 1971.

10. African Refugee Problems, UN Commission for Refugees, 1985; UNHCR, Global Refugee Statistics, March, 1994.

11. If the situation continues as it is today, it is going to be the largest migration or uprooting of the African peoples in modern times,

where the number of peoples leaving Africa will be nearly equal to the population of the Nordic Countries, i.e. the people of Denmark, Finland, Norway and Sweden combined.

12. This may be explained in different ways, but to put it into the context of this discussion, in pre-colonial period many African countries had limited or small economies (and small populations) based on barter and common possession of land. During the colonial period, many of the period worked for the colonial masters and the only possessions they had was their labor. After decolonialization came the period of neo-colonization with its many-sided attempts to tie the new nations as closely as possible to the economic and strategic interests and needs of the industrial nations. In independent Africa, what is left over from the external powers goes to the state, often dominated by an elite clique or a clan that possess the entire wealth of a nation. There may be a few rich people in some African countries attached to the ruling clan or clique but do not constitute an independent and broad sector of society to bring about democratic change.

Part Two

Focus on Ethiopia

Chapter Four

POVERTY AGGRAVATED BY INTERNAL FACTORS

In the previous chapter, we discussed the features of poverty taking into account both external and internal aspects. In this chapter the study goes one step further and attempts to illustrate, with the help of concrete examples from Ethiopia, how the factors earlier identified can deepen poverty.

The Ethiopian case serves first, to understand how poverty could be home-brewed through feudal misappropriation of resources, lopsided social structure and feudalistic methods of solving problems of poverty. The long-term traditions of Ethiopia were unable to absorb new technology and were able to adapt to improved methods of work. Later, when the country attempted modernity it did so at the expense of its indigenous practices.

Secondly, Ethiopian fixation on Westernization followed by "imported socialism," which were both failures, perhaps could throw light on certain problems and serve as lessons to other African countries that have experienced more or less similar economic, political and social development.

In the Ethiopian case poverty is generally re-enforced through misappropriation of resources, i.e. land. The negative landholding pattern together with the feudal political system methodically exploited the productive sector of the society the Ethiopian peasants.

This is presented in the first part of this chapter. The last part of this chapter, deals with how peasants and others in different walks of life, could not bear the extent of poverty they were exposed to, and rose up against the *ancient régime*, hoping to change their living conditions for the better.

FEUDALISM: THE GREENHOUSE OF POVERTY IN ETHIOPIA

The purpose of this section is to illustrate the postulation, which states that it is not only external impacts but also internal factors, which may play negative roles deepening poverty. In order to properly expound this theme, a non-colonized African country namely, Ethiopia is presented. More generally, Ethiopia is a country whose historical heritage, and culture, traditions were not directly disordered by colonialism as is the case with other African countries and yet, the country is among the poorest on the continent.

In order to have a full grasp of the poverty in Ethiopia; a historical summary of the roots of Ethiopia's feudal state is essential. Without a description of how this feudal political and socio-economic system prevailed in the country it is almost impossible to properly explain poverty in Ethiopia.

From time immemorial to the present, the people of Ethiopia have always been at war amongst themselves, on the one hand, and against foreign aggressors, on the other. In the country's history, it is difficult to find a single decade devoted to peace and civil economic activities (Tirfe Mammo, 1991). One single historical account may illustrate this point clearly. In what is known as the Era of the Princes, (locally referred to as *zemene mesaffent*)[1] which lasted for almost nine decades (1769-1855) the monarchy and nobility of northern Ethiopia were continuously engaged in civil wars. In these and similar internal conflicts between the feudal gentry, many peasants suffered and lost their lives. This is documented by an Ethiopian author of the era, Professor Afework Gebre Yesus (1908, cited in Pankhurst, 1967:174).

> ...the entire [feudal system]...which has no idea of work but only of pillaging and oppressing the population lives on the back of poor [peasants]. The latter, unable to bear the continual vexations of the former [the monarchy, the nobility and the feudal army] emigrate no matter where and abandon their lands [farm] without any hope of returning. With war and poverty, which annihilate the population, how can the country prosper?[2]

A strongly peasant-affiliated person, outside both the monarchy and the nobility, known as Kassa [later to become Emperor Tewodros (1855-1868)], led a revolt against the then existing chaotic political and socio-economic order. He is best known for two major efforts, i.e. passing a law that prohibited soldiers' rights of dispensation over peasants, and for unifying the northern part of present-day Ethiopia. In so doing, he pulled the country out of the chaotic era of regionalism.

The process of the unification of the Ethiopian Empire which was initiated by Tewodros was then followed by Emperor Yohannes (1869-1889), who succeeded in regaining the Red Sea coastal ports of Massawa and Arkiko, which had been taken by the Ottoman Empire. The expansion of the Ethiopian Empire reached its climax during Emperor Menelik (1889-1913), expanding the country to the south. The last emperor, Haile Sellassie (1930-1974) completed this process by incorporating Ogaden in 1948 and Eritrea in 1959 (Bahru Zewde, 1991).

Though the creation of the Ethiopian Empire may not have been different from any other state building process based on right of conquest, this process however affected the social structure of the country as a whole. For example, those people who were defeated in the wars, lost their land and with it, their earlier status with resultant poverty. Those who conquered elevated themselves to higher social status and became rich.

Prior to this northern conquest, the southern regions had lived under different social structures. For example, the kingdoms of Kaffa, Jimma, Walayeta, Yam, Konso, Gamo and Goffa, etc. trace their origin back to the fourteenth century (Trimingham, 1976; Bahru Zewde, 1991). Mohammed Hassen (1990) states, that the Oromo communities along the Gibe river such as, Limmu, Simma, Gomma, and Guma, had in their kingdoms, settled agricultural and a socio-political organization called *gada*.[3] By the same token, there were monarchical types of social organization in Wollega and the Muslim emirates in Harar. All possessed flourishing cultures and local organizations till the day they became victims of feudal conquest (Trimingham, 1976; Mohammed Hassen, 1990; Bahru Zewde, 1991).

After the conquest, some of the soldiers of Northern Ethiopia transformed their social status from that of ordinary soldiers to that of landlords; they began to live, not on their own labor, but on the labor of others, by the collection of taxes from the local peasants.

In discussing conquest and poverty in Ethiopia many people tend to focus only on the south, as if the peoples of northern Ethiopia lived in harmony and prosperity. This is not, in fact, the case. The worst kind of material poverty prevailed northern of Ethiopia. This is illustrated by the seemingly constant rebellions against the feudal system by the peasants. Peasants of northern Ethiopia were often massacred by the central government. In fact, the feudal system of surplus appropriation was born in northern Ethiopia. In the last quarter of the nineteenth century,[4] this social and economic order was later imposed on the egalitarian societies of southern Ethiopia.

LANDHOLDING DOMAINS AND SOCIAL CLASSES

More generally, before the 1974 revolution, the Ethiopian landholding pattern resembled what is termed "landholding domains" by Wolf (1966), who are patrimonial, prebendal and mercantile.

According to Wolf, patrimonial domain is where social relationships are typically feudal, and where the control of land is placed in the hands of landlords. In patrimonial domain, land is inherited within a kinship (called *rist* in Ethiopia). Patrimonial domain also denotes transfer of land within a lineage with a right of receiving tribute from peasants. This type of landholding, with some variations, is called *gult* in Ethiopia. As Wolf (1966:50) explains:

> such rights can be pyramided, with lords of higher order exercising inherited rights over lords of a lower order and lords of a lower order-exercising domain over the peasants who work (till) the land. The peasant is always at the base of such an organizational pyramid sustaining it with its surplus, which are developed in the form of labor, in kind or in money.

Unlike patrimonial, prebendal domain is not hereditary but granted to office holders, warlords, etc. who in turn collect tribute from peasants. Such domains are granted for services (or loyalty) rendered to the state and were known as *rist gult* in Southern Ethiopia. Wolf also notes another type of prebendal domain in which state officials are given rights to collect tribute in lieu of salary, which was similar to the practice termed *maderia* in Ethiopia.

The final type of domain according to Wolf is called mercantile, in it land is private property to be bought and sold by the holder at a profit. This was also called *private landholding* in Ethiopia. And all these domains co-existed in pre-1974 Ethiopia.

Landholding in pre-Revolutionary Ethiopia

Though the feudal Ethiopian landholding pattern is complicated and known for varying from region to region, I find it more convenient to discuss it in the following manner: (a) kinship owned land, (b) land possessed by the government, (c) privately owned lands, and (d) land possessed by the Ethiopian Coptic Church.[5]

Exhibiting few differences, the northern regions of Ethiopia also exhibited kinship landholding patterns or *rist*.[6] Rist was based on specified kinship, with hereditary rights based on blood ties. Therefore, a plot of land passed from one generation to the next. The person who inherited the plot, however, was not allowed to transfer it by sale, mortgage, or lease outside his family. A *rist* holder had the right to possess the plot as long as that person was alive and when that person passed away, the plot of land was divided equally among his/her children. If the family had no children, the plot was passed to the nearest relatives according to his or her will. One peculiarity of this tenure system was that any member of a family, even one who did not reside in the area and whose livelihood was not agricultural had the right to claim possession of a plot of land based on blood ties.

In Southern Ethiopia much of the land was owned by the crown. This part of the country was conquered in the later years of the nineteenth century and Emperor Menelik remunerated his warlords and soldiers wife by expropriated lands. It should be stressed that the emperor remunerated his warlords with expropriated lands. It should be noted that the emperor remunerated his warlords with land-use rights and did not grant them private ownership (Markakis, 1975a). Privatization of these lands took place during Haile Selassie's regime. During the latter, southern estates were gradually transferred into the hands of members of the royal family, military officers, warlords and local gentry, depending upon their loyalty to the crown.

In Northern Ethiopia, apart from *rist*, there was a landholding pattern called *gult*, denoting land ownership usually granted by the crown, and sometimes by the local ruling gentry to persons with proven loyalty. *Gult* land-holding rights can also be hereditary, but holders of *gult*, known as *guletnga*, enjoyed their privileges only as long as they were loyal to the ruler. According to Göricke (1979), *gult* land holding patterns were dispensed for a limited period to the beneficiaries by their immediate superior in the power hierarchy as a reward for services rendered. He further states,

> In the absence of a money economy, this dispensation of political and economic privileges to officeholders was the only way of rewarding them for services, while at the same time securing the loyalty of the elites (Göricke, 1979:10).

In Southern Ethiopia, differing from the *gult* system of the north, private property and freehold rights were known as *rist-gult*. Different from the traditional *gult* landholding *rist-gult* meant that the land could be sold, hired-or leased. This step by step granting of land titles to individuals in Southern Ethiopia, enacted into law by Haile Selassie, gave landlords the right to evict peasants from the land of their ancestors (Cohen and Weintrabu, 1975; Markakis, 1975a).[7]

The *gult* owners were, for the most part, absentee landowners who held government posts such as administrators, military officers, or members of the royal family and their associates. Such misappropriation created a class of absentee landlords as is shown in Table 4:1. From the table, it becomes evident that in five of the ten southern provinces, absentee landlords controlled over 40 percent of the arable land (in Southern Ethiopia) and these estates were farmed by tributary peasants called *gabbar*.

TABLE 4:1
PERCENTAGE SHARE OF ABSENTEE LANDLORDS AND ABSENTEE HELD LAND BY REGION, 1970

Region	Absentee Landlords	Land Held by Absentee
Arssi	28	27
Bale	15	18
Gomo Goffa	10	42
Harar	23	48
Illubabor	42	42
Kaffa	18	34
Shoa	35	45
Sidamo	25	42
Wollega	29	28
Wollo	26	13

Source[8]: Ministry of Land Reform and Administration, 1971.

Apart from the *gult* landholding rights, the other common type of private tenure system, especially in Southern Ethiopia, was known as *maderia* which literary means to support oneself from the land allotted. *Maderia* land was awarded by the crown or by the warlords to soldiers in lieu of salaries. The *maderia* landholding system was especially common in southern Ethiopia where new settlers took extensive arable lands from the local inhabitants. Feudal warriors made vast land claims formally in the name of the crown and then amassed fertile lands as a *gult* right for themselves first and then divided the rest as *maderia* to their soldiers. Any remaining estates became the crown's property. It was earmarked as state or government land, *ye'mengist meret.*[9] These so called state lands apart from being rented out to tributary farmers were also used to recruit local inhabitants by redistributing them, bit by bit, to the local gentry and other military and civil servants based on their loyalty to the crown.

Church land were lands possessed by the Ethiopian Coptic Church and were comprised of large estates throughout Ethiopia. In traditional Ethiopia, as in medieval Europe, the church was an adjunct of the state. The political establishment needed the support of the church and vice versa. For example, the king declared in the *fitha negast* (the traditional constitution-like document) his divine powers, he was a representation of God. And, thus, as no human has a right to question God, the same applies to Kings. The medieval understanding of the social stratification by the church and the state were as follows: on top is the king (*negash*), then the clergy (*kedash*) and lastly a class of farmers or peasant (*arash*) (Gebru Tareke, 1991:64-67).

The church was the disseminator of ideology of the time, the major institution for taking messages to the people and the authority for interpreting earthly and heavenly laws. According to the church's interpretation of the *fitha negast*, for example, the job of the king was to rule his people and the task of the church was to remind the people that the king's rights were divine and to be feared and respected as one respects and fears God. As a reward for this service, the church was given large amounts of land, which were exempted from taxation.[10] Peasants farming church lands, however, were not exempted from taxes. They paid their dues to the church instead of to the state (Göricke, 1979).

The system of land tenure in church holdings was called *semon.* The clergy and parishioners serving the church possessed *semon* land from which they derived income. Occupied with church services, the clergy normally could not farm the land and were allowed to lease the land, or collect tribute from the peasants farming their plots of land. Church or *semon* landowners were not allowed to sell or mortgage their plots, but they could transfer them to their successors provided the latter also served in the church.

Social Class in Feudal Ethiopia

Feudal social formation took place in Ethiopia first through force and acculturation. Prior to the 1974 revolution, feudal class formation in Ethiopia was roughly speaking, pyramidal, comprising three categories. At the top were the monarch and noblemen (*messafent,* which was hereditary), followed by warlords (usually acquired), then soldiers and finally peasants, called *gabber.* Let me begin with the last group.

A peasant, or *gabbar,* in Northern Ethiopia means one who pays tax and/or rent on the possessed land. Apart from the prime 10 percent, or tithe, to the church or to the state he may have had no other obligations.[11]

In contrast, landless peasants, or *gabbar,* in Southern Ethiopia, were categorized on the basis of oral agreements enforced by the landlords and sometimes no agreement at all. If there were agreements—they could work the land and keep one-fourth of their produce—as *irbo-arash.* In cases when the gabbar took one-third of the produce, they were called *siso-arash* and half, *ekul-arash,* or without land use right at all.

Traditionally, the landowner provided farming equipment and seed, but as land became scarce, *gabbar* often had to provide their own seed, oxen, and other implements of production. As Markakis, 1975a; and Bahru Zewde, 1991, note, the agreements and the conditions under which the *gabbar* worked prior to the land reform (1974) made Ethiopia as a coercive feudal system.

Prior to the 1974 revolution there were on one hand, landowners who themselves were engaged in farming (owner-farmed land) and on the other, landowners who rented, leased, share-cropped or had some other arrangements for tilling land but who were not directly engaged in farming themselves.

These types of landowner are referred to as absentee landlords (not living in the rural area and/or not farming).[12] The two tables below clearly depict the differences between the land farmed by the landowners and by the *gabbar.*

TABLE 4:2
PERCENTAGE OF OWNER-FARMED, *GABBAR* AND MIXED-FARMED HOLDINGS IN NORTHERN ETHIOPIA, 1966

Province	Owner-farmed	*Gabbar*-farmed	Mixed-farmed
Gojjam	13	7	80
Shoa	51	16	33
Tigray	7	18	75
Wollo	17	23	60

Source: Central Statistic Office, Addis Ababa, Ethiopia, 1966.

From Table 4:2 we see that in northern administrative regions (except Shoa which in many respects is also considered to be south), between 60 and 80 percent of the land was farmed (also was possessed) by owner-farmers. Thus, from this it may be stated that land ownership in the north differs from the south in that (a) land was fairly distributed to the tillers and (b) the landlords could not evict tenants who had *rist* rights. However, we must note that this does not imply, by any means, that the peasants of the North were better off than the Southerners. Rather we have to note, as Gebru Tareke (1991) remarks that the northern land tenure system was mostly known for its landlordism through surplus extraction, corvée labor and tribute—paid to the upper class till the advent of modern administration and introduction of a cash economy. When this occurred, forced peasant corvée labor in some places was replaced by tax.[13] Additionally, in the north, it is often mentioned that land was available to all "born in a given region," but this was not true as Muslims and craftsmen considered to be "low casts" (known by different cast names such as *ketekach* for metal craftsmen, *fugga* for those doing pottery, etc.) were segregated from the majority Christian communities and all the benefits that this entailed.

TABLE 4:3
PERCENTAGE OF OWNER-FARMED, *GABBAR* AND MIXED-FARMED HOLDINGS IN SOUTHERN ETHIOPIA, 1966

Province	Owner-farm (%)	*Gabbar*-farm (%)	Mixed-farm (%)
Arssi	48	45	7
Gemo Goffa	53	43	4
Harar	46	49	5
Illubabor	25	73	2
Kaffa	38	59	3
Sidamo	61	37	2
Wollega	41	54	5

Source[14]: Central Statistic Office, Addis Ababa, Ethiopia, 1966.

In the south (Table 4:3), with the exception of two provinces Sidamo and Gemo Goffa, the peasants were tributaries or *gabbar* to the absentee landlords (farming in rental, lease, or crop-sharing agreements). Note also that the differences in mixed farming, which was far more less than Northern Ethiopia (Table 4:2).

The Upper-class and its Methods of Recruiting New Members

Class formation of the warlords usually took place after every military conquest. The head of the military forces was traditionally the crown, but he used to delegate the right of governance to warlords or members of the royal family. If the governor was related to the royal family the designation could also be *le'ul* a hereditary title equivalent to duke. However, the highest designation was *ras*, literally means head or viceroy (it could as well mean head of the army, commander-in-chief of the designated area; Member of the royal family of the same designation is referred to as *le'ul ras*).[15]

The *ras* further delegated power downwards in the hierarchy to generals or the commander of the vanguard called *dejazemach* and *fitawrarie*. Then came commanders of the left and right brigades called *gerraazmach* and *kegneazamach* respectively (see glossary). Thus, the governor (called locally *enderase*) together with his rank and file residing in Southern Ethiopia were referred to as *neftenga*, which simply means riflemen.[16]

As there was hierarchy between the crown and his warlords, there was also clear division of labor from the warlords to the grassroots. The two grassroots level representatives of coercive methods were the *nech-lebash* and *chika-shum*. Their official tasks were collection of tributes and taxes and the passing of orders for corvèe works. The *nech-lebash* (literary means those who had clean or white clothes) in some areas, especially in towns and cities, also served as undercover security agents, and in some other places they also combined this with police activities. The *chika-shum* were village local administrators, (or headmen) who mainly collected dues and ordered corvèe labor.

Hierarchically speaking, down from *chika-shum* and up to *ras* were the major *maderia* landholders. Later on the pattern granting *maderia* land was expanded to other groups such as loyal rural elite, and influential local gentry. Some among the native or former landowners who had proven their loyalty to the warlords and especially to the crown were renamed (reconfirmed) as local gentry known as *bale'a-bat*, (meaning those who have valuable fathers of substance). Depending on their loyalty to the new order their right to possess land could be reinstated. Thus, these local gentry or *bale'abat* together with the *neftenga* (or *melkengna*) constituted part of the rural upper class in pre-Revolutionary Ethiopia.[17]

The Process of Acculturation

Perhaps one interesting sociological point in the upper-class social formation is the mechanism by which this class strove to widen its base. This process usually took place through the method of promoting an individual from what they call "common person" or *balager*, to a "refined citizen" with possession of land as *bale'abat*. The process from *balager* to *bale'abat* was pure socialization in a sense that it injected new learning and lifestyles to overwhelm the old roles and self-conceptions. We have to bear in mind that such socialization goes hand-in-hand with social control.

The process of acculturation of the "common persons"—*balager* into the cultural sphere and lifestyle of the ruling elite (of the Amhara and Tigray) was mainly carried out through complex processes of softening and acclimatizing. It could start with learning the *amarinja* language (a language spoken by the majority of the ruling elite, *amhara*) and this could be accomplished, for instance, through a religious conversion and becoming a member of the Ethiopian Coptic Church. The converted person acquires a God-father or mother (often a Christian Northerner) and becomes a member of that family and the family relations is known as *abe'lej*. In some cases, family ties from different regions are cemented through the process of taking adoptive sons and daughters of certain families called *gudefficha*. In both cases a fictitious kinship relations is formed. For many, such relationships are as strong as actual blood kinship.

Another process of socialization could take place through the symbolic sharing of the same breast of one mother, called *ye'tut lej* (almost the same as the blood brother of North American Indian culture). However, the commonest of all socialization processes was through marriage. Through these and many other systematic socialization processes, many from the south have hybridized and mixed with the highest classes *(mesafent* and *mekuanent)* of Northern and Central Ethiopia.[18]

PERMANENTIZATION OF MASS POVERTY IN ETHIOPIA

The Period of "Modernization/Westernization"

Though the process of Westernization began long ago, it did not materialize until the reign of Emperor Menelik[19] followed by that of

Emperor Haile Selassie. Haile Selassie's government, which ruled the country for nearly half a century played a prominent role in transforming Ethiopian from a predominantly feudal into a semi-feudal/semi-capitalist society. It was during the latter reign that formal Western oriented schools and administration as well as economic, political and military organizations were widely introduced into the country (Lipsky 1967).[20]

Haile Selassie's reign presented here, is divided into four periods: (i) from early 1916 to 1930—from the time when he was governor and care-taker of the government (as *ras* Tefferi) to his coronation as emperor Haile Selassie, (ii) from 1931 to 1941—a period of some reform disrupted by colonial Italy's intervention (1935-1941), (iii) from 1941 to 1960—a period of political reform, but also the subduing of regional opposition directed against his authority. In the latter period the emperor undertook harsh measures against peasants who opposed his grant of lands to warlords and new land taxes. These and other unpopular measures resulted in an abortive military coup in 1960, (iv) the last period between 1960 to 1974 which was marked by extensive opposition by the people and which resulted in a revolution that displaced him from power.

In general, Haile Selassie not only expanded the scope of modernization in terms of education but also introduced Westernization as the primary task of his government. Roughly speaking in the first two periods, i.e. up to the Italian invasion, his government had shown improvement. After the 1960s, his regime appeared to be a retarding factor to further social development. However, measured against earlier periods of Ethiopian history, the epoch under Haile Selassie was, indeed, different.

Concerning progressive aspects, Haile Selassie's government especially in the early years as Bahru Zewde (1991) notes, struggled to abolish the slave trade in the 1920s, and in the 1930s passed decrees to abolish corvèe and taxes in kind. Lipsky (1967) also writes that upon Haile Selassie's ascent to power in 1931 there were only two secondary schools, one general hospital and a small number of clinics, a very weak military organization, limited foreign relations, very backward inter-regional contacts and insignificant urbanization. It was during the reign of Haile Selassie that many schools were opened and young Ethiopians were sent abroad to receive advanced education. From 1931 to 1968, the number of formal (government) primary schools increased from two or three to about a thousand. Secondary schools increased in number from one to nearly fifty. A university and various colleges were also opened for the first time.[21]

Clapham (1969) discusses how Haile Selassie played a central role in modernizing the Ethiopian army, improving the administration and extending communications during this earlier period of his reign. Moreover, his government's material and moral contribution to the liberation of many African states from colonialism during the 1950s and early 1960s, and later the role he played in forming the first African forum—The Organization of African Unity (OAU) in 1963 were other breakthroughs credited to Haile Selassie's Government.[22]

The turning point of his regime from progressive to retrogressive appeared to occur when land became increasingly the property of the crown and the nobility, and when general rights were gradually revoked in favor of the privileges of the selected few.

The misappropriation of land in Ethiopia by Haile Selassie's government, as earlier stated, further disrupted land ownership patterns and this in turn fundamentally changed the social structure and economic orientation of the people. The government's policies mainly established by the crown and the warlords were essentially geared to the strengthening of their own positions. As Gebru Tareke (1991:29) notes,

> ...the new state never completely destroyed the basis of [feudal] local power nor did it fully penetrate and control the rural population. Failing to control it directly, the state was never able to reorganize and regulate rural social relationships.

What Gebru meant, to my understanding, is that the Haile Selassie government failed to by-pass the feudal lords and establish a state-peasant relationship and in so doing curtail the rights of landlords over peasants. Haile Selassie failed to create a peasant-state relationship because he built his power on the landlords rather than the peasants. He used the landlords and their *netch-lebash* i.e. paramilitary forces, to control the peasants.

Despite these inequalities the government continued its policy of modernization. Modernization was first attempted under a grandiose ten-year industrial development plan, stretching from 1945 to 1955. Since the country had neither material nor human resources to undertake such an ambitious industrial venture, the plan remained only on paper. Instead, a series of five-year plans were introduced, demonstrating the government's priorities of transforming Ethiopia from a traditional into a modern state through the establishment of industrial manufacturers.

If we take for example the first five year plan (1957/58 -1961/62) we find that among the planned investments that was earmarked for manufacturing (20.5%) was greater than for agriculture (14.5%) (Befekadu Degefe, 1981). According to the same source, the period of the first five-year plan was devoted to enacting legislation to encourage Ethiopian industrialization through foreign investors.

In the second five-year plan (1963/64-1967/68) foreign investment was clearly favored by the government's investment policy through relief on income tax, import and export duties and a generous policy of foreign exchange remittances. This period helped to bring forth a close relationship between the feudal and international capitalist economic systems and further strengthened the semi-feudal and semi-capitalist development.

The third five-year plan (1968/69-1973/74) was launched with great hope (by the government) of integrating Ethiopia into the capitalist world economy. However, this was difficult to put into practice as there were too many domestic and international constraints. Though this third five-year plan was extended for one year, in order to achieve its planned objectives, it finally failed to attain its set targets all together.

Haile Selassie made significant progress in the initial stages of his reign in order to profile himself as progressive and win support against his archenemies, (Zeweditu and Iyassu—both were "legitimate successors" of Emperor Menelik). Such positive image was essential to him because, although he belonged to the nobility (the son of a *ras*), he was not "a legitimate successor" to the crown by birth and thus, needed the support of the nobility to promote his ambitions. In light of this background, though Haile Selassie tried to 'modernize" Ethiopia, he could not abandon the feudal system and promote progressive measures in favor of the majority, especially the peasants.

After winning the palace intrigue, as noted above, Haile Selassie himself appeared to support the old system. This becomes clear when we closely examine both the Constitution of 1931 and the Revised Constitution of 1955, which imposed the indisputable power of the monarch, and benefits for the warlords at the expense of the peasants. The constitution, parliament, the judicial system and many similar public institutions became, more or less, window dressing to attract Western influence. The parliament could debate on certain issues for years, the judicial system could undertake measures in compliance with the constitution but this activity came to nothing. What mattered was the emperor's personal approval through his palace court (called *chilot*)—a situation where there was a government within a government.

Such an autocratic political organization could not cope with modern times. Firstly, the emerging intelligentsia and the introduction of "modernity" which he was forced to introduce partially at one point, needed more areas of operation and more freedom. However, the system as it was, was not in a position to accommodate this and therefore, change became unavoidable. Secondly, the excessive exploitation of peasants by the upper classes and the misuse of extracted surpluses in non-productive consumption left the country economically bankrupt. Haile Selassie's half a century attempt at transformation did no more than create a semi-feudal, semi-capitalist system. These half-hearted reforms became the stumbling block for further social, economic and political development and this impasse lead to the 1974 revolution.

An interesting point that may be raised here is how could the people, finally, raise up against the system that had ruled them for centuries? Many writers have interpreted the revolutionary actions of the people in many different ways. However, for the purposes of this study, the root causes of the 1974 revolution are presented on two levels. Level one—the longstanding poverty as explained so far finally forced the peasants to revolt, the military to attempt coups, the students to stage series of demonstrations and ethnic groups to wage armed struggles. The second level of understandings is found in the cumulative response which finally reached critical mass and exploded in uprisings triggered by food price increases, famine and ethnic wars as illustrated hereafter.

HAILE SELASSIE'S GOVERNMENT: POLITICAL AND ECONOMIC CRISIS

The Longstanding Causes of the Revolution

As we have observed, prior to the 1974 revolution, landholding patterns were complicated, rigid and invidious. The possession of land by the peasantry in the north and south of the country varied considerably. While the peasants of the north, by and large, possessed farmland the southern peasants in most cases, were displaced from their lands. Though the northern peasants owned their own plots, they did not have better living conditions. This was because excessive population density led to extensive fragmentation (smaller and smaller plots of arable land). This resulted in difficulties in producing enough food to sustain a household, let alone a surplus for market.

Government land grants in the south, were for the most part, given to members of the royal family, high ranking civilian and military officials, warlords, local gentry and loyal elites and not to the peasants. These people who did not have direct attachment to rural life often rented the land to agricultural entrepreneurs, who in some cases introduced mechanized farms and evicted peasants from their plots. The land grants, in effect, widened the gap between the haves and have-nots. Finally, the majority of the peasants became serfs working to support the luxurious lifestyles of the upper classes and this became one of the fundamental causes of the peasant revolts.

Peasant Revolts and Urban Unrest

As a route of escape from poverty, peasant revolts have a long history in Ethiopia. Two recent studies, one by Gebru Tareke (1991) who studied peasant rebels both in north and south Ethiopia (*Weyane, Gojjam* and *Bale*)[23] and Andargachew Tiruneh (1993) who added the nomadic movements of the Ogaden and Eritrean Sahel plains, enrich the knowledge on Ethiopian peasant rebels prior to the 1974 revolution.

According to Gebru, the *weyane* movement that began around 1941 was a combination of peasant dissatisfaction and political motivation. The political motivation stemmed from the dissatisfaction of the local gentry who were side-lined by the central government of Haile Selassie in the aftermath of the Ethio-Italian war.[24] The peasants, especially the nomadic community *Raya Azebo*, rebelled, against the new government policy of centralization which they saw as a threat to their communal style of living. The Tigray settler peasants joined *weyane* for both economic and political reasons, i.e. (a) poverty arising from the infertility of land due to hundreds of years farming without replenishing the soil (ecological degradation), (b) the high density of population per arable hectare, which together resulted in recurrent famine, and (c) the Tigray gentry was pushed from the center of power by Haile Selassie's government (Gebru Tareke, 1991:91).

For the reasons stated above, the movement received wide support from peasants and challenged Haile Selassie's Government. Additionally, the British force, which was located near Tigray (in the neighboring Eritrea), provided indirect support to this uprising. This was due to the fact that Britain then held the option of the coalition of Eritrea and Tigray unless the Ethiopian central government somehow remained in the British domain. After some time, Haile Selassie confirmed his absolute loyalty to the UK and then Britain used its air force to demolish the *weyane* revolt in 1943.

The *Gojjam* administrative region is also known for its sporadic peasant revolts against central government. The first series of revolts were between people who favored regional power and those favoring centralized power. Like the *weyane*, the *Gojjam* movement was against the central political power, plus the local gentry wanted to be reinstated to its traditional position.[25] However, some revolts such as that of 1967, were solely based on peasant dissatisfaction against high levels of taxes on agricultural production (Bahru Zewede, 1991; Gebru Tareke, 1991).

The other peasant rebellion was in one of the southern administrative regions called *Bale*. The *Bale* movement which extended from 1963 to 1970 was totally different from the earlier revolts. Unlike the Northerners, who by and large were Christians, the population of *Bale* and its adjoining areas were Muslims. The *Bale* revolt was directed against new settlements in the region and the resultant shortage of arable land and high taxation by the central government and the landlords. The causes of Bale rebellion is best explained by one of its leaders,

> Ours [history] has been of deprivation and misery, a story of endless tragedy. In our own country we have lived as aliens and slaves, deprived of our lands and discriminated against on the grounds of our tribal and religious identities (quoted in Gebru Tareke, 1991).[26]

The *Bale* peasant movement was integrated with the pasturalists of Ogaden and Borana, who also were affected by the central government's restrictions on free movement in search of water and visiting markets at the borders adjoining Somalia. The movement obtained the support of the local people and the struggle continued for seven years.

When discussing the peasant movements certain precautions must be taken. One, there should not be a direct inference made between the Ethiopian peasant movement and the 1974 revolution—the peasant movements were not the forces which brought about the revolution in 1974. These movements, though referred to as peasant because of the large-scale participation of this group, were lead by the local gentry whose interests were adversely affected by the central government. As Gebru Tareke correctly notes, peasant revolts in Ethiopia *per se* did not bring about the social change of 1974. What they did was to "sap the energy of the old regime and inspire a generation of radical students who served as a catalyst in the revolution" (1992:122).

The 1960 Military Coup and its Impact

In December 1960 an abortive coup was staged against the government of Haile Selassie. Though the attempt did not succeed as planned, it did serve as a turning point for the country.[27]

The 1960 coup for the first time questioned the power of the king to rule without the people's consent and in so doing openly challenged Haile Selassie's government. Worse, the divine right of kings and misuse of power by the emperor and his court was openly condemned by the son of the emperor, the crown prince himself in a radio and broadcast aired throughout the country. This was the first time in the history of the country that the power of the king or "the earthly God" was officially questioned. Thus, the coup suggested to the Ethiopian people that the power of the king is subject to question (Greenfield, 1965; *Tatek*, 1970).

Moreover, the coup provided an impulse for the intellectuals, especially the students, to chose sides, i.e. to support the system or serve as the mouthpiece of the poor. From then onwards students chose the latter, and became more radical, articulate and determined to change the situation of the poor, especially the peasants.

The Ethiopian Student Movement

The Ethiopian student movement, it could be asserted, was born from the 1960 coup. Their first street demonstrations and distribution of opposition leaflets took place in support of the 1960 coup (Balsvik, 1985). Prior to this coup though the students discussed the sufferings of the poor, they had not become the defenders of the poor. In this regard, the 1960 coup helped them to make their choice. Balsvik notes that the coup gave to the students a new life, an intellectual life aimed at openly and loudly supporting the poor. A leader of the university student association explained this new life as follows:

We didn't know what a coup d'état was—we had never demonstrated before, we hardly understood what it meant. ...They [the
coup makers] came and spoke to us about our own ideas, however unexpressed these had been. It was like Jesus healing the
cripple. We had the same feelings of joy the cripple must have
had. The incredible, a miracle had happened ... We felt [at last] the
country was oppressed, and we disliked the government very
much (Balsvik, 1985:95).

From then onwards the rift between the elite and the government
widened until the system collapsed in 1974.

The Ethiopian Student Movement was strong because the students were organized both in and outside Ethiopia. The student
movement in Ethiopia ran the day to day opposition against the government while the student unions abroad (USA, West and East
Europe, the Middle East etc.) served as "ambassadors of the people"
by disseminating information and staging organized demonstrations
in many cities of the Western world.[28]

Dissatisfaction that Underpinned the 1974 Revolution

In discussing the long-term causes of Ethiopian poverty (which ultimately led to the 1974 social change) we have seen how the government of Haile Selassie consolidated its power with the help the
church, the upper echelons of the military establishment, landlords,
the local gentry and the civil servants, all of whom were beneficiaries of the system. The economic interests of the royal family, the
higher clergy, the nobility, the senior military and the well-situated
public officials were spread deep and wide in the fiber of Ethiopian
society. These same people owned the fertile lands, ran modern agricultural undertakings and operated commercial and industrial enterprises. The collected earnings from these diverse economic activities, however, were not sufficient to fulfil the aristocracy's ever
growing demand for luxury goods, such as expensive cars, fancy
clothes and extraordinary tastes in food and drink. In order to meet
all these extravagances, the landlords had to levy more taxes on the
peasants, increase rents, and freeze wages. In short, for every increase
in the luxurious consumption of the ruling classes, the peasants were
forced to bear the cost.

On the eve of the 1974 revolution, the agricultural sector, the
primary livelihood of the country that was to bear all these costs,

101

was in a state of crisis. One of the central reasons for this crisis, to repeat, was the retrenched land holding system, which favored not the laboring peasants, but the royals and their subordinates, the high clergy and the landlords.

As favorable prices could be gained for commercial crops on the world markets, landlords began to increasingly invest in the cultivation of cash crops instead of locally consumed food grains. In order to obtain more arable land for these cash crops, large numbers of peasants were forcibly evicted from their farms. As taxes were not fixed by law, landlords levied taxes geared to their own personal demands and not based on the level of production of the peasants. Under such conditions no peasant became willing to produce surplus that went as a greater share to the landlords. Ultimately the fall in food grain production resulted in severe famine.

Moreover, the major commodities the country exported were (and still are) unrefined agricultural products—such as coffee, hides and oil seeds and the prices of these commodities are low compared to industrial goods. They are also determined by the international market. In the 1970s, profit from the sale of these products was insufficient to cover the skyrocketing prices of imported consumer goods, including the military hardware used to fight the prolonged war against Eritrea and to suppress peasant rebels in different parts of the country.

The combined effects of peasant eviction, high taxation, natural disasters, such as famine, and civil wars made life very hard in rural Ethiopia and many peasants left for urban areas. Since there was not enough work in urban areas to accommodate the exodus, young girls became prostitutes, boys were thrown into delinquency and the already dispossessed adults remained unemployed and destitute. In general, the lack of food, shelter and the high prices of basic consumer goods, accompanied by a high rate of unemployment increased the scope and depth of the economic and political crisis that finally contributed to the outbreak of the 1974 revolution.

Immediate Causes

Though the outbreak of the revolution was believed to be the cumulative effect of long standing socio-economic and political crises, as presented so far, there were also certain immediate factors that prompted the outbreak. These included, (a) the new education policy adopted by the government, (b) international economic crises caused by the 1973/74 oil price-shocks, (c) the total dissatisfaction of the urban workers and the middle and low-ranking military corps, and most importantly, (e) the outbreak of famine in many provinces (Bondestam, 1975; *teglachen*, June, 1977, No.3; Harbeson, 1988; Ottaway, 1990).

The new education policy, *The Educational Sector Review*, called for minimization of higher education (universal education up to fourth grade followed by vocational training) because the economy of the country was already on the verge of collapse and could not provide meaningful work for its graduates. The report was categorically rejected by students and teachers. One of the precipitators of the 1974 revolution, the Ethiopian Teachers Association (with about 18,000 members), went out on strike against the sector review and demanded better educational standards and a corresponding budget increase to improve the quality of education, including revised curricula and the banning of various indirect school expenses. Subsequently, the students who had stayed tuned from the 1960s onwards-boycotted classes in support of the demands put forward by their teachers. The students, the teachers and other opposition groups together formed a sort of front against Haile Selassie's regime and intensified their rally around the popular slogan *meret la'rashu*, meaning land to the tiller (*Teglachen*, 1977; Pausewang, 1983, 1990).

Additionally, the *international economic crisis* triggered by the increase in oil prices served as one of the immediate destabilizing factors to the political and economic structure of Ethiopia. With the increase in oil prices, the prices of many imported industrial products also increased. At the same time, the price of exported agricultural products and other raw materials fell rapidly. At the beginning of 1974, as Bondestam (1975) notes, the price of cloth increased by 11 percent, food items by 20 percent, gasoline by 30 percent and imported goods increased by 17 percent and all these increases in prices were accompanied by a wage freeze and increased unemployment.

Later, the rebels were joined by the taxi drivers. As the Arab oil embargo forced a sharp increase in the price of gasoline, discontent among taxi drivers grew as the cost of fuel and spare parts for their cars became very expensive and living expenses generally, increased astronomically. Thus, taxi drivers supported the demands of teachers and students and together they took the issues to the streets of cities and provincial towns.

With each passing day the revolt grew broader and broader, and eventually the factory workers joined the forces of the revolution. The Confederation of Ethiopian Labor Union (CELU), with 85,000 members, demanded compensation for increases in the cost of living caused by inflation for its members and urged an end to the master/servant relationship with their employers and for this to happen, with immediate effect, it called for a general strike.

Thereafter, the revolution was joined by the unemployed and people from every sector of society including the lower clergy. Strikes, boycotts, demonstrations and the distribution of clandestine newspapers became the order of the day. The struggle took shape and the battle lines were drawn between the rulers and the ruled. The flame of the mass struggle grew brighter and finally erupted when the armed forces joined the side of the people and the revolution.

Over and above the political and socio-economic crises, the most shocking experience for the people was famine. Over two hundred thousand people perished in one province (Wollo) alone. While the people died by the thousands, the government of Haile Selassie categorically denied the existence of famine in Ethiopia. However, the reality was, as Harbeson, (1988) reveals, that the government was fully aware of the shortage of rainfall in the previous years. The Ministry of Agriculture, for example, had produced an internal document in March, 1973, in which it stated that food grains from the major cereal producing areas had drastically decreased. This was followed by another report issued by relief and rehabilitation activists disclosing that over one and half million people were in famine zones. The Ethiopian Grain Corporation reported to the government that its supplies had virtually run out (Harbeson, 1988).

In spite of all these early warnings, the government did not wish to respond, because that year the Organization of African Unity's (OAU) annual session was to be held in the capital, Addis Ababa, and the Emperor was hosting the African heads of state. Thus, all the grievances and sufferings of the people should be kept silent so as not to tarnish the Emperor's image as benevolent and wise. To this effect arrangements were made to prevent starving people from entering the capital, Addis Ababa.

However, as the suffering increased, some of the famine-stricken people could not bear their hunger a day longer and managed to pass the government barricades and appear in the capital. The residents of Addis Ababa and its suburbs witnessed these horrible events and took what ever they had at home—water, food, clothing and medicines—and met the starving people on the streets with open arms, leading small children and old men and women into their homes. These scenes were relayed through the international media and reverberated around the world.

The events partially described above brought a deep political crisis within the ruling class. As Andargachew Tiruneh (1993) states, the government's initial response the only organized body, the army, entered the political arena and claimed power.[29]

To sum up, the participants in the 1974 popular uprising were the armed forces, the teachers, the students, the trade unions and the civil servants. Among them, it must be boldly stated, it was the long political agitation of the students, later supported by the mutiny of the armed forces that brought the government to its knees.

CONCLUSION

The feudal landholding pattern favored the crown, the nobility, the higher clergy and the modern rural and urban elite and in so doing it clearly hindered the development of the peasants. The peasantry, the basic supporter of the Ethiopian society, was misrepresented and dispossessed which in turn meant that they were excluded from the only source of income and determinant of social status—land. This led to a decline in the production of food grain that ultimately culminated in famine. The more land was concentrated in a few hands, and the more farming was mechanized, the more frequently peasant eviction occurred. This exodus placed further strain on already overburdened urban areas. Thus, objective socio-economic conditions were synchronized with the subjective or political crisis by the slogan of land to the tiller—a principle that students and the intelligentsia had supported for decades.

The forces of the Ethiopian revolution included people of all types and from all walks of life, not only the army and the middle class as many people assume. This participation of all sectors of the society against the ruling monarch and his court explains why the 1974 Ethiopian social change is called a revolution and not a coup d'état. In the early stages of the revolution the participation of the Ethiopian people was whole-hearted, broad and intensive. Based on such facts, many argue that the Ethiopian revolution was one of the genuine revolutions of our time. This is because the revolution was not only the first social revolution in Ethiopia but also the first of its kind on the continent of Africa.

The revolutionary forces who struggled to bring forth the 1974 revolution achieved their most important goal, i.e. to abolish the age-old feudal system with its last feudal king Haile Selassie. He had ruled the country for over a half century. The revolution also paved the way for better relations of production which could be used for constructing better lives for all Ethiopians. In short, it could be asserted that the first chance of real social revolution against poverty was set in motion by this popular uprising.

NOTES

1. The word *mesaffent* is a plural form of *mesfen* meaning, son of a noble and/or or a monarch. See glossary.

2. In fact, the people of Ethiopia have never experienced a period without wars (including conquest, feudal expansion, peasant rebels, civil wars, and major riots). In the country's long history it is difficult to find "a golden age" for all its peoples at the same time, marked by peace and development. Afework's critique appeared in a book called Gude du Voyageuren Abyssinie, Rome, 1908.

3. *Gada* is a politico-jural system especially practiced by the Oromo people. It entails rights and obligations, mainly based on age groups. For further information, see Asmaron Legesse, 1963.

4. There is a debate among Ethiopians whether to call this incident a "conquest" or "feudal expansion." The problem is using the former is that it denotes a colonial type of occupation (external power such as the European conquest of African countries) while the latter, according to some writers, hides the economic exploitation, the cultural domination and the suffering of the conquered people.

5. Sorting out certain confusing terms may perhaps help. Landownership means possession of land or a plot that was transferred, hired, leased or mortgaged by the owner—private landholding. Land-use right denotes usufructuary rights, that is to say farming a plot of land without privately owning it. Finally, landless peasants (*gabbar*), especially in Southern Ethiopia, were those who sold their labor, based on different, temporary contracts. For a detailed account of the landholding pattern and class formation in Ethiopia see Markakis, 1975:73-104.

6. The village land ownership pattern exercised in part of Tigray and Eritrea by the name of *deissa* is not dealt with here. *Deissa*

means a land tenure system where land is owned by the commune (village). Rist a system, which is kinship, differs from the communal pattern of *deissa*. For further discussion, refer to Kidane Mengisteab, 1990, Görick, 1979. Moreover, Northern Ethiopia comprises Begemder, Gojjam, Tigray, Wollo and Northern Shoa. Southern Ethiopia comprises Arssi, Gemo Goffa, Harar, Kaffa, Illubabor, Wollega and Southern Shoa.

7. Cohen and Weintraub (1975:28-61) describe land tenure patterns prior to the 1974 revolution and especially how these government land grants affected the peasantry in general (pp. 59-61). They describe how the grants made by Emperor Haile Selassie (first in 1934, then in 1936, 1942, 1945, etc.) favored the upper class, especially the local elite. Through these land grants the crown further expanded its social base to include the nobility, the landlords and the local elites.

8. Caution must be applied in interpreting the tables, especially that from Ethiopia because 9a) the figures are usually very old, (b) the process under which the data was collected was controversial and (c) they were mainly issued by government authorities and may be biased for political reasons. However, they can serve as indicators rather than determinants.

9. One ought to remember that there was not distinction between state and crown ownership of land the king owned the state lands as his private property. Until land reform legislation (1975) the state (i.e. the crown) was the single major agricultural landholder in Imperial Ethiopia.

10. That may be why it was common to refer to the church as "one-third government" (or *siso-mengist*). According to the available evidence, church holdings were 10 to 12 percent of the total available arable land in Ethiopia (Dessaleng Rahmato, 1984).

11. This avenue was correctly explained by Bahru Zewde (1991) as follows, "The ruling class appropriated not only surplus produce from the *gabbar* but also surplus labor. The chief expression of this forced labor, or corvée, was farming on state or governor's land (*hudad*). This generally took about a third of the *gabbar's* labor time. The *gabbar* also ground grain for the *melkegna* [landowner, rural bureaucrat]. He was engaged in the construction of granaries and fences for the governor or the *melkegna*. He was custodian of any state prisoner, with liability to take his place if a prisoner escaped. He also provided transport service, carry-

ing the personal effects of the governor or an official in times of peace and provisions in times of war" (p. 87).

12. These were people mainly engaged for example, as government functionaries, i.e. local military officers, soldiers, priests, local gentry, etc. The term *gabbar* is confusing: after 1965, the law recognized *gabbar* as "owner"—in the sense of freehold, i.e. the one who had paid the tax. So, typically, the absentee landlord could claim to be the owner, because he had the tax receipts. The point here is that in some cases the people themselves did not know whether they in fact were "owners" *gabbar*, or both. It is with this reservation that the tables should be seen.

13. For example, *gult* landholding was abolished in 1960 in northern Ethiopia and in so doing Haile Selassie succeeded in attacking the economic basis of the northern nobility, as they then had no right to collect tributaries from their gult.

14. The original source used the term "tenants" instead of *gabbar*, but tenants and *gabbar* are not the same. Tenants hold or possess land by some kind of title or agreement protected by law. Many of the Ethiopian *gabbar* lived at the mercy of the landlords without any legal protection. Therefore, I prefer to use the term *gabbar* instead of tenants.

15. A governor of a province was also known as *enderase*, who looked after or ruled the area as the representative of the crown. *Le'ul* (prince) and *lej* were also names of high designate and especially the former one is equivalent to prince and used only for members of the royal family.

16. The term *neftenga* is generally misused when relating it only to the Amhara/Tigray ethnic groups. It is worth noting also that all *neftenga* were not landlords, there were poor *neftengai* as well. For further discussion, see Markakis, 1975.

17. The *bale'abat* were mainly indigenous people whose fathers were local chiefs, or owned land and still remained loyal to the crown, while the *mekuanent* mainly were for example, warlords. *Mekuanet*, unlike *bale'abat* and *mesafent* were not necessarily born into the local gentry but they could acquire the title through distinguished work such as being good warriors and exhibiting loyalty to the crown. The *mesafent* were descendants of local kings and princes and were direct members of the royal family or their near associates.

18. These processes are applicable to date, not only between south and north or rich and poor, but throughout the whole fabric of

the society and even across religious borders. In this respect, one may say, it can be contributed to the foundation of a common identity.

19. Menelik is referred as *chief creator of the modern Ethiopian Empire* (Lipsky, 1952; 17) and he was the one who laid the groundwork for Ethiopian modernization. In the period between the death of Menelik and the emergence of Haile Selassie, the country was affected by historical eclipse marked by palace intrigues between Haile Selassie, *Lej* Iyassu (1931-1916) and Empress Zeweditu (1916-1930).

20. This does not mean that Ethiopia had no contacts with Europeans prior to these periods. In fact, Ethiopia had earlier contacts with European powers of the time, for example, with the Portuguese in the 15th century; and with the British, the Italian and the French, etc. in the 18th and 19th centuries. With many of these European powers, Ethiopian kings and princes exchanged letters, gifts, and Ethiopian and European representatives visited each others country for further discussion and examination of the letters exchanged, refer to Rubenson, 1975, *The Survival of Ethiopian Independence;* Various studies of Tekle Sadek Mekuria, (Grahgn, Tewodros, Menelik,—all in Amarinja).

21. I referred to the modern schools as formal schools just to differentiate them from the traditional schools run especially by the Ethiopian Coptic Church for many hundreds of years. Note also that these numbers exclude schools opened by private persons, by missionaries and schools run by the Ethiopian Coptic Church.

22. See Lipsky, G., 1962, *Ethiopia: Survey of World Culture*, pp. 5-28; Markakis, J., 1974, *Ethiopia: Anatomy of Traditional Polity*, pp. 143-0182; Clapham, C., 1969, *Haile Selassie Government.*

23. Gojjam and Bale are administrative regions, while *Weyane* is a Tigrayan movement and according to Gebru Tareke (1991) it denotes statelessness with strong group solidarity.

24. Within the Tigray ruling class there were two factions. On the one hand, there was a family led by the adopted son of Emperor Yohannes, *le'ul ras* Mengesha and his son *ras* Seyum. On the other, there was Emperor Yohannes' real (biological) son, named Araya Selassie and his son *ras* Gugssa. The Haile Selassie government strategy was to play them against each other by favoring, for example, Seyum and Mengesha who were less of a threat to the crown rather than Gugssa and Aray Selassie who had a

direct claim to the throne. For further analysis see Gebru Tareke, 1991.

25. Gojjam had a regional king called Tekle Haimanot (former *ras* Adal Tessema 1873-1909) and his successors, especially his son *ras* Hailu, wanted to re-establish his rule after 1941, but this was strongly challenged by Haile Selassie.

26. Though the name of the two brothers, namely Cherri and Wako Gotu of Bale, were popularized, there were many other radical leaders like, Ibrahim Lemmu of Goba, Kahin Abdi, Mohammed Abdi of the regions of Wabe and Deno, etc.

27. The main architect of the coup was a civilian elite member by the name of Germame Neway. Germame was a political scientist from Columbia University (USA) and popularly known as able administrator. The association of this coup with the military was because of Germame's brother, General Mengistu Neway, then commander of the Imperial Bodyguard. The other key associate with the two brothers was colonel Workneh Gobeyehu, Chief of Security. These three were believed to be the ringleaders of the 1960 coup (for a detailed account. See Greenfield, 1965). For further analysis of the 1960 coup's contributions and weaknesses, see *Tatek*, April, 1970.

28. The student unions abroad not only disseminated information on poverty in Ethiopia but also provided a forum for political and socio-economic debates among the intelligentsia abroad and documented the results of the debates and other theoretical inputs in different journals such as *Tatek* (meaning get armed, a theoretical debate journal) and *ye'teglachen Zena* (News of Struggle) and *Challenge*. These journals, though printed in Europe and the USA, their destination was home. Such intensive and compact opposition activities by the Ethiopian students took place until feudalism was wiped out of the country. It is also important to note here that towards the end of the 1960s, the student movement advocated Marxist Leninism as the correct ideology to solve Ethiopian poverty. This of course could not be seen in isolation from the international socialist movement of the time that was underway in Latin America, Indo-China, Western Europe, Palestine and in the Algerian struggle for self determination.

29. A stick, because, in desperation to meet the challenge the government arrested over five hundred taxi-drivers and many other individuals. A carrot, because the king announced the suspension

of the sector review, ordered the reduction of petrol prices and increased the payment for the military first to USD 9 followed by USD 15 then USD 20 in a period of less than two months. However, all failed to convince them.

Chapter Five

THE ATTEMPT TO
ESCAPE FROM POVERTY

The main preoccupation of this chapter is to examine the major
political, economic and social changes brought by of the 1974 revolution. This is done first by examining genuine efforts to change
the living conditions of the poor, such as agrarian reform. This
chapter also makes an attempt to identify the negative impacts of
the revolution. However, it is limited to recounting the state of
affairs as they occurred. Analysis and identification of lessons
learned will be dealt with in the next chapter.

THE 1974 REVOLUTION AND ITS OUTCOME

The Ethiopian revolution attempted to bring fundamental social
transformation in three phases. The first lasted from mid-1974 to
mid-1976. This was the period marked by a search for identity, legit-
imated under slogans of *hibretesebawenet,* and *ethiopia tikdem*—meaning egalitarian socialism and Ethiopia First, respectively. It is also
worth noting here that one of the important achievements of the
revolution—land reform legislation took place in this period in
March, 1975. The second phase was when the new democratic
forces announced the National Democratic Programme (NDP), the
attempted implementation of which lasted for about two years
(1976-1978). The major characteristic of this period was its procla-

mations in favor of the people. Many of the efforts, such as organizing the peasants in local self-help administrations, also took place during this time. The final phase lasted from 1978 to 1991 and was a period characterized by a non-capitalist path of development. This was a period when the government ruled with aid from USSR, and is a period marked by the policy of collectivization.

Although I make the above distinctions for the purpose of clarity, I am not going to present a review of these periods as this has already been done in various studies. Instead, I will focus on some examples of genuine efforts undertaken to affect poverty, and also try to identify some of the bogus results.

Before going any further, let me examine, in brief, how the army, consolidated power and how the intelligentsia, especially the students, played a crucial role in bringing the revolution to rural areas and succeeded in sowing the first seeds of revolution in the history of Ethiopia.

THE ESTABLISHMENT OF THE MILITARY GOVERNMENT

Search for Ideology and Legitimacy

In forming the first armed forces committee, each army division sent representatives to the capital to create a military administrative body. Consequently, a hundred and twenty middle and lower-ranking officers, in June/July 1974, established a committee, it later became Provisional Military Council (PMC) or *derg* (which means a committee).

During the initial months of the revolution the PMC conducted the struggle which the Ethiopian students' journal referred to as a *creeping coup* (*tatek*, 1974, and 1975).[1] The armed forces however, further consolidated their position by deposing the Emperor and in September, 1975, proclaimed itself as the Provisional Military Administrative Government (PMAG). Thereafter, the *derg* abolished the crown, threw out the constitution and closed the parliament. It promised to introduce a sort of *egalitarian* socialism *(hibrete-sebawenet)* based on a somewhat vague idea of Ethiopia Forward and popularized as *ethiopia tikdem*—marked by its strong connotation of territorial nationalism.[2]

Of its own will in December 1975, the *derg* issued a ten-point program as the basis for its egalitarian socialist Ethiopia.[3] It is interesting to mention some of these points in order to form an idea of the general development of the military government. Some of these points were (a) that the Ethiopian people had hitherto been divided along ethnic lines but the Armed Forces Committee promised to do everything in their power to create a spirit of unity, equality and brotherhood, (b) that they (the *derg*) could achieve change without bloodshed, (c) that they would remove allegedly corrupt officials, (d) that they would act as a watch-dog to ensure public security and property (*Addis Zemen*, No. 505, 13 September).[4] This ten-point program contained statements against the old regime with which many Ethiopians agreed. It failed, however, to serve as a new ideology or as blueprint for what the *derg* called Ethiopia *tikdem.*[5]

Guided by its twin principles of *hibretesebawenet* and *ethiopia tikdem*, the military government nationalized many production units— ranging from small private enterprises to additional family houses. The ownership and control of important means of production were transferred from the individual to the state. According to the armed force's political proclamations (1975) *hibretesebawenet* was said to be a model of government which did not allow for personal gain and which instead, emphasized the moving priorities towards the interests of the community. The interests of the community in turn, could only be safeguarded by the government. Therefore, in its Economic Declaration of February 1975 the *derg* proclaimed

> ... those resources that are crucial for economic development and are of such a character that they promote an indispensable service to the community [are to be] transferred to government ownership (Addis Zemen No. 34/598, January 2, 1975, Proclamation of 1975, Article 4:1).

The major landmark of *hibretesebawenet* was definitely the adoption of the land proclamation in March 1975 in which private land ownership was prohibited (Proclamation No. 31 of 1975). To enforce this new land legislation and to describe the purpose of the revolution to the rural areas of Ethiopia a mobilization known as Development Through Cooperation, Enlightenment and Work Campaign locally known as *zemecha*, was launched.[6]

The main objectives of the campaign were to redistribute land, to explain, teach and propagate the tenets of *hibretesebawenet* and *ethiopia tikdem* to the rural peasantry. The *derg's* initial ideas or thoughts focused on how to "be free from age-old exploitation, corruption, selfishness, egoism," which they believed that the majority of the Ethiopian masses had been beset by for centuries.

115

The task of carrying these messages to the rural peasantry was assigned to enlightened youth in general and to students and teachers in particular. They in turn, accepted this responsibility and went out to rural Ethiopia without much hesitation.

The students became involved in the mobilization of distribution of land based on the provisions made. This first campaign or *zemecha*[7] mobilized over 60,000 university and high school students and their teachers and all were immediately dispatched throughout the rural parts of country with the task of organizing the peasants, explaining the nature of the revolution and more importantly, implementing the new land legislation.

Keep in mind that a campaign of this magnitude took place without any sort of concrete guidelines, meaningful orientation to the problems they might encounter or any preparatory training. Some students were not acquainted with life in rural areas and were generally inexperienced for an undertaking as serious as the allotment of land. As a consequence, many of the students were confronted with various difficulties and some even lost their lives. At any rate, the work of the students and others who participated in this campaign laid down the necessary corner stone for the organization of the peasants. During a short period, from January 1975 to July 1975, about four million peasants were organized into 16,000 associations. Though later on the task of redistribution of lands was performed by the peasants themselves, the first initiatives were taken by the *zemecha*, and thus it remained the first campaign of its kind in Ethiopia.

Generally speaking, the Ethiopian students were among the earliest groups advocating change. They had struggled for decades against Haile Selassie's regime and stubbornly agitating for land reform under the famous banner of "Land to the Tiller." This was one of the primary reasons as to why the students accepted the call from the *derg* and went out to rural Ethiopia. For the students, the land legislation was the noble cause for which they had sacrificed their lives fighting against the imperial forces.

Harbeson (1988:141) is right when he states, "... their loyalties [the students] were to their revolutionary ideology and to land reform, which they took as its realization, rather than to the government." When they joined the peasants they continued agitating for a civil government. As a result, they were finally labeled "enemies of the revolution" by the *derg* and exposed to terror. Against

116

this background, many were imprisoned, tortured, killed and forced to flee the country.[8]

One important point is that the students did not accept the members of the *derg* as the political leaders of Ethiopia. They joined the campaign to implement their ideas for reform issue. In this way, they were caught between the devil and the deep blue sea. On one side, they fought against the feudal landlords (when confiscating their lands for the peasants), and on the other, against the *derg* which continuously demanded recognition which the students were not willing to give. In the end, they also became victims of different political factions led by organized groups.

What I would like to underscore here is that the students seemed to live up to their word, and many proved their love for the Ethiopian peasants and did whatever possible to improve the lives of this poorest sector of Ethiopian society.[8] Another point which may also be underlined here is that the Ethiopian students were the advocates of change and the moving force behind the outbreak of the 1974 revolution. If any credit for efforts towards social change and the provision of land in Ethiopia is given, it should go to the students. The Ethiopian students then, had proved to be what Balsvik (1985) said they were, "champions of the underprivileged," an assessment with which I totally concur.

GENUINE EFFORTS

There were, initially, many genuine efforts and positive results that came out of the Ethiopian revolution. Some of are irreversible and have positively affected the lives of millions of Ethiopians. The abolition of the age-old feudal system and the distribution of land to the tillers are examples. Another major achievement of the revolution, which is difficult to quantify, is the improvement of the level of awareness of the people in general. These achievements, of course, cost many sacrifices and without exaggeration they were obtained in exchange for the lives of many young Ethiopians.

Land Legislation and the Abolition of Feudalism
In Ethiopia, where the majority of the population and the economy depend on agriculture, necessary changes for the betterment of individual life and increased well-being depend on man's relationship to land. Thus, land reform is the major tool for tackling the multiple problems of poverty.

117

In a predominantly rural society like Ethiopia, landholding determines the political, social and economic status of an individual or a family. However, prior to the revolution, the right to hold land was restricted to a selected few and thus, in order for socioeconomic reform to have any chance of success this situation must first be revolutionized. One can also argue that it is not the a succession of *first* the revolution, then the social-reforms - the social reforms *are* the revolution.

The effective launching of political, social and economic transformation therefore, called for at least two fundamental criteria to be fulfilled. First, the redistribution of land to the tillers. This in its turn, it was hoped, would bring political, social and economic equity. Second, the rural or local peasant organizations were established to implement and sustain the land provision and, ultimately to create local governments.

The shift of ownership of rural landholdings from the landowners to the real tillers was seen as a symbol of the transformation of Ethiopian society from age-old exploitation and would result in the elevation of the standard of living of the poor. Against this rationale the military government's proclamation of public ownership of rural lands in March 1975, was very much welcomed and justified. What were the aims and the contents of this land reform?

One aim of the land reform was to make all rural landholdings into the collective property of the masses. The proclamation clearly stated that "no individual or group or organization shall own land in private ownership" (*Negarit Gazeta* No. 26, 29 March, 1975).

The Ethiopian land reform of 1975, by prohibiting purchase, exchange, mortgage or lease of land, broke the old feudal character of production and called for a new social, economic and political structure. Since it broke the landlord/peasant economic relationship, it was an unquestionable blow to the feudal class and destroyed the very base on which this class was constructed. More importantly, rural lands were to be divided according to household needs irrespective of sex, religion or ethnic group. The land legislation facilitated social revolution because it supported the struggle of the landless peasants against the land owners and thus became the force of agrarian economic transformation. As Pausewang (1990:46) states, the 1975 land reform, "... did actually redistribute resources, giving peasants more to eat, by allowing them to keep

118

those parts of their produce which earlier had to be delivered to landlords."

What prompted such radical land reform in 1975? Though different reasons are given as to what prompted the revolution, generally speaking, the long-standing agitation for land to the tiller by students and many progressive individuals remains one of the primary factors. Apart from this, Kidane Mengisteab (1990:89-90) for example, points out, "The reason for this was that the urban masses and the working class were, in most cases, first-generation urban dwellers with strong ties to the peasantry." Though I agree with Kidane in principle, I would add that the first generation migrants to towns or cities are often more estranged from rural life then the second or third. For first generation migrants, everything is new, fascinating, more "civilized" and modern. Only the later generations see the disadvantages of town culture and the value in rural life.

Kidane also notes as the land question was the main focus of transformation in the south, "it was clear that the Oromo Liberation Front (OLF) was going to make the land issue a rallying point for the Oromo masses, the largest single ethnic group in the country, if the derg failed to address them." It is true that if the land reform had not been radical and geared especially to satisfy the peoples of the southern Ethiopia who, by and large, were victims of the old feudal structure, the reform would have been failure.[9]

Harbeson (1988) also reasons in the same manner when he states that the 1975 land reform was indeed the *derg's* direct response to the large-scale rallies staged for many years by university and high school students who had long struggled for the slogan of land to the tiller.[10] Therefore, the military government was well aware of these facts and addressed the issues directly. Thus, the armed force's decision with regard to land reform had the full support of the predominant sector of Ethiopian society—the peasantry. Whatever reason prompted it, the 1975 land legislation was the death blow to the feudal system of Ethiopia.

The Formation of Peasants Associations (PAs)

Following the proclamation of the public ownership of rural lands other important legislation was issued (*Proclamation No.71 of 1975*). The proclamation allowed peasants to organize and defend their rights. According to this proclamation, it was considered necessary to organize the peasants, *inter alia*, to safeguard their own interests, to make the peasants aware of their rights, to inform them of the basic need for self-administration and self-reliance and to encourage their awareness in social, political and economic issues. Having these as objectives, peasant organizations were established on the local to the national level (Chart 5:1). This, of course, created a political dilemma for the *derg* at a later stage.

The organizing of peasants into associaons was one of the significant achievements of the revolution along with the abolition of feudalism and distribution of land to the peasants. As Brune (1990) also observed, though the Ethiopian peasant organization had some resemblance to Chinese and Tanzanian peasant organizations, Ethiopia's movements were unique.

CHART 5:1
ORGANIZATIONAL STRUCTURE OF PEASANT ASSOCIATIONS: FROM VILLAGE TO NATIONAL LEVEL

All Ethiopia Peasant Associations

14 *Provincial* Level Executive PAs
|
102 *Awraja* Level Executive PAs
|
571 *Woreda* Level Executive PAs
|
23,500 *Kebele* Level PAs
|

Grassroot sub-committees: Producer and Service co-operatives, Women and Youth Associations, Judicial Tribunes, Revolutionary Squads, Resettled Societies, etc.

Since peasant settlements tend to be dispersed, associations consisted of about two hundred households, in an area of eight hundred hectares. This figure appears to be *arbitrary* as there was not enough arable land for this number of households. Almost all adults became members of the peasant association in their jurisdiction. These members constituted the assembly which became the only legal body for the election of its executive committee at all levels. The term of holding office for elected administrative members was two years.

The organizational structure of the peasant associations, extended from the village level (formerly called *cheka* later *kebele*)[11] to the national level. The total number of PAs in all the *kebele* were

about 24,000 in 1981, i.e. they comprised over seven million households or around thirty five million people (Chart 5:1).

The real foundation of the organizational capacity of the peasants lies in the various grassroots committees in their respective
kebele (Chart 5:1). From the level of the *kebele*, in the next hierarchi-
cal level upwards there were five hundred seventy one sub-regions
called *woreda*; above which were a hundred and two administrative
regions called *awraja*. These were succeeded by fourteen provincial
or *kefle hager* levels, and finally, the national level called—All
Ethiopian Peasant Association (AEPA) (Table 5:1).

TABLE 5:1
NUMBER OF PEASANT ASSOCIATIONS, THEIR MEMBERS PER HOUSEHOLD AND AVERAGE MEMBERS PER ASSOCIATION, BY REGION, 1976

Region	Association	Members	Average Members
Arssi	1,104	256,384	232
Bale	793	110,792	140
Gamo Goffa	281	96,151	342
Gojjam	1,828	316,004	173
Begemder	1,672	266,348	159
Harar	1,807	549,495	304
IllLubabor	1,008	176,342	175
Kaffa	1,571	385,161	245
Shoa	4,450	1,029,136	231
Sidamo	1,497	619,461	414
Tigray	1,289	380,071	295
Wollega	2,007	372,737	186
Wollo	2,191	557,110	254
Total	21,498	5,115,192	242

Source: Ethiopian Ministry of Agriculture, 1981.

At the *kebele* level a major task of the peasant organization was, to
execute land reform legislation by distributing land among themselves, to administer and conserve public properties within their
jurisdiction, to collect taxes, fees and tributes, to establish and execute judicial tribunes in matters especially dealing with land reform
and local disputes, to organize and manage co-operatives (producer as well as service co-operatives), organize and support women's
associations, youth associations and defense squads. Later on these
organized bodies were forced to participate in the different collec-
tivatization programs. More importantly, with regard to the powers

and duties of peasant associations the purpose of the proclamation was:

> ... to enable peasants to secure and safeguard their political, economic and social rights, to administer itself, [and] to participate in all activities concerning the development, etc. (Proclamation No.71, *Negarit Gazeta*, 14 December, 1975).

The All Ethiopia Peasant Association (AEPA), was initially established to coordinate the different activities of peasant associations at all administrative levels (vertically and horizontally), to coordinate the work of peasant bodies with government institutions, and above all to seek ways and means by which self-government and self-reliance on the part of peasantry could be implemented and sustained in rural areas.

The Declaration of the National Democratic Program

One of the basic ideological underpinnings of the Ethiopian revolution was the proclamation of the National Democratic Revolution Program of (NDRP) of April 1976. This program, though short-lived, provided a clear ideological rationale for the Ethiopian revolution.

Upon the introduction of this program, all earlier confused and generalized terms such as Ethiopian socialism or *hibretesebawenet* and other political jargon was avoided. The aims and immediate tasks of the revolution were explicitly defined as were the primary and secondary problems. The "enemies" of the Ethiopian revolution were identified as "feudalism, imperialism and bureaucratic capitalism," and the "friends" as "the broad peasantry, the working class and the left intelligentsia" (NDRP, 1976). The latter are encouraged and supported to establish an alliance and form a common and united front against the former. In the immediate tasks section of the National Democratic Revolution Program it was stated that:

> The revolution can advance forward only if the popular masses are made politically conscious, and are organized and armed. But in order to do all these all sectors of the oppressed classes must be furnished with the opportunity to learn, to teach, to organize and be organized (*Negarit Gazeta*, No.26 1976).

It must be stressed here that the National Democratic Revolution Program called for a political and economic struggle against what it called the primary enemies of the Ethiopian people. It focused on the common cause against domestic political and economic struggle and adopted a position against injustices imposed by external forces. This attempt avoided ethnically-based political and economic conflicts on the home front, which could perhaps have changed the course of the social revolution. It is also important to note that the program's main focus on political transformation was based on the rights of different political groups to organize themselves and openly participate in the social transformation. In this context the program states,

> For all these it is imperative to put into practice unrestricted exercise of democratic rights for all anti-feudal and anti-bureaucratic capitalist forces. These forces will be immediately accorded full freedom to speak, to write, to assemble, to demonstrate peacefully, to organize and be organized...therefore, all progressive forces will be accorded the freedom to organize and be organized in political parties and in mass organizations (*Negarit Gazeta*, No. 26, 1976).

However, it has to be stressed here that the NDRP only embraced, what was called "the friends of the revolution" namely, those who were defined as anti-feudal, anti-bureaucratic capitalist and anti-imperialist forces by the program. Generally speaking, the NDRP, was important because it not only cleared up the ideological ambiguity of the *derg* like, *hibretesebawenet, ethiopia tikdem* (Ethiopia First) etc, but it also laid the groundwork for the civil-military alliances which played significant roles in the overall development of the revolution.

The First Civil-Military Alliance

Mid-1975 to early 1976 was full of uncertainty and confusion, created by the political power vacuum left after the Emperor. Internal and external struggles intensified and various internal civilian groups on one hand, and external powers on the other, tried to pull the *derg* towards their respective sides and all found ways and means of inducing the *derg* to take their advice.

In early 1976, after the triumph of one wing in the struggle within the *derg* the first civilian military alliance began. The members of the *derg* who emerged on top in this internal power struggle sought to carry out sound and populist measures that would influence the people and thereby win support. In an effort to accomplish this, the *derg* called for the support of both politically organized and unorganized leftist intellectuals.[12] Some groups responded to the call and agreed to set up a politburo, A Provisional Office for Mass Organization Affairs (POMOA). POMOA was established by the *derg* in May 1976. It consisted of about fifteen left-wing intellectuals, including some representatives from the *derg* itself. Its main tasks were to gain a better grip on the ideology of socialism, to replace the ambiguous idea of egalitarianism or *hibrtesebawenet* with tangible ideas, organize, politicize, and produce politically-conscious cadres. To these ends a political school—a cadre training center—was opened under the guidance of POMOA.[13]

It was at this juncture that some left-wing intellectual groups such, as The All Ethiopia Socialist Movement (AESM, or locally known as *meison,* decided to ally themselves with the armed forces. This alliance was based, according to the groups, on the principle of *critical support*—which simply meant to create a temporary alliance to advance the revolution as long as the *derg* followed the general popular line.[14] For the *derg,* this alliance meant it could come out of its isolation and also receive services from these intellectuals.

The politburo drafted the National Democratic Program in April 1976, and this provided the required guidelines for the revolution. In so doing, the intellectuals in the politburo became directly accountable for many of the popular declarations issued until 1978. However, this does not necessarily imply that the groups were whole-heartedly in favor of the *derg.*[15] As Ottaway notes,

> ...their [civilian members of the politburo] relationship to the Military Government was similar to that of the students. They were radical intellectuals who disliked the military and had agreed to collaborate with it in the hope of eventually being able to seize power (Ottaway, 1990:177).

It may be added here that the civilian groups in the politburo indeed disliked the *derg.* For instance, they did not refer to their co-operation with the *derg,* as an ally or as a collaborator, as Ottaway stated, nor did they say they had merged with the *derg* as many mistakenly imply. To them, their co-operation was only what they called *critical support* and did not admit full support for the *derg* to maintain and sustain political power over the Ethiopian people.

Be that as it may, the alliance showed both positive and negative aspects. Positive because it accomplished many popular provisions in a short span of time that could otherwise have taken many years. Negative because it marked a major watershed between the various factions of the Ethiopian left-wing intellectuals, especially between the AESM and the Ethiopian People Revolutionary Party (EPRP)[16] both of whom had, for over two decades, struggled together against the old regime of Haile Selassie (under the banner of land to the tiller). Ultimately, not only did both left-oriented organizations became victim of the Military Government, but their disputes caused the revolution to be diverted in a direction that both organizations did not want.

At a later stage, four allied civilian organizations including a part of the *derg*, tried to establish a front[16] against EPRP, and also aimed at the establishment of an alternative political leadership but it failed. It failed because (a) the *derg* was not willing to step down from its position and (b) the intelligentsia outside the *derg* had disintegrated. The intelligentsia, in turn, failed to stand against the *derg* because of its internal weakness and the severe repression imposed on them from the *derg*. Ultimately, the most severe blow to both EPRP and AESM came from the *derg's* new ally, the Soviet Union.

This failure to provide an alternative leadership on the part of the intelligentsia, brought a chaotic situation which lead the armed forces to apply mass extermination known as the Red Terror in the major cities and towns of the country (from the end of 1977 through 1978). The *derg* was determined to silence all opposition forces. House-to-house searches took place and anyone who opposed the military regime was either shot on the spot or thrown into prison without any due process of law. Thus, many of the democratic forces/opposition groups were forced to go underground. Many joined the various liberation fronts, some fled the country, others went underground and many others languished in the crude jails of the military junta. From this historical turning point onwards the military ruling clique began to follow a non-capitalist model of development led by the Soviet Union and the Eastern European states.

BOGUS RESULTS

Impacts of Foreign Intervention and Civil-Wars
Ethiopia had been one of the strongest allies of the USA and remained under America's sphere of influence for over three decades, from early 1950 till the outbreak of the 1974 revolution.

The Soviet Union's entry into Ethiopia was accentuated by the war between Somalia and Ethiopia (1977/78) over the Ogaden region. In 1977 Ethiopia and Somalia went to war, the Soviets took an active part in support of the Ethiopian regime and gained much influence in the country.[17] One example may illustrate this point. In the Higher Committee for the National Defense of Ethiopia (also called the Supreme Military Strategic Committee—SMSC), there were eight Soviet officers, three Cubans and seven Ethiopians (Kessing Archives, 1978). Because the regime was forced to rely heavily on the Soviet and its allies' resources to sustain itself in power, the *derg*, as shown above, became a minority in its own government's military committee that influenced the direction of its war. It was really amazing to consider how the Soviet Union, which had helped the Eritrean secessionist in the northern part of Ethiopia for far more than a decade and had supported the Republic of Somalia in its territorial claims over the Ogaden region of Ethiopia, did an about face overnight and stood on the side of the Ethiopian armed forces against its two former clients.[18]

Their strategy was simple. It was to gain better control over the horn of Africa and ensure a central position in African affairs, to which Ethiopia had access. Following this line, the Soviets leadership worked hard to consolidate its grip on the *derg* and made sure that the *derg* remained under their control for a long time. After that, the leadership of the USSR persuaded the *derg* to make a fundamental change in the political transformation of the country, towards the socialism. This process did not take place under Russians influence alone, but with the help of a portion of the intelligentsia.[19]

The Second Civil-Military Alliance and the Deterioration of the Political Situation

After the failure of the first attempt to create a government with the members of the different political organizations connected with the politburo, the *derg* looked for another opportunity. This was a second attempt, but this time with the help of the Soviet Union and its trained cadres. For this to happen the *derg* established the Committee for Organizing the Party of the Working People of Ethiopia (COPWE) in 1979. The purpose of COPWE was to play the role of the former politburo, which was dissolved after the collapse of the first alliance between the military and the left-wing intelligentsia. COPWE also took on the task of preparing the Ethiopian people for the creation of a socialist party.

The Attempt to Escape From Poverty

It is important to bear in mind that there were fundamental differences between the politburo from the first civil-military alliance and what was called the committee for organizing the party, which I here refer to as the second civil-military alliance. The former incorporated civilian groups of left-wing intellectuals who tried to build a democratic state in Ethiopia based on the principle of the existence of democratic opposition forces (a civilian government with the help of military rule). In contrast, the committee for organizing the workers party (COPWE), was dominated by officers and advocated democratic-centralism under one party. In practice, the latter served against civilian rule in favor of military dictatorship.

COPWE's primary task was to dissolve all semi-open and clandestine political organizations and thus become the major policy-making body, with a small group of closely-knit military officers and Soviet advisers wielding the real power. It was carefully tailored to suit to the Soviet model. COPWE adopted an organizational structure that comprised a general assembly, a central committee, and an executive committee. The executive committee, acting as a politburo, replaced the *derg*'s standing committee and became the real source of power in Ethiopia. The central committee and its alternates acted as a quasi legislative body, giving rubber stamp approval to executive committee decisions (New Africa, 1982). Other forms of decentralized power, for example, regional representation and grass-roots participation, at least on paper, were assured within the structure, but were never practiced. In short, as Harbeson (1988:180) states, COPWE "... was an instrument for introducing some measures of civilians rule on the basis of established military foundations."

Most of the key positions in COPWE were divided among the former *derg* members. For instance, former *derg* position holders all became members of the central committee of COPWE too. All in all, of ninety-three available posts in the central committee, military personnel took seventy-nine seats. According to the report of the first assembly proceedings, (1979) except for those officers holding military command positions, the military titles of other members of COPWE were replaced by civilian names (Generals, Colonels, Corporals, etc., became prime ministers and deputy ministers, political commissioners, governors, experts and resource persons in various political, social and economic fields). Thus by 1979, COPWE had in practice assumed the functions of a party in its own right. As the New African Year book (1981/82:18) puts it, "...thus far from representing the civilian masses, COPWE simply reflected the existing military dominance."

Later on, when the establishment of the Workers' Party and The Socialist Republic of Ethiopia was made public (1984) it was by and large, composed of the same members of COPWE (that is to say, the former *derg*) who had successfully transformed themselves into the new role of leaders of The Socialist Republic of Ethiopia. What, then, were their policies for poverty?

The *derg*, in its own way, had made efforts to change the situation in Ethiopia. It had made numerous efforts in urban as well as rural areas. The concern of this study is only to focus on rural areas.

RURAL TRANSFORMATION THROUGH COLLECTIVIZATION

The non-capitalist or the socialist oriented path of development through the use of collectivization as means of "socialist" transformation was believed to fundamentally alter the old Ethiopian political and socio-economic system. Collectivization comprised here, (a) co-operatives and state farm schemes, (b) villagization (inter-regional settlement), and (c) resettlement (intra-regional settlement) programs. It must be stated from the outset that though, for the sake of clarity, (a), (b), and (c) are described separately, they all are integral parts of the collectivization program having their roots in the non-capitalist theory and practices of development. A brief review, is presented below.

Co-operative and State Farms
Versus Household Farms

In the land legislation and its consolidation proclamation (*Proclamations No.31 and No.71 of 1975*) the need for and the importance of co-operatives and state farms were clearly stated. However, except for modest mention of co-operatives, it was the peasant associations and household farming that were mainly encouraged in the period prior to 1978.

Thereafter, the military government regarded cooperatives and state farms as essential components of further transformation to socialist oriented agricultural production. In light of this, a good number of different co-operatives were introduced. A few among them were agricultural producer and service co-operatives, artisan producers, savings and credit, housing co-operatives etc. Service cooperatives mainly bought and distributed consumer goods and production inputs, provided facilities for grain storage, gave services in mills and instruments of productions and ran retail shops where the peasants bought their daily consumption items. However, agricultural co-operatives referred to also as *producer co-operatives* are the main subject of discussion below.

Producer Co-operatives

The first proclamation establishing producer co-operatives was issued in 1978. The proclamation stated that the goal is "to put the means of production under the control of the masses through organized form ... and transform them gradually to collective property" (*Negarit Gazeta, Proclamation No.130 of 1978*). Thereafter, co-operatives were considered to be the major instruments through which socialist transformation could be achieved. Economically, co-operatives were taken as shortcuts to increased agricultural production, expanded industry, and accumulated capital—all through mobilization of rural resources. Ideologically, co-operatives were identified as vehicles for accelerating socialist orientation and raising the political awareness of the peasantry.

Later on, to strengthen the progress of socialist transformation, three stages of development of producer co-operatives were introduced. Stage one, was called *meleba*—this was the primary stage of co-operative development, where the majority of arable land and oxen could be pooled together for the common use of the co-operatives. In this initial stage of socialist orientation, private ownership of oxen, small agricultural tools and a piece of land for family use remained in the hands of the household. In the second stage, *welba*, distribution of production was based on socialist principle of *from each according to his ability, to each according to his work*. In this stage members were asked to transfer all their major tools of production to the co-operatives as their common property. In the third stage, *weland*, the co-operatives were expected to attain an advanced, socialist technological level and be transformed into large-scale, mechanized agricultural production units (Fassil Gebre Kiros, 1982). In brief, these were the stages of agrarian development set forth by the government as a path to the socialist transformation of Ethiopia.[20]

The co-operative farms were the *derg*'s favored agricultural organizations. This is evident when examining the facilities the state agricultural sector enjoyed viz credits at low rates of interest, fertilizer supplies, oxen, improved seeds and extension services which were easily available for co-operative societies (Cohen and Isaksson 1986, Dessalegn Rahmato, 1982 and 1984; Kidane Mengisteab, 1990; Alemneh Dejene, 1990). Of the total amount of fertilizers nearly 90 percent went to the co-operatives while only less than 10 percent was allotted to household farms in all the administrative regions except in Gomo Goffa and Harar, where household farms acquired over 50 percent fertilizers. One of the reasons perhaps was that, in these two regions, there were less registered co-operatives (Kidane Mengisteab, 1960:150).

As all the sources named above agree, in spite of all this support, production from co-operatives accounted for only 2-4 percent of total food production. In contrast, over 94 percent of food grain production were provided by smallholders (Table 5:2).

TABLE 5:2
PERCENTAGE DISTRIBUTION OF TOTAL CULTIVATED AREA,
TOTAL YEARLY CROPS PRODUCTION AND TOTAL YIELD BY TYPE
OF FARM, 1979/80 - 1985/86

	Private farms	State farms	Co-op farms
Area (hectares)			
Cereals	94.7	2.8	2.5
Pulses	97	0.5	2.5
Others	90.4	5.6	4
All Crops	94.8	2.6	2.6
Output (quintals)			
Cereals	94.1	4.2	1.7
Pulses	98.4	0.2	1.4
Others	94.5	3.3	2.2
All Crops	94.6	3.7	1.7
Yield (quintal/hectare)			
Cereals	11	15	8
Pulses	10	3	5
Others	4	2	2
All Crops	11	7	7

Source: Compiled from *Statistical Bulletin* 56, Tables 1-15, 1987, Addis Ababa, Ethiopia. One quintal is about 100 kg.

State Farms

The other means of transforming the socio-economic situation of Ethiopia was through *state farms*. State farms were also favored and encouraged by the *derg*. For instance, prior to nationalization (1975/76) state farms covered an area of around 70,000 hectares. Less than three years after nationalization they covered an area of between 200,000 and 245,000 hectares (Brune, 1990; Cohen and Isaksson 1986). From 1980 onwards the average annual expense of the state farm was recorded as 80 million *birr* (USD 1=2.07 *birr* then).

The Attempt to Escape From Poverty

The bulk of what is known as the state farms today were first owned by private individuals of both local and foreign origin as commercial farms, but after 1974 all were nationalized by the *derg*. These commercial farms were situated in rain rich, fertile areas and had better access to local as well as international markets. Moreover, they were relatively mechanized, farming fields acquainted with modern agricultural techniques and produced both cash and consumption grains. After nationalization these farms were directly transferred to government undertakings and became state farms (Haile Yesus Abegaz, 1982).

Kidane Mengisteab (1990) revealed that in 1981/1982 state farms were allocated over 94.8 percent of improved seeds and 80 percent of all the agricultural credit facilities (1990:148). On top of all these advantages of availability of fertilizers, expertise, mechanization etc. the state-owned Agricultural Marketing Corporation (AMC), which was the sole buyer of all agricultural produce, paid over 50 percent more for production from state farms than from private farmers. The wonder is, despite all this support, state farm production never rose above 2-4 percent of total food production (Brune, 1990) (Table 5:2).

Peasant Household Farms
With the establishment of government sponsored cooperatives and strong state farms the *derg* began to shift away from the traditional household/family type of farming, which was mainly based on free and independent peasant associations. This shift was a political priority rather than a decision based on productivity. The two state sponsored undertakings were taken as socialist path prototypes and thus simply awarded special favor.

Household farms, meanwhile, were neglected. As Desalegn Rahmato (1984); Kidane Mengisteab (1990); Brune, (1990); and many other's findings reveal, household or family farms were clearly discriminated against and discouraged in the "socialist" agricultural development strategy of the Military Government. Despite the poor support by the state, family farm performances were much better than the two state sponsored activities, as is shown in Table 5:2.

Household farms achievements with regard to working on areas of thousands of arable hectares (94.8 percent), in producing thousands of quintals of food grain (94.6 percent) and better productivity per hectare (11 quintals of grains per hectare) proved that household farming performances were much better than state sponsored ones.

Peasant household farms, also produced far greater yields of essential food grains like *teff* (staple crop), sorghum pulses and oilseeds

131

in absolute terms than the state farms—not to mention the cata-strophic agricultural performances of the co-operatives. However, it should be noted that due to the high degree of mechanization and the generous application of fertilizers state farm's yields of barley, maize and wheat per hectare were better than that of household farms.

It also became evident that in such a socialist transformation—through huge state sponsored cooperatives and mechanized farms—greater human as well as financial resources were required. To meet this demand villagization and resettlement schemes were introduced.

Objectives and Extent of Villagization
In pre-Revolutionary Ethiopia, villagization within rural areas was practiced on a modest and small-scale basis. Groups of families or individuals moved to new places, say from densely to sparsely popu-lated and fertile areas. However, movements were small in number, on a voluntary basis and usually initiated by local authorities, families or individuals. The main reasons for internal migration prior to 1974 were economic preferences or other advantages as seen through the eyes of the individuals or member of the families concerned. However, after the *derg* became convinced that agrarian reform was only possible with collectivization, villagization became an integral part of the socialist transformation.

TABLE 5:3
NUMBER OF NEW SITES OR CENTERS, VILLAGIZED
HOUSEHOLDS AND POPULATION BY REGIONS, 1987

Region	New Sites or Centers	Villagized Household	Total Population
Arssi	1,160	181,850	1,002,819
Bale	562	129,283	851,974
Gamo Goffa	41	4,175	15,068
Gojjam	1,221	97,445	501,137
Begemder	296	7,642	31,675
Harar	3,466	416,809	2,212,839
Illubabor	876	51,607	56,341
Kaffa	1,097	78,199	397,814
Shoa	3,130	170,293	719,458
Sidamo	76	19,222	86,433
Wollega	1,106	46,524	211,905
Wollo	52	1,491	3,200
Total	13,083	1,204,540	6,290,663

Source: Kirsch, et al., 1989:115.

The official objectives for villagization were (a) to increase agricultural productivity through enhanced extension services, promote land-use knowledge and conserve natural resources, (b) to build rural socialist societies by providing access to schools, clinics, safe drinking water and (c) to provide *security for the local people* who were threatened by the Somali invasion (Dawit Wolde Giorgis, 1989).[21] By late 1985, villagization schemes were extended to over eight of the administrative regions. It was only thereafter that the government officially disclosed that it intended to escalate the scheme to a nationwide villagization program in which over thirty three million rural people would be villagized in less than a decade (Cohen and Isaksson, 1986). Consequently, by 1986 more than five million people, 15 percent of the country's total rural population, had been displaced from their original villages.

Later, when Ethiopia was said to be transformed into a socialist state (1984), the scheme was already on a scale never before seen or practiced on the continent of Africa. For instance by the end of 1989 more than twelve million people (about one third of Ethiopia's rural inhabitants) were displaced from their original settlements into new villages (Alemayehu Lirenso, 1990, and Table 5:3 clearly shows the magnitude of this program).

The Resettlement Program and its Rationale

Prior to the 1974 revolution, under the Third Five Year Plan (1968-1973), over seven thousand households were resettled in twenty resettlement sites. The cost of this undertaking was said to be MUSD 8 million (Alula Pankhurst, 1990). Compared to the military government's resettlement program in later years this pales in significance.

The first large-scale resettlement program in Ethiopia was motivated and designed purely from a famine rehabilitation view point and began after the famine of 1973/1974. This program was supposed to resettle a population of approximately 520,000 over a period of ten years, but by 1983 only 103,500 persons, or 31,506 households (Eshetu Chole and Teshome Mulat, 1988) had been relocated.

Later on, the resettlement program was found to be essential, not only for famine rehabilitation programs but also for many other reasons such as (a) redistributing population from densely overcrowded areas to sparsely populated areas, (b) redistributing underutilized and unused land to new land hungry labor forces, (c) checking ecological imbalance through the control of land degradation, (d) changing the life of pastorals by making them settler agriculturists and (e) controlling the recurrent famines (Dieci et. al 1992).

The largest resettlement program according to Cohen and Isaksson (1986) was disclosed in November 1984, when the government declared its intention of resettling about two million famine affected rural people.[22] This plan envisioned moving over 200,000 settlers per year at a cost of hundreds of millions US dollars (Alula, Pankrust, 1990). One year after this declaration the *derg* "succeeded" in resettling some 600,000 people in the regions of Kaffa, Illubabor and Wollega.

The fully-fledged integration of resettlement programs however, was intensified upon the establishment of the Working Party of Ethiopia in 1984. Thereafter, the tasks of resettlement together with villagization, were definitely confirmed as integral parts of the socialist transformation of Ethiopia. Shortly after the creation of this party, a budget of 123 million Eth. *birr* was set, and the party's cadres fully assumed the task of organizing, financing and directing the resettlement program (Alula Pankrust 1990; Dawit Wolde Giorgis, 1989).

The structure of the resettlement program according to Alula Pankrust (1990) was twofold—conventional and integrated. Alemayehu Lirenso (1990), however, argues that it can be seen in three distinct forms: large-scale, integrated and low-cost schemes. However, leaving aside the low-cost schemes, which were very few in number and more or less merged with the new ones, what are left—are two settlement schemes, conventional (large-scale) and integrated.

Conventional schemes accounted for 53 percent of the total resettlement programs and were implemented in the fertile low lands of Gojjam, Illubabor and Wollega. The settlements were equipped with mechanized agricultural instruments. They had tractor services and the use of chemical fertilizers. In these settlements new reclamation of large estates were common. Each resettlement site, for example, contained 10–20,000 households and the settlers lived in relatively well-built houses. Moreover, they had on-site extension staff, better health care facilities and more food. There were nearby schools, shops and mills, craft workshops and cultural centers. The people were organized in co-operatives and were led by political cadres. This could be proof that conventional schemes were really designed as prototypes or examples of socialist villages.

In comparison, integrated settlement schemes were located in the Highlands of Kaffa, Illubabor and Wollega. The settlements were scattered and comprised 44 percent of the total resettlement scheme.[23] Integrated resettlement schemes were smallholdings, not mechanized and predominantly using oxen for ploughing. Settlement sizes were small and members were widely dispersed. Each settlement site comprised about fifty households. The dwellers lived in low quality huts and had no special services. They had less food and were organized under the leadership of peasant associations.

CONCLUSION

It is true that, in the earlier stages of the revolution, many positive political and economic decisions were taken by the military government. Among the measures taken—the abolition of the feudal system, the 1975 land reform and the establishment of peasant associations (PAs) were credits on the *derg's* account.

The political transformation sought to operate under the National Democratic Program and attempted to address many questions posed by the revolution it did, however, possess shortcomings. First, though it had raised the right of nationalities to self-government (regional autonomy), it seemed to fail to suggest a proper mechanism for implementing its own recommendations.[24] Later on the *derg* found the NDP to be too radical and replaced it with non-capitalist path of development which was of an altogether different orientation and strongly influenced by the ex-Soviet Union.

The implementation of non-capitalist path gave legitimacy to the creation of a military dictatorship under a cover name of Workers Party of Ethiopia. The policies of this party as applied in collectivization produced bogus results. The priorities given to state sponsored co-operative and state farm were lop-sided, and the performance of the co-operatives especially were catastrophic. In the villagization and resettlement programs, for example, over six million peasants were displaced and for many life was completely altered. The program disoriented and disengaged the use of local knowledge and traditional practices.

Lastly, though the Ethiopian revolution was initially positive in its political achievements, abolished the old feudal system and yet, its efforts towards agrarian reform have not helped reduce poverty or check the people's chronic problems famine and meeting basic needs, even after two decades of application.

NOTES

1. An early assessment of the revolution was made by the journal of the Ethiopian students in Europe, *tatek*, in two volumes, June 1974 and October, 1975 (Hamle, 1966 and Tekemet, 1967 Ethiopian Calendar) under the pen Feleke Ewnetu, who was the late Haile Fidda, one of the central leaders of the All Ethiopia Socialist Movement.

2. A deep-going ideological debate had been put forward both by The All Ethiopia Socialist Movements (AESM) in its organ *Voice of the Masses (ye'sefew hizb demt)*, especially in No. 10, 22 October, 1974 and No. 19, 27 January, 1975, citing the essential differences between what was called then Ethiopian socialism *(hibrtesebawenet)* and scientific socialism. The Ethiopian Revolutionary Party (EPRP) had also often commented at length on *derg's* ideological vagueness in reference to *hibrtesebawenet and ethiopia tikdem* (see *Democracia*, No.20, 25 September, 1974). For a comprehensive analysis of the differences between *derg's* socialism and scientific socialism see also *Tatek*, No.1, December, 1976 (all in Amharic).

3. Revolutionary Party (EPRP) had also often commented at length on *derg's* ideological vagueness in reference to *hibrtesebawenet and ethiopia tikdem* (See *Democracia*, No. 20, 25 September, 1974).

4. For a comprehensive analysis of the differences between *derg's* socialism and scientific socialism. See also *Tatek*, No.1, December, 1976 (all in Amharic).

5. At this point the ideas of the armed forces did not contain any concrete political or economic policies. One simple example may serve to illustrate this. After deposing the Emperor, a highly placed military officer was asked by an international journalist what kind of policy or principles the *derg* was following. The person answered that their policies were based on their ideology, which was mainly *anti-communistic, anti-imperialistic, anti-capitalistic and anti-socialistic*. In stating this, the representative of the *derg* had neither left room for any existing ideology and political guidelines nor brought forth a new one. For a critical review

of the *derg's* ideology and "scientific socialism" see *Tatek*, No.1, December, 1976.

6. Proclamation of Development Through Campaign Programme, November, 1975.

7. From this period onwards, Mengistu (head of the state and the military force) ordered many campaigns (*zemecha*) and somehow seemed to enjoy huge displacement of men and resources. A point made by Dawit in regard to Mengistu's love of campaigns runs like this: "Mengistu loves campaigning, and this was something he could sink his teeth into—creating new committees and agencies, launching campaigns [and] emergency measures that would mobilize the entire nation with himself at the top" (1989:290). Since the land reform was so radical even to the people of Southern Ethiopia many accepted it with joy and acclamations.

8. The students openly fought with the landlords, in some areas even against their own parents and relatives. This genuine commitment of the Ethiopian students especially from the late 1960s and the 1970s will no doubt be noted in history with honor and it always remain in the minds and hearts of any student of agrarian reform in Ethiopia in general and the peasants in particular.

9. Since the land reform was so radical, to the people of southern Ethiopia, it was accepted with joy and acclamation.

10. Pausewang (1990) also argues in the same vein in his several studies including his article - *meret le arrashu*, see Ethiopia: Rural development Options, 1990:38-48.

11. *Cheka* was the lowest administrative unit in rural areas. Today it is common to use the term *kebele* instead of *Cheka* both in urban as well as rural areas.

12. In fact some of them were personally approached by the then vice-chairman of the *derg*, Colonel Mengistu.

13. The members of the politburo were both members of political organizations and independent individuals. For example, among the fifteen members—four were from All Ethiopia Socialist Movement; two from The Ethiopian Oppressed People's Revolutionary Struggle *(Echat)*; four from Revolutionary Flame *(seded*—members of the *derg)* and five independent individual members. The other major left-wing intellectual group organized as the Ethiopian People's

Revolutionary Party (EPRP) categorically rejected the idea of the alliance with the armed forces.

14. For a detailed discussion on "critical support" and more events in the Ethiopian revolution refer to *AESM's Struggle in the Ethiopian Revolution, 1989*, unpublished document (in Amharic).

15. Many of the progressive proclamations made during the early stages of the revolution were later on reversed by the *derg*.

16. The difference between AESM and EPRP began in the early 1970s in student organizations in Europe and North America and was then transported to Ethiopia. For a background and detailed account of their differences see the journal, *teglachen* under a tilled "Our Differences" *(leu'netachen);* then the same journal No.1, and No.2 January 1976; No.1. October, 1977 (AESM's version) and a response to it, by EPRP was entitled "Our Line" *(mesmerachen)* in *teglachen*, March, 1974 No.3 and No. 2 October, 1975 (EPRP's version). This alliance was between left organizations—*meison, echat, seded,* The Ethiopian Marxist-Leninist Revolutionary Organization *(malerid)* and The Workers League *(Woz)*. The front or alliance also had a common publication (gazette) called *Voice of Unity (ye'hibret demt)*. What happened was the Revolutionary Flame *(seded)* succeeded in eliminating most of the leaders of other political groups, banned their organizations, and advocated a one party system á la Soviet. Finally *seded* (1984) transformed itself into the Working Party of Ethiopia.

17. Soviet aid—which included 80 aircraft, 600 tanks, and 300 Armed Personnel Carriers (APC) had an estimated value of USD 1,000. In a matter of months this amount, for example, surpassed the total sum of US aid to Ethiopia over a period of twenty-five years. One-fourth of this total military aid was a grant, and a small part was reportedly financed by the Libyan Government—the rest is debt. As a result by the mid-1980, the total value of debt to be repaid in hard currency, became equivalent to MUSD 1,700. In the same period Ethiopia was repaying an additional commercial debt equivalent to MUSD 30 to the Soviet Union for other items such as cranes and trucks *(Ethiopia : A Country Study,* 1980:262).

18. During the 1978 conflict which was started by the Somali leader General Said Barre and the Ethiopian leader Colonel Mengistu, the leadership of the Soviet Union persuaded its allies Cuba, South Yemen and East Germany to contribute

material, financial and human resources to Ethiopia against its former ally, the government of Somalia.

19. Soviet documents appeared first in 1979 for establishing the Committee for Organizing the Party of the Working People of Ethiopia (COPWE). The revised version appeared in 1984 establishing the Working Party of Ethiopia (WPE). The final document was adopted on the ten year anniversary of the revolution and upon the establishment of the military dominated party (September, 1984), and thereafter it became the first basic "constitution" to legitimate Mengistu's first Socialist Military Government of the Republic of Ethiopia.

20. A detailed account of producer co-operatives is found in Producer Co-operatives Guide, June, 1979, Addis Ababa, (in Amharic). A summary of this guide is reported in Fassil G. Kiros, "Mobilizing the Peasantry for Rural Development—the Ethiopian Experiment in Progress, a paper presented at the Seventh International Conference of Ethiopian Studies held in Lund, Sweden, 1982.

21. The villagization program of the *derg* started long before the outbreak of war between Somalia and Ethiopia and about one million people were already settled in new villages in the regions of Bale and Harar.

22. According to Dawit Wolde Giorgis, in the earlier plan of 1984 Mengistu decided to move 300,000 households (about one and half million people) from Wollo and Tigray alone to southwestern Ethiopia in a nine-month period.

23. The remaining 3 percent of the resettlements were mixed with the old settlement sites in different locations.

24. An example of this may be the options of federal, confederated or local governments for decentralized political power, but these were overshadowed by the debate focused mainly on "territorial integrity."

Chapter Six

LESSONS OF EXPERIENCE FROM THE ETHIOPIAN REVOLUTION

The attempts made to bring forth socio-economic transformation in Ethiopia through the reformation of landholding and the creation of independent peasant organizations have been presented in the preceding chapters. The *derg's* decision to facilitate change through collectivization is also discussed. The task of this chapter is to assess the impact of these efforts, which once sought to reduce poverty. The scrutiny below focus on (a) land legislation and problem of its implementation, (b) state domination of local self-help organizations, (c) impacts of collectivization, (d) parastatal monopoly, (e) lack of accountability and transparency and finally, (f) crisis in ideology and leadership. In reading through this chapter, bear in mind that the experiences recounted below are the results of genuine efforts of the people, though the *derg* played fast and loose in its application of the non-capitalist path of development.

LAND LEGISLATION AND PROBLEMS OF IMPLEMENTATION

One of the shortcomings of the land legislation, as earlier pointed out, was that it allowed access to rural land without permitting the right of the peasants to privately possess or individually own land.[1]

Secondly, the statement in the legislation, which says that *"land remains the collective property of the Ethiopian people"* (*Negarit Gazeta No. 26, 29 March, 1975*) was ambiguous since the proclamation did not go any further and elaborate how this collective ownership of land would affect peasant landholding. The other side of the same argument is that individual farmers had no fixed agreement or contract with the state to guarantee his landholding, which left peasants at the mercy of the government. This allowed the military government to experiment with state sanctioned collectivization at a later stage, regardless of how the peasants felt. Moreover, as Tenker Bonger (1994) notes, the failure of the legislation in prohibiting the hiring of agricultural laborers made rural labor mobility inflexible. The unemployed labor force in the north, for example, could not be hired for the harvest season of the south or vice versa.

With regard to the problems of implementation of land legislation, which partially led to the failure of the agricultural transformation in Ethiopia, I would like to briefly comment on some specific issues like, (i) imbalance in the proportion of arable land to peasants, which finally led to fragmentation of plots, (ii) shortage of instruments of productions namely, oxen and ploughs, and (iii) lack of appropriate institutions to execute agrarian reform in general and the land issue in particular.

Proportion of Population to Land and Problems of Fragmentation

Alula Abate *et. al.*, (1980) and Kidane Mengisteab (1990) state that the average number of households in a peasant association (members of a community among which land was distributed) were initially estimated at between a hundred thirty and two hundred, but in reality there were many rural settlements where the number of households were doubled. The significance of this point lies in the land legislation where provisions were made stating that a single peasant association had a fixed area of eight hundred hectares of land to be distributed to a maximum of two hundred households, i.e. a minimum four hectares per household. This, of course, was much less than ten hectares per household as stipulated in the land legislation (*Negarit Gazeta*, No. 26, 29 April, 1975).

Andargachew Tiruneh (1993) confirms that over 60 percent of farmers had less than one hectare each. The problem of proportion of population to land is also supported by Almenh's (1987) study of the Arssi region where he found that about 65 percent of the peasants had experienced a reduction of land-holdings after the land reform. According to the latter author, the negative land to person ratio often led to the fragmentation and it thereby reduces production.

Prior to the revolution, fragmentation of arable land was common in northern Ethiopia, where the population density on arable land was evidently higher, however, this had not been so common in the south. In post-revolutionary Ethiopia the fragmentation problem also spread to the south and according to Kirsch's, et. al., finding (1989) only 1.6 percent of the peasants had more than five hectares.

Fragmentation of land in general, argues Andargachew Tiruneh (1993), hinders the increase of production as it limits technological innovation. Kirsch, *et. al.* also state that subdivision of plots into smallholdings is unproductive as they could not absorb the available labor force, let alone mechanize as the *derg* later attempted (Cohen and Weintraub, 1975).

Shortage of Farming Implements and Essential Inputs

Another problem area in Ethiopia's agrarian reform was the shortage of farming implements and other essential inputs. After the redistribution of land, the previously landless, as poor as they were, lacked oxen to farm their plots. They also had no hand-ploughs and crop seed. Furthermore finance for necessary investments was not easily available.[2] The national percentage of farmers with no oxen is 38.1 percent. The availability of oxen was (and still is) crucial to the production of food grain. While a pair of oxen is a minimum for farming, it is only 24.4 percent of farmers who owned two oxen.

Thus, what can be observed above is that in regions like Gojjam, Arssi and Wollega more food grain production is possible. This is because they need relatively better percentage of landholding and better distribution of oxen. It may be, perhaps, due to these facts, among others, that these regions are less vulnerable to famine. The combination of availability of oxen and sufficient land appear to affect peasant food production to a considerable extent. The point which I would like to address here is that since the arable land portioned out to households became fragmented and many of the peas-

143

ants lacked oxen, it become difficult to reduce the level of famine and poverty as anticipated.

TABLE 6:1
AVERAGE SIZE OF LANDHOLDING IN HECTARE, PERCENTAGE OF LAND AND OXEN HOLDINGS BY REGION, 1977

Region	Landholding Average in ha.	Landholding more than 5 ha.	Oxenholding 3 or more per withheld
Arssi	2.16	3.0%	8.1
Bale	1.18	0.0%	11.9
Begemder	1.90	1.5%	5.4
Gamo Goffa	0.86	1.3%	2.4
Gojjam	1.80	8.3%	9.9
Harar	0.91	0.0%	1.6
Illubabor	1.09	1.5%	8.5
Kaffa	0.86	1.7%	4.7
Shoa	1.39	0.0%	5.2
Sidamo	0.58	0.2%	3.1
Wollega	1.59	5.5%	11.2
Wollo	1.57	0.0%	5.3

Source: Compiled from Alemneh Dejene, 1987:22; Kirsch *et. al*, 1989:130, 135.

Lack of Local Institutions

Another major problem of implementing the agrarian reform in Ethiopia was the lack of appropriate institutions to carry out land distribution in an orderly fashion (be it traditional or modern institutions). Despite the general consensus that land reform was essential to the country, there were no studies undertaken to enable organized analysis, and the local people were not consulted. When the revolution suddenly made land reform possible there was not enough preparation to accommodate such a sweeping and radical agrarian reform (Cohen and Weintraub, 1975).

For instance, the Ministry of Land and Settlement, which was reorganized during the land reform, did not have sufficient resources to execute and supervise the land legislation. The task of ex-appropriation of land from the landlords and allocation to the landless peasants needed well-organized, experienced and resourceful local institutions, but these were absent in certain areas and ineffective in others. The wide geographical extent, the large population—more than 50 million, (1990 census) of which well over 80 percent are peasants, spread all over the country also added more problems to the tasks of agrarian reform activities.

The point of emphasis here is that either the previous governments or the new ones have disregarded the utilization of local institutions in development activities. Despite the neglect, it was the peasant's effort that ultimately implemented the land legislation.

STATE DOMINATION OF LOCAL SELF-HELP ORGANIZATIONS

Problems of Peasant Associations

As often stated, in the initial period of the Ethiopian revolution the importance of agrarian reform was understood and accordingly, land reform was undertaken. This land reform in turn, presupposed many other chains of activities such as implementation of land legislation and the establishment of rural self administrations to secure improved living conditions for rural inhabitants. For these, and many other similar activities, organized peasants were found to be essential and to this end provision was made (Proclamation No. 31 and 71, 1975). Peasant associations were thus formed and began to exercise their stated political, economic and social rights administering themselves. For example, they organized themselves into associations and distributed land among themselves according to the prescribed provisions of the land legislation and even adapted it to best suit a peasant household situation.

They established local judicial tribunes, enforced law and order within the jurisdiction of the relevant peasant association. In many places peasant associations successfully assumed the duties of local government functionaries and rural bureaucrats. The peasant judicial tribune, consisting of people elected from the villages, brought many advantages to the peasants. For instance, they put an end to the peasant's enforced travel, often over considerable distances, in search of government judicial tribunes. This saved the peasants from wasting their time on matters that might easily be solved locally. More importantly, the judicial tribune elected from and by the peasants became more favorable to the people as it possessed a basic understanding of the issues brought before it.

During the early days of the revolution 1975 to 1978, the peasant associations were beginning to develop self-administration and wield rural power. As Pausewang (1988:7a) argues, there was an attempt to implement participatory rural democracy and involve the peasantry in decisions that affected their lives. His observation that "During the first years, until 1977-78, central authorities had in reality very little control or influence over local decisions" was very true. However, Pausewang's observation of some peasant associations in early 1975, in which he witnessed elements of rural democracy in practice differed considerably from his second visit in 1987. His second series of observations clearly illustrate the rapid transformation undergone by the peasant associations. Let us hear what he says:

> It appears to me the peasants today [1987] feel controlled from above, they complain they have no influence whatsoever over their own local affairs ... peasant associations are becoming increasingly a tool of the government and lose their function of local discussion and local action. Elections are in practice decided by the officials who select candidates which peasants have to endorse through their vote. The control committees, established to avoid abuse of local authority, are evaluating the performance of peasant leaders according to the criteria of the administration ... in collecting taxes, in applying orders, and in organizing peasants for any activity that is initiated from above (1988:6b).

The issues of self-help, self-administrative and participation on equal footing i.e. rural democracy were gradually reduced to their lowest level and leaders of peasant associations increasingly became instruments for implementation of government directives. In short, they were bureaucratized. Step by step, the military government succeeded in integrating peasant associations into its administrative organization. The independent judicial tribunes for example, lost their power to party cadres, the rural defense bodies became revolutionary squads whose task was, instead of defending decisions passed by the peasant judicial tribune, to defend the party line. Finally, the peasant leaders were left with multiple tasks such as collecting government fees and taxes, they were assigned to recruit militia men, feed soldiers and organize collectivization programs (Dessalegn Rahmato, 1984).

This gradual introduction of the old order, is conformed by a series of reports from peasants who fled these hardships. Such peasant testimonies have been reported by different humanitarian organizations, which gave shelter to them. A report from one humanitarian organization reads like this:

> Peasants are required to spend two to five days a week working for the militia and collective farms; the Mandatory General Assembly [PAs] meetings also take up considerable time. Since these duties limit the time available for working in their fields and protecting their crops from pests, the harvests have declined by two-third to three-fourth since 1974. Additionally, taxes, levied on a per-capita basis, have now had to be paid three years in advance, with the result that peasants are being dispossessed of their last remaining wealth. Imprisonment or threat of imprisonment during the harvest for non-attendance at meetings or a failure to pay taxes is a common occurrence (Survival International 1986:37).

The same source accounting for peasant grievances notes that many peasants believe that all these hardships levied on peasants to be part of a deliberate policy to undermine peasant agriculture so that the authorities could later state that peasant holdings were "low in productivity, primitive and individualistic" and should be replaced by modern and "effective" collective farms.

Where the Peasant Associations Go Wrong and Why?

The problem the Ethiopian peasants faced was double edged. Firstly, they were in confrontation with the government to determine their future in self-help local organizations or peasant associations. Through their organizations, the peasants demanded more participation than the government was willing to allow. Secondly, many of the goal-oriented and conscious peasant leaders were replaced by political cadres.

Realizing the pivotal position of the peasants' organizations, the military government created parallel parastatal alternatives and thereby paralyzed the peasant's power. The military weakened horizontal contacts within the peasant organizations and instead succeeded in creating one way, top-down, organizational forms which had the effect of bureaucratizing peasant association office holders through provision of financial and material advantage. Step-by-step, the leaders of peasant associations were designated to serve as civil servants and/or political cadres of the government and ultimately the association itself became the social, economic and political base of the *derg*.

According to reports from peasant refugees in the Sudan it was confirmed that in the later stage (especially after 1978), chairmen of PAs were appointed by the government and "they faced a punishment if they failed to implement government directives" (Survival International, 1986:36).

The peasants tried many times to obtain help (leadership) from external sources but this help was not forthcoming because the (left) intelligentsia, who were suppose to deal with such matters were involved in identifying a pie in the sky, i.e. promoting the needs of a handful of workers against over 80 percent of the population.[3] The cumbersome organizational structure of the peasant associations, from local to national level was also partially responsible for obliging them to become more bureaucratic. The huge expansion of their organization for instance, demanded a higher literacy level to run the office. Accounting and auditing skills became important as the organization's revenue and expenditure expanded. However, the people who possessed these skills were found outside the peasant community. They were either from among the well-to-do rural families—former landlords—or else from the government who had totally different agendas to the peasants.

Represented by about twenty-four thousand peasant associations, which comprised nearly eight million rural households, that is 35-40 million individuals, the peasants could have been one of the major political powers in the country and a power to be reckoned with. However, due to the lack of strong, independent organizations, aware of their power and clearly identified with peasant issues, the genuine participatory efforts of the Ethiopian peasantry produced unanticipated results.[4]

The lesson one may learn from this is that one of the decisive failures of the Ethiopian revolution, a failure that hampered political and socio-economic development, as argued here, was the transposition of the peasant association's power to the military government. Had the peasant association's time, labor and resources been geared towards their self-help, had the political situation been favorable to their empowerment, then the foundation of rural political and socio-economic development through peasant associations could have been properly cemented. The foundations of genuine transformation would have been laid and finally, the level of poverty would have been positively affected.

IMPACTS OF COLLECTIVIZATION

When the military government launched its economic transformation on a large scale, its first move was to institutionalize its command economy.

This was done by fusing its military structure with the country's economic development plan in the form of the National Revolutionary Development Campaign (NRDC) in 1976. The NRDC consisted of a Central Planning Supreme Council (CPSC) which was solely responsible for the overall development and planning of the economy. The members of the Executive Committee and the Chairman of the Supreme Council were largely from the army and thus, from this time onwards (1976) economic activities began to be addressed in military terms, geared to military purposes.

It was through the guidance and supervision of the Central Planning Supreme Council that gradually the intensification of the 1930s Soviet type collectivization, state farms, promotion of villagization and resettlement programs were adopted.

The Impact of State Sponsored Farms

The *derg*, instead of advocating private smallholdings, set out to establish huge state and co-operative farms. In discussing cooperatives in general many people argue, for example, that they had shown good performances in the *kibbutzim* of Israel; on the sugar plantations of Cuba; and that villagization and resettlement schemes too were made possible with the help of the World Bank in Tanzania. Many years previously, Dumont (1966) had suggested co-operatives like that of Sweden (*kooperativa förbundet*), the *kolkhozes* of Poland, *moshav ovdim* of the Yugoslavia and the Chinese *commune* be looked into carefully and lessons learned from their experience to be adapted to an appropriate development model for Africa.

TABLE 6:2
COMPARATIVE COST OF PRODUCTION, OFFICIAL OR STATE PRICES, AND FREE MARKET (WHOLE SALE) PRICES, SELECTED AGRICULTURAL PRODUCTS, 1985-86
(birr per quintal)

CROPS	STATE FARMS	PEASANT FARMS
Cost of production		
Wheat	73.0	36.0
Maize	59.0	29.0
Barley	82.0	41.0
Government sale price		
Wheat	47.0	31.0
Maize	31.0	20.0
Barley	40.0	27.0

Source: Central Committee for National Planning, 1987.

The principal point of the argument here is not whether such programs have or have not worked in some countries, but that as a consequence collectivization helped, not to transform the rural economy, but to serve the *derg's* vested interests. More importantly, the schemes were not based on the free will of the people concerned, they were planned at the center, hastily implemented, totally inhuman and finally resulted in the unnecessary loss of many lives.

Government action favoring co-operative and state farms was deliberate, open and commonplace. For example, the comparative cost of production for government sponsored farms were more expensive than the peasant farms. Despite household farming's better performance, the government paid them less for their products (Table 6:2). Finally many hard working peasants were labeled *kulaks*,[5] and as a result negative measures were taken against them.

According to Alemneh Dejene's study (1987) the performance of family farms was superior to that of co-operatives and state farms. Note also that these performances took place in a situation where resources were scarce and not more than two hectares per household was allowed. The findings of his study (Arssi region), reveal that around 75 percent of the peasants would have liked to remain within the peasant association as private farmers rather than joining state sponsored co-operatives.

Many studies conducted show that co-operatives and state farms, as implemented in Ethiopia under the *derg*, proved to be failures. In the co-operatives and state farms, the peasants mainly worked to produce surplus cash crops to generate foreign exchange, which was either used by the government to buy military hardware or to purchase luxurious consumer items to satisfy the ruling elite. What, then, were the major failures of the derg's agrarian reform?

Technological change and innovation to enhance *per capita* and total food production is often carried out in one of two ways—one is labor intensive and the other capital intensive. The choice between the two in the African context is considered advisable as elaborated below.

> In the rural areas of most developing nations where land parcels are small, capital is scare, and labor is abundant, the introduction of heavily mechanized techniques is not only often ill-suited to the physical environment but, more important, often has the effect of creating more rural unemployment without necessarily lowering per unit costs of food production. Importation of such machin-

ery can therefore be "anti-development" since its efficient deploy-
ment requires large tracts of land and tends to exacerbate the
already serious problems of rural poverty and unemployment
(Todaro, 1983:277).

Todaro's statement is supported in the Ethiopian case. For example,
the capital investments made in state farms and co-operatives were
costly and noted for their maladministration and lack of incentives.
In contrast to mechanization there were effective family/household
farms who were considerably more productive but paradoxically
they were denied any provision to increase their outputs. This, of
course, resulted in a negative trend in *per capita* food production.

Though the *derg* avoided employing them, there are at least two
commonly accepted agricultural development strategies, namely, *unimodal* and *bimodal* (Hulme and Turner, 1990). Unimodal strategy is
characterized by small-scale or household agricultural activities (e.g.
Tanzania, Taiwan, China etc). This model appears to be effective especially in producing food grains in short spans of time using local
human labor and other available inputs. In contrast, bimodal strategy
is large-scale and mechanized agricultural undertakings (e.g. USSR).

The point I would like to establish here is that the task of agrarian development in Ethiopia was clear. It was to provide food for the
millions who were (still are) threatened by famine using the available
human and local resources. To this end, the strategy followed by the
derg was the opposite. The state deliberately avoided small-scale
household farming and instead established mechanized farms, organized huge co-operatives and state farms and enforced bimodal strategy, which led to further famine.

Impacts of Regional and Inter-regional Settlement Schemes

Earlier it was stated that it was essential for the *derg* to control food
and other resources in order to resume the different wars and sustain
itself in power. To put this into practice it had to mobilize and control massive agrarian labor forces i.e. to grip the peasants and force
upon them the ideas of collectivization. As Habreson (1988:177)
observes, "Such centralized and comprehensive control and such
collectivization of economic life at the grass roots were virtually
without precedent in prior Ethiopian history."

Cohen and Isakssons (1986) also state that inter-regional settlement schemes, widely known as villagization was one of the means

of reconstructing Ethiopian rural society to fit into collectivization and allow the government to impose the necessary political control.

From its period of initiation, some time in 1985 this massive villagization campaign was undertaken without any sort of guidelines known to the people. It was simply implemented by the military government acting on its own advice. The leading organs of the scheme, the National Villagization Coordinating Committee (NVCC), and its various local branches were all established in 1986). But by the time these institutions were set up, more than six million rural people were already villagized or displaced Thus, from its very inception, the program was hasty implemented, and as Alemayehu Lirenso (1990:136) states, "...it was neither well-planned nor well-coordinated ... there were no feasibility studies available and implementation was enforced under time pressure."

Villagization programs, by and large, were imposed on peasant associations, however the peasant associations lacked financial and material resources to implement these enormous programs. When many people were assigned to one-host *kebele* resources had to be stretched further. The new villagers were to be equipped with a house and it was difficult to obtain building materials, they needed food and other facilities which the peasant associations of the host villages (*kebeles*) themselves lacked. The host peasants therefore, had to put aside their day-to-day farming work in order to construct the required facilities for these settlers without any sort of compensation for neither the lost working days nor the resources used. The long-term consequences of food grain shortage due to agricultural labor time lost appears not to have crossed the minds of the *derg*'s planners.

Another scenario showed that due to lack of any feasibility studies beforehand, some new villages were built on marshy and water-logged plains. Such conditions increased not only vulnerability to various illnesses but also difficulties in finding locations for schools, health centers, shops and other services. More importantly, because of such, settlement farm land was not available in nearby areas and thus the new settlers were forced to walk long distances from their villages carrying their heavy ploughs and driving oxen for a distance of between 2-6km, back and forth, every working day (Alemayehu Lirenso, 1990).

The points I would like to underline here is that, firstly, proximity to the fields is essential for protection of the harvest from wild animals, birds, pests and poachers. And farm fields so far from a residential village bring negative consequences. Secondly, because the farm fields were so far away from the villages they could not be used for grazing. According to the same source, it was revealed that due to the increase in distance, the grazing time of cattle was reduced by nearly 20 percent and thus, livestock mortality rates significantly increased (Alemayehu Lirenso, 1990:140).

In some areas villagization brought a different problem. For example, after their study of villagization in one administrative area, Arssi, Cohen and Isaksson (1986) noted that the heavy concentration of human and livestock during villagization had negatively affected the environment of the newly inhabited areas.

The failure of this program needs no further evidence, except the action taken by the participants themselves. After all this damage, with the fall of the *derg's* government, in May, 1991, the villagers (peasants) have abandoned their new villages and returned to their former homesteads.

Another undertaking of the *derg* was regional re-settlement or commonly known as the resettlement scheme. Time and again the government had stated that the resettlement scheme was on a voluntary basis. However, to find one and half million volunteers, in the short period of time the scheme was operational, makes this statement extremely suspect. As the report of Survival International puts it, although there is no dispute that some of the settlers willingly joined the scheme, "the overwhelming majority, without doubt, have been transferred from north to south Ethiopia by blackmail or force" (1986:13).[6]

In this resettlement scheme, people of the northern regions, from where most settlers were taken, complained that part of their population was moved in the name of resettlement while the true motives behind were political and were aimed at hindering recruitment of fighters against the central government by the different ethnically-based liberation movements.[7] The southern peoples, in whose regions the newcomers were settled, also complained that the plots distributed to the new settlers were not either unused or under-utilized lands as the government often said, but were taken from the local peasants.

In this manner the resettlement program brought ethnic conflicts between the newcomers and the local inhabitants on one hand, and between the different settler groups on the other. Confrontation between the local inhabitants and the newcomers appeared to be a typical characteristic of many resettlement schemes. In many of the resettlement areas, for example, the people had difficulties even in communicating with each other as some had no common language and also divergent cultures with regard to food, clothing, constructing houses, etc. Since they were distinctly different in many ways, living side by side in an environment free from hostility was difficult.

The heart of the matter is, the resettlement program had uprooted local people from their environment on which they based their knowledge and practices and this is non-productive in all of its aspects. Though the government time and again stressed that resettlement was motivated for "liberating the peasants from backwardness in agriculture through cooperatives, villagizations and state farms of a socialist character" (Alula Pankrust, 1990; Dieci and Viezzoli, 1992), as much evidence produced so far indicates, the entire movement was political—that is to say, the scheme was a cover to deport peasants from their homesteads in order to hinder their recruitment by the different ethnically-based guerilla organizations fighting against the central government (Dawit Wolde Giorgis, 1989).

Moreover, there is evidence to show that peasants were influenced to join the resettlement program by false descriptions of the living conditions in the new settlement sites—as areas of affluence where nobody needed to work hard, where land would be cultivated for them by tractors, houses would be built by the host peasants, enough food, clothing and farming equipment would be provided free of charge etc. (Dawit Wolde Giorgis, 1989:281-308; Kirsch et. al., 1989).

In some areas peasants were forced or intimidated into volunteering for resettlement. Reports from the drought affected peasants in Wollo, for example, witnessed that the these peasants only received food rations if they were willing to be registered as volunteers. There is a report made by Oxfam (the British Aid Agency) which states that food was not delivered to children because their parents refused to be resettled (Survival International, 1986:16).

With regard to resettlement Dawit Wolde Giorgis, revealed the coercive methods used by the military government. He testified that in 1975, close to one thousand members of political opposition groups and individuals, which the *derg* referred to as "trouble-makers," were rounded up in Addis Ababa and sent to resettlement centers. The resettlement center, according to the author, could be state farms and/or any war fronts within the country. According to Dawit again, in 1980 the peasant associations of Tigray, Wollo and Northern Shoa were asked to send a number of young peasants (based on an assigned quota) to the resettlement programs. Some among these peasants were later directly sent to war fronts and some were settled in war buffer zones, for example areas of Humera, Bale and Gode. The author further explains that of those people resettled in new areas against their will, a few escaped, some joined the different liberation fronts, many died from diseases and some were also executed for their attempts to escape from resettlement areas (1989:281-308).[8]

Colchester and Luling (cited in Görcke et. al., 1989) reported that the resettlement schemes were the equivalent of deportation. Dawit Wolde Giorgis supporting this allegation states that the understanding of the resettlement sites by some local authorities was as places to deport tax evaders, peasant associations critics, co-operative haters and all *trouble makers*. He explains the settlement program as follows:

> From the very beginning, resettlement for Mengistu [head of the *derg*] was not a development program but a solution to his social and national security problems. Any dissidents, anyone who created problems or was seen as a security risk, was packed off to a resettlement site. Resettlement programs became our Siberia. As a result, in the minds of the people they were equated with concentration camps (1989:285).[9]

The lessons we draw from villagization and resettlement programs are as follows. Peasants were forced to provide free labor as well as material contributions for construction of houses, provision of food etc. for the newcomers without any sort of compensation in return. This had negative consequences, reducing food production and exacerbating poverty.

Peasants, who were affected by these schemes, disliked displacement, they did not want to be removed from their home surroundings. In addition, they disliked working in collectivization, controlled by political cadres. In some collectivized settlements, peasant properties and possessions were seized by the *derg's* cadres in the name of "common use of all." This is not common to the tradition of the people when these peasants were free to own their property and sharing is common first, within the family, then within the kinship group. Implementing textbook principles of socialism directly without paying regard to the socio-cultural milieu resulted in hate rather than acceptance of the principle.

Moreover, villagization and resettlement schemes, as huge as they were, cleared the forests for cultivation, for building houses, for making utensils, for cooking, etc. As a result, deforestation accelerated, wildlife disappeared and the top fertile soil layer was removed by erosion. In Ethiopia the deforestation reduced the country's forests from 40 to 3 percent over five decades, including a period before the revolution, of course. According to one estimate, if the resettlement scheme had been executed as planned, about 62 percent of the remaining forests would have been demolished.[10]

PARASTATAL MONOPOLY AND INDISCRIMINATE NATIONALIZATION

There is no doubt that government intervention, especially in poor countries may be essential. One purpose of government intervention could be to help agriculture and other enterprises to succeed so that they can contribute to the overall development of the country. The main task, in general, is assumed to be to lubricate productive activities as much as possible. However, the lesson from Ethiopia contrasts starkly with this ideal. Instead of lubricating economic operative machinery it poured sand into their tanks. The *derg* prohibited private entrepreneurs and monopolized the purchase of agricultural produce and controlled marketable outputs. Agricultural products, by and large, were purchased by the state at low and fixed prices which provided no incentives. In return, the prices of basic consumer goods supplied by the *derg* to the peasants were expensive, if not highly inflated. Indeed, these profits were drained into the purchase of arms to sustain itself in power and/or ended up in the pockets of *derg* members.[11]

One of the main agents of development that would have exercised a prosperous effect on rural development but was severely hampered by the *derg* was private grain entrepreneurs. Grain merchants are important mediators in rural development and are especially important in a country like Ethiopia where neither the government nor non-governmental organizations could distribute food grain from where there was surplus to areas of shortage.

Prior to the 1974 revolution, grain-trading activities were undertaken by private entrepreneurs as well as landlords. The landlords used to collect their crop-shares and sell them to urban areas either directly themselves or through private entrepreneurs. However, post-revolutionary Ethiopia, in ostracizing the landlords, lost one wing of the local entrepreneurial group. Instead of injecting the idea of entrepreneurship into public life the government condemned private rural trading as capitalist practice and in its place parastatal monopolies, i.e. heavily state sponsored institutions, such as The Ethiopian Domestic Distribution Corporation (EDDC) and Agricultural Marketing Corporation (AMC), were established.

EDDC was established to supply consumer goods to both urban and rural inhabitants who were effectively embraced in their respective residential area organizations known as *kebele*. Over 70 percent of the people, especially in rural areas, depended on these consumer shops (Kirsch et. al., 1989).

The Agricultural Marketing Corporation (AMC), the subject of our discussion below, was another clear parastatal monopoly active in buying and selling food grains. According to the military government the reasons for implementing this state monopoly were, (a) to avoid the exploiting profits of middlemen, (b) to minimize local differences in prices of grain (by covering value-added costs such as transport, storage, labor inputs etc.), (c) to guarantee better production and supply of food and (d) to supply food grain at reasonable prices *(AMC Proclamation No. 105 of 1976)*. However, reality did not reflect the above statement. The government, driven by demand for food both from urban dwellers and its army, forced the peasants to sell their produce to the state monopoly (AMC) at fixed or farm-gate prices set by itself and these prices remained unchanged for over a decade (1980-1990).

While AMC paid higher prices for state and co-operative farm produce, the family smallholding sector received 20 percent less. By doing this, firstly, it forcibly extracted household farms to finance the losses from the state and cooperative farms. Secondly, by purchasing food grain at fixed low prices and selling at high prices to consumers, the AMC considerably increased its profit margins (Kirsch, 1989; Picket, 1991).

When, for example, the market consumer price for *teff* in 1985 was 200 *birr*, AMC paid the peasants around 60 *birr*. Naturally, under such circumstances the peasants could not be motivated to work hard and sell their produce at prices much lower than private entrepreneurs or consumer markets willingly offered. The peasants and the local grain traders, therefore, became unwilling to co-operate in AMC's price policy.[12]

Then, the government stepped in and introduced a quota system which forced peasants to sell their grain to AMC at fixed prices.[13] The measures taken against those peasants who could not fulfil the levied quota were extremely harsh and went as far as forbidding them from buying basic consumer goods from co-operative shops. As there were no other shops where the peasants could fill their daily needs, there was no way out except to purchase grain from other places and contribute their share to AMC (Befakadu Degefe and Tesfaye Tafesse, 1990). Confirming these malevolent measures of the *derg* Picket (1991:130) states," ... only in 1985/1986, perhaps one-third of the peasants were punished for no or late delivery of their quota."

Just as for the peasants, a quota was set for the grain traders and up to 50 percent of the private grain traders purchases (i.e., what they bought from farmers to sell in the free market) were forcibly resold to AMC at fixed prices. Merchants who failed to strictly follow this quota had their trading licenses withdrawn. Additionally, grain merchants especially from grain producing areas such as Arssi and Gojjam, were banned from buying directly from peasants and in this way the *derg* definitely strengthened its real monopolistic position and damaged rural entrepreneurs (Alemneh Dejene, 1987; Picket, 1991).

Such inappropriate measures and the overall polices applied by the *derg* towards grain producers and traders discouraged food grain production and distribution. Under these circumstances, the peasants found no incentive to produce more than what they needed. As a result, from 1982 to 1984, food grain production in regions such as Arssi and Gojjam fell between 15 and 20 percent (Picket, 1991:130).

The point here is, the *derg* did what was in its power to force the peasants, grains merchants and cash crop (e.g. coffee) producers and distributors to sell to its monopolistic establishments (AMC) at a deficit. This was damaging both for producers and distributors of food grain. Such policies of the government discouraged farmers from producing a surplus, and it also discouraged the development of an entrepreneurial spirit in the minds of local distributors. Instead, private ownership was disfavored and state bureaucratic capitalism fostered.[14]

It is through private profit makers, and voluntary associations or what the Ethiopian government labeled *capitalist dreamers,* that goods and services could effectively be transferred from place to place and from one economic or cultural sphere to another. This is particularly true in Africa where governments either have limited resources to carry out the task or use the process to enrich the state bureaucracy. In the latter case, as is stated above, it is evident that the new political elites of Africa, supported by a series of nationalizations were striving to become the dominant entrepreneurs, thereby completing their absolute political and economic dominance over their citizens.

Indiscriminate Nationalization[15]

Indiscriminate nationalization is mentioned here to indicate the *derg's* nationalization of small private enterprises. These enterprises were the major sources of earnings for local entrepreneurs—like renting of houses, transport services, small-scale manufacturing, commercial farms etc. To establish such enterprises take many years of work, and to many people even more than a lifetime. But all lost by a stroke of a pen.

After this irrational and indiscriminate mass nationalization many were left without any sort of income to sustain their lives. Private capital accumulation was officially condemned and only the state (the *derg* in this case) had the sole right of accumulating capital. This removed enthusiasm and spirit for hard work and the accumulation of capital from the ordinary people (Table 6:3).

TABLE 6:3
GOVERNMENT INVOLVEMENT IN THE ECONOMY, 1974-84.
PERCENTAGE OF GDP - SELECTED EXAMPLES

Sector	1974	1979	1981	1984
Industry	10.2	53.1	55.9	8.3
Construction	na	39.1	42.7	48.4
Electricity& Water	95.1	100	100	100
Transport & Communication	40.6	60	69.4	71.8
Administration	100	100	100	100
Banking & Insurance	51.0	100	100	100
Housing	1.0	36.2	35.9	36.4
Education	75.0	87.6	91.6	94.3
Health	51.3	78.7	83.6	87.6

Source: National Committee for Central Planning.   na - not available

Indiscriminate nationalization (1974/75) of small private farms, which were in the preliminary stages of introducing modern agricultural development, negatively effected to the development of agriculture. Without contradicting what was stated earlier. There were modern private farms run by feudal landlords who evicted peasants to introduce mechanized cash-crop farming. In light of these facts,

the measures taken against these groups or individuals in expropri-
ating the land once belonging to the peasants was understandable.

However, the subject now under discussion is that a few of the
modern agricultural entrepreneurs had started working in the regions
of Awash Valley, Tendho and Setit Humera, borrowing large sums of
money from domestic and foreign financial sources. In most of the
cases these people had cleared areas not previously inhabited by
peasants. These agricultural entrepreneurs could have been tolerated, as they were small-scale capitalist-oriented agricultural entrepreneurs.[16]

It was true that due to the lucrative prices of cash-crops, these
mechanized farms concentrated their production to oil-seed, fruit,
sugar cane, cotton, tobacco, etc. and produced less locally consumed
food grains. However, this should not have been a major problem for
the state as it could easily have utilized price mechanism to encourage them to produce food grains. Moreover, the government should
have reinforced their motivation and concentrated on protecting the
agricultural laborer's benefits and rights by e.g. fixing a minimum wage
level and other legislation to secure better living conditions in the
farming areas.

It is important to emphasize here that these were different
agricultural development initiatives taken by private Ethiopians
side by side with traditional agriculture. They could have been tolerated, at least, on the basis of pilot projects for new agricultural
production. Had the state been a little more tolerant of these
entrepreneurial undertakings instead of declaring war on them in
the name of socialist revolution, the country might have benefited from their experience in improving agricultural development.

The lesson here is that, in the post-revolution period, ideology was served before pragmatism and all private farms were
nationalized without any preliminary study of their advantages
and disadvantages. The former owners of these commercial
farms were forced to step down and the *derg* assigned its political cadres to manage the farms and to ensure that benefits were
directly channeled to the *derg*. In this process the country lost two
essential inputs at one stroke. One was the long managerial and
technical know-how of the farm owners and the other was the
revenue from these farms. After seventeen years, the balance
sheet of this nationalization process exhibited rusting tractors
and invading wild grass.

CRISIS IN IDEOLOGY AND LEADERSHIP

The crisis of ideology in the Ethiopian revolution, according to discussions so far presented, exhibits two phases. The first confusion of ideology and leadership was after the emperor was deposed. It took about two years (1974-1976) for the *derg* to establish an ideology—from *hibretesebawenet* to the National Democratic Program (NDP). On the proclamation of the latter, we have also seen that one wing of the left intelligentsia (EPRP) dropped out of the open forum and intensified its underground struggle, whilst the other wing (AESM/Meison) stayed with the *derg* and determined to support NDP. This situation brought forth the most debated ideological twists within Ethiopian left-wing intellectual groups. The debates, however, were far from the people's everyday reality and so self-consuming that they finally boomeranged on the groups themselves.

After marching for a while along the path of NDP, the *derg*, with the help of the Soviet Union, shifted course and adopted a non-capitalist way of development. Civilian progressive forces tried their best to pull the *derg* into their domain and tried to stitch up their "unity," however, this failed. It failed because it was not accepted by the *derg* and the USSR and thus, the second phase of the ideological and leadership crisis became unavoidable.

When the non-capitalist path entered into effect, the left-wing intellectuals who were earlier connected to the derg (under the banner of NDP) could not be tolerated by either the *derg* or the USSR. Instead pro-soviet and socialist forces had to enter into the political arena. The important factor to pay attention to here is how the Soviet Union leadership isolated the *derg*.

Left-wing organizations in Ethiopia (AESM, EPRP other political groupings and progressive individuals) were in the Soviet's eyes, believed to be anti-Soviet (pro-China an ideological archenemy of the Soviet ruling party then) and they did not wish to see these people involved with the *derg*. This happened at the time when the *derg* was in desperate need of military assistance from the USSR.

True, many Ethiopian disapproved the type of socialism advocated and applied in the Soviet Union and its Eastern European allies. It was also true that Soviet leadership wished to sideline these individuals and, in their place, to train massive forces of pro-Soviets. This was necessary as the USSR at that time did not have enough of a social base to fully extend its sphere of influence into Ethiopia.

The strengthening of their social base was assisted by the military. As noted earlier, the outbreak of hostilities between Somalia and Ethiopia (1977/78) helped the USSR to push through its strategy, which was an essential ideological instrument, which enabled control over the *derg* and the Ethiopian people. The dispute helped the *derg* to mobilize the people in nationalism through emotionally loaded slogans such as *defense of the mother land and territorial integrity*. This, in turn, shifted internal alliances from civilian to military. The new alliance had succeeded in isolating the *derg* from civilian forces, which advocated the establishment of democratic pluralities and civil society. Instead, it helped the *derg* to self-style itself as nationalist and a unifying factor at this time of "national crisis," and thereby paved the way for the officers clique to assume pivotal positions.

This last point becomes evident when the earlier status of the *derg*, that of Provisional Military Administrative Government (PMAG), was dropped and the National Democratic Program altogether abandoned. POMOA was also transformed into what is called A Commission for Organizing the Party of the Working Class of Ethiopia (COPWE) in 1979 and later in 1984, the same COPWE (or the same *derg*) was again transformed into the Workers Party of Ethiopia (WPE), which propounded the official ideology of non-capitalist path of development.[17]

Finally, the establishment of this single, dominant party definitely curtailed any hope of participation, open dialogue and a democratic forum to ventilate differences and had the effect of forcing opposition groups to armed struggle.

The Failure of the Intelligentsia to Assume Leadership

The groups of intelligentsia referred to below are mainly the left-wing intellectuals outside the government (i.e. those who were in opposition at one time or another). Since the officer core in power (*derg*) is extensively dealt with throughout the preceding chapters, it will not be discussed again.

The majority of the Ethiopian intelligentsia had struggled for decades against the semi-feudal, semi-capitalist government of Ethiopia. They had facilitated and accelerated the successful breakdown of the government of Haile Selassie, both at its base and in its superstructure, which by itself is no mean feat. During the revolutionary period of early 1974, they had actively participated in distributing land to the landless peasants and struggled for popular legislation in favor of the people. Against this background, many anticipated that the coming period would mark the turning point of the longstanding political and socio-economic crisis of the country.

Those political forces which sought to bring forth such a change however, failed conspicuously to assume political power and transform Ethiopian society for the better. Thus, without denying the Ethiopian intelligentsia's positive contribution, I think, it is possible to point out its fatal flaws.

Members of the intelligentsia's core often claimed tolerance and readiness to participate in open dialogue, however their methods of approaching and solving problems in practice did not reflect such claims. Judging from events that took place from the beginning of the 1974 revolution, it was noted how difficult it was to be able to keep a cool head about differences of opinion. For example, long-term allies were betrayed for short-term political gains. Thus, one of the main reasons for the disintegration of the intelligentsia, is a *lack of democratic tradition*, that is to say, lack of open dialogue, tolerance or willingness to entertain new and divergent ideas.

The other major reason for the failure of the civilian intelligentsia can be found in the civil political groups that mushroomed after the revolution which lacked experience and above all, were not legitimized by the people. They were too new and inexperienced in protracted political struggle to lead a nation-wide uprising of that magnitude. They also lacked organizational strength. When they did manage to organize themselves, timing failed them, i.e. the period of working for political organization and self-consolidation coincided with solving the day-to-day problems of the revolution. The revolution took place at a rapid pace and demanded intense leadership and guidance. It needed cool-headed problem-solving rather than heated arguments between groups. The revolution demanded the accomplishment of so many things over such a short span of time and so many of the civilian political groups were overtaken by events. In short, they were not prepared to assume power.

Many argue that the Ethiopian intellectuals who actively participated during the 1974 social revolution were victims of the 1960s and early 1970s world socialist movements. For instance, the debate that dominated the political life of the Ethiopian intelligentsia during the late 1960s and early 1970s were to a greater extent, one-sided i.e. socialist oriented. The theories of Marx, Lenin and Mao (even Stalin) were taken as the central methodologies the application, which could solve Ethiopia's problems.[18] Except for a sector of the intelligentsia i.e. a handful of university and high school students and perhaps, middle class office employees, the majority of the Ethiopian people were unaware of the idea of socialism and their endless debates in search of the "vanguard of the 1974 revolution" or the application of the "dictatorship of the proletarian" were extremely tiresome to the ordinary people. Such debates, by and large, were signs of self-absorption and were detached from Ethiopian reality.

The lessons that I would like to draw here is that firstly, during the early period of the revolution (1975-78), the intelligentsia seemed to be carried away by the idea that they had emerged victorious, without realizing that real political power had remained in the hands of the army. It is doubtful that the intelligentsia were given enough time to rationalize and digest the nature and the speed of the revolution in relationship to its own force, the army and the options left to them.

Secondly, the intelligentsia who were organized into Marxist-Leninist parties, movements and groups, developed antagonistic attitudes among themselves, which boomeranged, damaging them badly, and instead allowed the *derg* to buy the time it needed and finally to dispose of them all (Ottaway, 1990).[19]

Lastly, let us also take the groups of intelligentsia who join the party at a later stage (1978-1991)—here referred to as the groups of the second alliance. With massive assistance from the Soviet Union and its allies, these civilian groups helped the *derg* to organize and establish a single party in the name of Ethiopian workers. This party, with the help of extensive nationalization, promoted state capitalism led by a dictator. Thus, the intelligentsia who collaborated in this period helped to facilitate the *re-creation of a neo-feudal despot.*

The efforts of the civil intelligentsia around the Ethiopian Workers Party did not succeed in stabilizing a functioning political administration, and thus failed to sustain and maintain power at the center. Militarily, they could not succeed in defending the sovereignty of the country. Had it not been for massive assistance from Cuba and the USSR the civil/military government of the *derg* would have lost the Ogaden region to Somalia in the same way as it completely lost Eritrea. The party and the government created by the *derg* finally proved to be hollow, a house built of cards, one hard push and it all collapsed.

CONCLUSION

The economic transformation of the *derg* resulted in disaster because of the simple fact that it was based on rigid militarist commands, and denied the participation of the people in general and the peasants in particular. The collectivization carried out by the *derg* was seen by many as deportation and coercion and had very little to do with rural development. As priority was awarded to political activities, fruitful economic undertakings were frustrated, agricultural development particularly was hindered and the net result was accelerated famine.

The political tug-of-war between the central government, which endeavored to exercise more power and control over the resources of rural areas on one the hand, and the peasants who wished to liberate themselves from this central domination on the other, ended in the defeat of the peasants. Inevitably, the peasants lost this conflict with the *derg* as they had no assistance from other sectors of the society in general.

The fatal flaw of the military government stemmed from its being one dimensional, i.e. it believed that only ideology would solve all problems encountered by the Ethiopian people (socialist hallucination). They considered that traditional undertakings were obsolete and could provide no contribution to the new "revolutionary Ethiopia." They wanted everything to be new, but not born from the old, nothing from indigenous knowledge, traditional practices nor from local institutions. The answer they adopted to this dilemma was to import "new hybrid" from outside Ethiopian society. They brought one and inserted it in the womb of the old society to be reproduced, but what finally happened was that the offspring was a monster, which, of course, the majority of the Ethiopian people did not want to survive.

NOTES

1. For detailed discussion on the shortcomings of the land legislation see Cohen and Koehn, "Rural and Urban land Reform in Ethiopia," in *African Law Studies*, 1, 1977 pp., 3-62; Bruce, "Ethiopia: Nationalization of Rural Lands Proclamation," in *Land Tenure Center Newsletter*, No.47, 1975.
2. After the land reform there was a serious lack of the most essential tools of production such as oxen, ploughs and seeds. In

illustrating these facts, Dessalegn Rahmato (1984) revealed that in some areas up to 50 percent of the peasants lacked oxen. This partly explains why the famine prevailed long after the land reform.

3. Instead of joining the masses (i.e. the peasants) the left intelligentsia were so busy in reciting the different socialist theories to convince each other as to who led the 1974 revolution, and debating how to establish a proletarian party without the proletariat, and preaching for a dictatorship of the working class in a predominantly agrarian/peasant society.

4. These happened because the prevailing social institutions which might have been useful for improving the peasant's living standards were dominated by the political elites and other socially better-positioned individuals. These powerful sectors of African societies viz. landlords, merchants, police officers, judges, etc. utilize the peasants as their tenants, housekeepers, wage laborers, etc. Any development or economic betterment of the peasants' condition threatens their comfort and social status and therefore, socio-economic development of the peasants is unacceptable to them (Holmberg, 1977).

5. A term originally applied in the 1930s to rich farmers in the Soviet who opposed the policy of collectivization of family farms.

6. This statement is confirmed by refugees living, then, in one of the refugee camps in Sudan. According to interviews conducted by Survival International (1986), some people were beaten with sticks and rifle butts ... some were forced to run over thorns with bare feet, ... lie down on their back on a thorny bush, ... crawl on their knees, because of protesting against their resettlement.

7. With regard to the Northern rebellion groups, on one occasion the leader of the Military Government, Mengistu said, "Why should people have a right to be fed when they won't listen to what we tell them is best for them? The people have an obligation to obey programs and policies designed for their own benefit. If they think they have a right to wage war on us, why don't we have the right to stop it and to move them to areas where they have less chance of rebelling?" (Dawit Wolde Giorgis, 1989:298).

8. According to Dawit Wolde Giorgis, of the 700,000 people moved by the end of 1986, it is believed that close to 20,000 died either during the movement or at the new settlement sites. Almost 500 people were executed while trying to escape and an estimated

1,000 were lost while attempting to go back to their villages. Over 500,000 people managed to get back to their homelands and over 10,000 people crossed the border to Sudan. The rest continued to toil away under great hardships to satisfy the dreams of Mengistu (1989:304). Another source, Survival International quoted estimates that as many as 100,000 people have already died due to the resettlement program (1986:20).

9. Dawit Wolde Giorgis has more to tell to illustrate the unpopularity of the resettlement program. One case is taken up here which occurred in the Ogaden region. Some nomad people from this region were mobilized and put in shelters to be resettled in a new fertile place called Gode. Some elderly leaders from the group were invited, before hand, to visit their new would-be village. On their return, these elderly leaders of the clan were advised to convince the others over that night and all the necessary arrangements were made to move the people the next morning. After discussing the matter, out of 11,000 nomads over 10,500 of them successfully escaped (1989:284).

10. Environmental degradation is one of the acute problems in Africa today. In some parts of southern Sahara about 16 km of land per year is added to the desert. Soil erosion or degradation of land is another common problem of sub-Saharan Africa. Salinization, alkalinization, water loss aggravates land infertility. In Ethiopia it is estimated about 2,000 tons of fertile topsoil per square km are washed away each year. However, minor efforts such as terracing, laying of heavy stones across slopes, reduction of overgrazing, nursery measures could prevent this human disaster. For further discussion of the ecological impact of resettlement, see Alemayehu Dejene (1990:174-186).

11. There is a book (in Amharic) that reveals how the wars were much in the interests of the high military officers in the *derg* and high government functionaries in order to accumulate wealth in shorter periods of time. For further discussion see *Atfeto Metfat*, Yohannes Mulugeta. Moreover, in a recent publication of the journal of Addis Ababa University Teachers Association, Dessaleng Rahmato states, "There is sufficient evidence, though much of it is still hidden from the public, that some of the money raised by means of such "contributions" or levies ended up in the pockets of party and government officials" Dialogue 3rd. Series, March 1992, Vol. I No.1. p.50.

12. To make the point clear, let us take one concrete example. In 1985 the price for *teff* (the staple food grain) in Gojjam administrative area was 60 birr per quintal (about 100 kg), however the AMC price of *teff* in Addis Ababa, was 200 birr while the cost of transport was only 20 birr per quintal. AMC used to pay, including transport, 80 birr for a quintal of *teff* (Picket, 1991:123). Then, let us say for the sake of convenience, all costs including labor in loading and unloading, fuel and the like, amounted to 10 birr per quintal plus an extra 10 birr for other (unforeseeable) expenses. Now the AMC's total expenses were generously estimated at 100 birr per quintal and yet the profit made was an extra 100 birr per quintal. It was such lucrative profits that encouraged the *derg* to ban other competitive traders operating in the market.

13. Peasants who failed to fulfil their quotas, for example, could be prohibited from buying consumer goods from local shops or even forced to leave their plots of land (see Befekadu Degefe and Tesfaye Tafesse, 1990:116).

14. The events that are described in Ethiopia also have resemblance to other African countries regardless of their political coloring. For instance, Sandbrook (1985) illustrates how the marketing boards in Kenya and Ivory Coast paid peasants below the world price for their cocoa, coffee, cotton etc. Chamber (1983) also points out how the Zambian beekeepers are exploited by the government departments in paying them much less than market prices. With regard to this he indicates the situation as "... where government was already exploiting poor people so much, and so much more than any private trader might have dared" (Chamber, 1983:196). And this was exactly what happened in Ethiopia through AMC.

15. This should not be confused with nationalization earlier discussed such as the nationalization of properties that had either been owned by colonial powers or feudal landlords.

16. According to Makonen Getu, for example, mechanized farming intensified particularly in the 1960s and early 1970s and he states that "... the number of tractors, for example, increased from 200 in 1960s to 2 500 in 1970s while the area of land under commercial farming went from 6 500 to 350 000 hectares in the same period". (1987:51).

17. The steps taken by the military to consolidate its power, in short were: *derg* or a committee (1974-1975) —Provisional Administrative Council (1975-1977)—Provisional Administrative

Government (1977-1980)—Commission for Organizing the Party of the Working Class of Ethiopia—COPWE (1980-1984) Workers Party of Ethiopia (1984-1991).

18. Many were very committed to these theories and there was, for example, a schism in the early 1980s with those who had diverted from the general line and accepted the Russian (then called "revisionist") line of socialism. Such divisions among the Ethiopian intelligentsia (especially those residing abroad) did not stem from the Ethiopian reality, but were as a result of the Sino-Soviet conflicts prevailing then.

19. This period, especially after 1978/79, was the second mass liquidation, harassment, imprisonment and flight of Ethiopian youth. As we have seen earlier during the campaign *(zemecha)*, thousands of students, teachers, and youth from every walk of life who were ordered to serve the revolution perished in rural Ethiopia or fled to neighboring countries.

PART THREE

WHICH OPTIONS REMAIN? OUTLOOK FOR THE FUTURE

Chapter Seven

THE ROLE OF INDIGENOUS KNOWLEDGE, TRADITIONAL PRACTICES AND LOCAL INSTITUTIONS

In the introductory part, it has been pointed out that the focus of this study is on what has been named the bottom-up approach to governing—approach here meaning path or route. The bottom-up route, therefore, is conceived as efforts of people in the spirit of self-help and self-employment using their own local knowledge and resources. It indicates the use of indigenous knowledge and practices to carry out day-to-day activities. It also incorporates the use of local institutions and informal economic activities. By the same token, what is meant by top-down here is procurement of resources by state and parastate and/or foreign development agencies through line departments.[1]

Though my emphasis is placed on the bottom-up approach, this does not exclude the top-down approach as a desirable method. In fact, these approaches are complementary to each other. The point is, how these complementary ingredients could be infused to give better results.

Arguing this line, some authors indicate two fallacious approaches. The first is paternalistic, one which assumes that rural people are incapable of improving their lives and therefore many activities must be done for them by governments (top-down). The other equally erroneous stand is a populist one, which seems to argue in favor of poor people but in actual fact works against them. This approach assumes that rural people are capable of doing everything by themselves and, thus, should be left alone with no assistance (bottom-up). In this regard, examining both approaches may finally help us to identify a balanced solution to attack poverty.

Though the purpose of this chapter, and the following, is to assess which options remain and what is to be done to alleviate mass poverty, I have to confess, this assessment has become difficult. It is difficult, because there is no ready-made formula to follow to attain a given goal. Development needs mobilization of all resources, and the activation of every sector in a given society. In short, it needs a combination of all positive efforts.

If we take, say, developmental activities carried out by members of a given community without the support of government or any external inputs, they are bound to encounter difficulties in attaining significant results. Their efforts may be enough for survival but not enough for significant development of the magnitude we have discussed so far.

Not only communities', but also governments' efforts may not always exhibit significant results, however much political and economic good-will it may demonstrate, because poor states do not have enough resources to enforce their will. Additionally, even if there are sufficient resources that a government would like to allocate, there are so many bottle-necks to overcome before achieving the reduction of the level of poverty in a country, (e.g. lack of improved technology, skilled personnel, appropriate institutions; low level of education, insufficient political and economic infrastructures etc). In connection to this if a certain society has been able to mobilize its human and natural resources, development could become a difficult task unless local knowledge and traditional practices are open and adaptable to innovation to support their efforts.

The task that awaits us hereafter is to expound the postulation—local people's efforts in their day-to-day activities (bottom-up) supported by the efforts exerted by states and parastates (top-down) could produce better, coherent and significant results. The mechanisms to do so as argued below, are first and foremost, participatory activities. Participatory activities in turn entail democratic practices—accountability, transparency, tolerance and dialogue (political participation). The balanced combination of these ingredients, I believe, could bring about sustainable development and thereby reduce poverty.

Bottom-up Route: People's Initiatives

As I have stated above the bottom-up approach is used to identify efforts mainly contributed by local people. It may be efforts to execute a given piece of work needed by a community or it may as well be long-term commitments to change local conditions of lives. In both cases, however, it is assumed that local people employ their indigenous knowledge and traditional practices. Let me examine them in detail.

Indigenous Knowledge and Traditional Practices

From the early evolutionary stages of the Paleolithic era to the emergence of modern man, human history has been nothing more than a struggle for survival. The struggle has been carried out through physical labor supported by the improvement of tools. In this struggle to sustain life, human being and her tools improved significantly, and daily activities became routines or common practices. Thus, here practice is defined as actions taken regularly, or work performed frequently to meet individual, family or community needs. Practice, as employed here, has a connotation that has determining effects upon human actions. As Sherry (1984) notes, it shows how actions and interactions "may have changed in the past or be changed in the future" (p.146).

Practices that are proven to sustain local needs are repeatedly carried out over time and passed down from generation to generation, eventually becoming the customs and traditions of a given society. Normally, only those actions which, as a result of trial and error, are proven to serve a given society's needs, and which are based on the prevailing available resources are preserved and handed down. It is essential to stress here that the customs, traditions and beliefs transmitted to new generations are generally those that have been tried, filtered and accepted by societies as guarantees of their survival. Thus, for the purpose of this study, we can say, traditional practices are actions, values, attitudes and patterns of performed exercises, inherited from the past, and accepted as useful in the present.

The process of preserving useful practices and transmitting them down through generations has its own established process.

Some may be carried down in written or documented form, but the bulk of them are transmitted through oral traditions and repeated performance of the practice. Many people today carry out their daily activities of farming, fishing, building huts, eating, dressing, etc. in a specific manner (tradition) without much thought given as to why they dress the way they do, eat this but not that and build their huts in a particular way. However, in the actions performed there are often explanations as to why they should be so done.

Not only physical practices, but also beliefs, can become part of traditions and be transferred down generations. These beliefs can be useful in protecting vital resources and lives. For example, in some parts of Africa certain animals are declared "sacred" with the help of religious prohibitions, and slaughtering them is forbidden. However, the explanation of this behavior is of a more secular nature, the reality behind this practice is—if people consume certain useful animals (scarce resource), there may not be enough left for farming, transport, in short, for sustaining life in general.

Traditional practices also incorporate protecting the lives of fellow community members. With regard to protecting lives, in Ethiopia, for instance, there is an injunction against eating pork, the main reason behind it being that the highlanders eat raw meat, a practice that is potentially deadly if one eats raw pork, therefore eating pork is forbidden altogether. In many traditional societies such explanations are often given in association with religion or some other supernatural power to create the required sense of fear and respect towards practices which are potentially harmful either to human lives or to scarce resources. This may be said to be sub-rational, however, it is rational. In Western societies similar protection is imposed with the help of the law or dissemination of information through appropriate institutions.

Identification of Local Knowledge and Practices

Traditional practices and indigenous knowledge are dependent on each other and it is difficult to draw a clear line in between them. However, while already prevailing knowledge is used for present practice, from that particular exercise society may gain new stocks of knowledge useful for the future. In this manner both are complementary and interwoven. Let me give some examples to identify some of this indigenous knowledge and point out to what extent they are useful to local communities.

Rural inhabitants' indigenous knowledge covers many fields of activity essential for the sustenance of life. This knowledge includes, *inter alia,* farming techniques that extend from terracing, irrigation and crop rotation to soil conservation; indigenous knowledge of traditional medicines is worthy of respect; they are well versed in folksongs and historical tales and also enjoy an interest in physical fitness and sports, they have a comprehensive knowledge of animal husbandry, forestry, and preservation of food and crops.

As a means of protecting the forests and farm lands, a form of soil conservation is established knowledge among peasants. Many foreign experts would assume peasants do not have knowledge of soil conservation, but farmers in general are able to tell which soil, red or brown, is suitable for a certain kind of crop. Bee-keeping is another area of well-established practice in many parts of Africa. Artisans, e.g. fisherfolk, are remarkably knowledgeable on the relationship between lunar inclination and tides and the resultant increase or decrease of catch (Titze, 1985). A traditional medicine man can identify a number of herbs useful for alleviating headaches (some for ordinary and some for migraine) and can also prescribe various herbs for combating intestinal worms both in humans and animals.[2]

Rural inhabitants are well aware that, for example, wild plants are homesteads for different species and provide food for animals and people and attract rainfall. They are aware that forests provide them with medicines and materials for building their houses, boats and utensils and they are also conscious that care should be taken. They are also aware and capable too of maintaining ecological balance. However, the severity of the poverty under which they live today has forced them to cut down forests in order to be able to cook their daily food, burn it to make charcoal for sale, or clear for farming in order to survive. Many development experts seem to have difficulty in understanding the actual level of their poverty, which forces them to act in this what might be called "irrational manner."

Apart from their knowledge of sustaining life through taking care of scarce resources, rural poor people are also good at economics, marketing, local credit and savings systems, food processing etc. For example, Gladwin (1980), explains how west African women dominate fish marketing and how their knowledge of preserving fish (through smoking, sun drying, salting) is efficient. These women also practice well developed credit and saving systems. I may also point out here the industrious *gurage* women of Ethiopia who dominate business in Markato, Addis Ababa. Their sharp entrepreneurial

177

minds and their well-developed credit system (*equb*, forthcoming) can indeed merit them as well-qualified carriers of African indigenous marketing and commerce capacities to date.

Indigenous knowledge and traditional practices also extend into the areas of handicrafts and manufacturing enterprises. Ethiopian women, for example, are outstanding in handspun soft Ethiopian cloth, locally known as *shemma*. The handspun thread is also used for making cloth by skilful weavers called *shemane*, whose technical knowledge and instruments of production, though they have been used for millennia, are very similar to early European hand weaving devices. The process of making local liquor (*katikala*) and the scrupulous steps taken to filter and condense it, though indigenous, are in principle similar to laboratory filtering.

One essential question that may be posed after this catalogue is how to demonstrate that the use of indigenous knowledge and traditional practices help to foster development? Before answering this question, however, we have to draw the line between the incorrect position taken by many development experts and agencies, who presuppose that traditional knowledge and practices are unfit (obsolete) for modern innovations. My point of departure is antithesis to this errors postulate.

Erroneous Assumptions and How to Overcome Them

A number of studies show that what are generally referred to as traditional societies' knowledge and practices are not as completely played-out as Western development practitioners have often described them to be. In addition to their methods of protecting vital resources and human lives (as described earlier), traditional societies, for example, are rational (Scott and Gormley, 1980), technically minded and experimental (Chambers and Howes, 1980). They are good at conceptualizing their world outlook (Swanson, 1980), and are endowed with empirical and technical knowledge (Richards, 1980).[3]

Many development promoters seem in a hurry to pass judgement on, or label, certain traditions as backward without investigating why the people stick to their traditions and are skeptical of *change* (here change means Westernization). Poor people are often reluctant to accept practices or ideas forced upon them. This is because, by experience, they know that they often do not have much to gain from what is called *new*. The source of this skepticism is perhaps that when foreigners and some foreign influenced local development practitioners attempt to implement new ideas, they often forgot to think of how to communicate with the local people (inter-cultural communication). As a result of such neglect, experts proposed undertakings may fail to receive a positive response from the local people. This frustrates the foreigners (and even national experts) and invites them to pass all kinds of unfair judgements concerning the abilities and understanding of the local people and their practices.

In relation to the point raised above, one often hears how traditional societies in general are conservative and anti-innovative, but few to explain the reasons behind this resistance to rapid modernization and innovation. *Change* to the poor means perhaps the loss of a plot of land from the weaker to the stronger person, or from the poor to the rich—a step towards destitution.

Example: take a certain rural household who is against birth control. They are against it because it means minimizing labor in the family and loss of income and security in old age for the parents. More children means maximizing chances and safeguarding the individual from many possible eventualities. Many children must be born into the family because some will die early, some may become busy with their own family and will not find time to spare for their old parents. The traditional way of thinking therefore is, the more children, the more chances of receiving help in bad times and old age (compare this to the different types of savings in banks, insurance, bonds, stocks etc. of the Western societies—geared to safeguard individuals and their families). Therefore, there are several reasons for local (traditional) people not to simply abandon what has been done for generations, which they know for sure has helped to sustain life, in exchange for something *new* and unproven, without any guarantees.

It has been stated that retaining traditions means preserving knowledge for coming generations. Following this line of thought, if a certain practice is lost to some thing new which at the end of the day proves to be a failure, perhaps the link not only between the past and the present but also to the future will be lost forever. This happens because traditional knowledge is usually preserved orally through story telling. The passing down of traditional practices is, by and large, through show and do processes. Thus, if this practice is interrupted for a while, as nothing is documented, the generation that follows will be left empty handed.[4]

Without attempts to understand the reasoning of local people, the proponents of African modernization argue that traditional practices are not conducive to development. What I would like to say here

179

is that the problem does not lie in the obsolescence of traditions as they tend to believe. For example, African development activists, so far, have neglected African indigenous knowledge and social institutions. The major reason for such neglect as Ake (1990) also argues, is due to the fixation on the wrong goal, namely Westernization, which is something new and not based on African reality.

The underlying problem is that many foreigners (the introducing agents of this new technology) coming into Africa do not make any attempt to understand that it is the environment, local needs and poverty, which have caused the people of a given area to act and live according to a certain pattern, and that has nothing to do with "ignorance or behaving in a savage fashion." These and many similar faulty and self-created concepts of outsiders lead them to dictate their agenda without taking into account the stocks of knowledge preserved in a manner that foreigners could not understand. Therefore, under such circumstances, outsiders shall make extra efforts to allow time to learn how the rules of nature dictate the generations-old practices of various localities.

To sum up, the message I would like to convey is that the effort of development ought to be geared towards cultivating, enriching and transforming local values, traditional knowledge and practices.[5] For this to happen, respect for the historical heritage of a society is the very cornerstone. Such heritage is the ground on which the people stand and from which their forward movements can be directed. To repeat, development efforts that are not based on a given society's cultural and historical heritage and that do not take into account the extent of indigenous knowledge and traditional practices cannot be expected to bear the anticipated fruit. In this line, important to the argument perhaps is to ensure that, in the future, outsiders understand that the traditional bodies of knowledge are useful to the people, and thus that mutual respect is essential to be able to start afresh. As Chambers (1983:101) also suggests on the complementarity of the two experiences:

> The two types of knowledge complement each other; and together they may achieve advances which neither could alone ...
> For that to happen ... one first step is for the outside professionals [experts], the bearers of modern scientific knowledge, to step down off their pedestals, and sit down, listen and learn [from the local people] .

After establishing this and clearing our path to start afresh we have to ask ourselves—in what manner can these stocks of indigenous knowledge and traditional practices be put into practice? Are traditions adaptable to innovations? What is the extent of modernity and invention of traditions?

ADAPTABILITY AND MODERNITY OF TRADITIONS

As earlier stated, because of the fixation on becoming Westernized, some development activists maintain that African culture, social institutions and indigenous knowledge, are not, and could not adapt to modern development. However the question to be answered here instead is—what kind of development? Development for whom? If the answer is development aimed at the reduction of the poverty of the African people then it seems reasonable to argue that the knowledge, practices and other potential of the poor cannot be neglected but have to be mobilized.

Most development efforts applied thus far have been heralded as change or new phenomena—a scrapping of the old and introduction of the new without any appropriate continuity from the past. As repeatedly demonstrated in the Ethiopian case this is faulty thinking. Such a notion from the outset is not only anti-traditional, but it fails to explain on what foundation this new change is to be built. As Swanson (1980:67) also notes, the Western attempt at change runs counter to the reality that "every culture is dynamic in that it is always in a process of change, always in a process of self-redefinition."

In the preceding sections it is argued that traditional knowledge and practices are not static, and we have also noted that practices are handed over from one generation to the other and through such a process each generation adds some new and meaningful knowledge to the previous store and this new addition demonstrates the adaptability, or what I would like to call the modernity, of tradition.

An interesting point concerning the adaptability or modernity of tradition is found in Rudolph and Rudolph's (1967) study of Indian traditional societies on how different traditions adapted to modernity. The authors analyze variations in the meaning of modernity and tradition, and suggest how these two infiltrate and transform each other (p. 3). The main theme of the study is to show how traditional values, such as the caste system and Brahmin Sanskrit law, are slowly being transformed and modernized.

Hobsbawm and Ranger (1983), enrich our knowledge by examining traditions from another perspective. The author state that old tradition can die and new will be born from it, which they referred to as invention of tradition (see Chapter One). In the invention of traditions we see how new knowledge and experiences intertwine with each other as a result of working or living together. Many Latin American and some African countries are vivid examples of this phenomenon.

Though the above examples are given to achieve clarity, my concern here is mainly with the modernity of traditions as manifested by local initiations and it is to this type of local organization and institution that I now turn.

Local Organizations and Institutions: Meaning, Types and Functions

Before going into detail some distinctions must be made between what is referred to as local organizations and local institutions.

An organization may be conceived as a process wherein individuals are assembled as units to accomplish common objectives. More generally, there are two types of organizations. One is formal and the other informal. The former denotes situations where rules and tasks are officially and strictly observed. The latter represents situations where beliefs and behaviors are not authoritative, and it is to these organization I refer below.

Local organizations as used in this context incorporate different kinds of peasant associations, co-operatives, and other forms of village organizations. To understand the discussion in this study, perhaps, it may be easier to illustrate local organizations in terms of double-layered structures. On one layer, for example, there are locally operating branches of government agencies, parastatals, line departments and party branches. Such local organizations tend to be strictly formal and centrally steered, supported by state (and/or donor agencies), and their loyalty and accountability are often to the forces behind and above them. On the other layer, we find organizations locally initiated, and their loyalty and accountability are to their community—informal or voluntary.

Voluntary organizations may also be defined as those local organizations mobilized for a specific period directed towards specific activities by the local people themselves (they may be organized by external forces, yet their loyalty and accountability is to their community). The life span of such voluntary organizations may extend over years, or can be brief, depending on the task that the community wishes to accomplish. Apart from formal and informal organizations, we may also come across the term institution.

Institution implies on one hand, an established custom and practice and on the other the act of instituting, establishing and founding. The latter types could be enacted or consciously created by governments, e.g. organized bodies of law, education, research institutions etc. and can also be highly systematized with carefully designed roles. Institution that implies custom and practices, entails a fundamental behavioral pattern of cultures and traditions. Such institutions are stable, as they are part of a web of long traditions and tend to remain meaningful social organizations.

Local institution referred to below are less formal social structures that have served communities for longer periods, and through which local people's indigenous knowledge and traditional practices were (and still are) manifested. Since they have proved their importance to communities, they often are preserved and passed down from one generation to another (e.g. *mahaber, equb, eder* of Ethiopia). It is such types of institutions that I would like to discuss.

Though I try to give working definitions above, in the discussion hereafter, there are places where local organizations and institutions are used interchangeably, but they always remain the type of local organization where their loyalty and accountability are to the members of a given community. Below some examples from Ethiopia are given that may help us to obtain a better picture.

Local Organizations and Institutions:
Some Examples from Ethiopia[6]

Before going into detail the following points should be mentioned. The local organizations or institutions and their methods of work described below by no means represent an exhaustive list, and are only used to indicate their capacity as agents of transformation. It is also equally important to mention here that the structures and performance of indigenous social organizations presented below are not uniform throughout the country. For example, some had written regulations and elected leadership, whereas others lacked such characteristics. A few of these organizations may have functioned in some areas relatively well and in other areas poorly. However, on the whole, they are useful to rural societies.

For the purpose of this study, I have categorized the examples into three groups. These are: (a) local institutions mostly associated with social functions known in many regions of Ethiopia as *mahaber*, which simply means association (b) socio-economic and welfare affiliated local organizations, represented here by *debo* and *meredajas*, and c) *equb and eder* are identified as examples of traditional financial institutions.

The types of local organizations and institutions named above may have different functions. Some can serve as a local level democratic forum and pressure group, others are purely used for advancing economic benefits, and yet others are used to sustain social-networks. In certain communities, one local organization could also be multi-functional. Dealing with all these in detail, however, is beyond the capacity of this study, instead I shall concentrate only on brief presentation of their places in Ethiopian society and attempt to demonstrate in what capacities they could serve further development.

Local Institutions Associated with Social Functions

Among many different associations dealing with social functions, *mahaber* is a common one. The word *mahaber, per se*, means association or local organization, and is used for both religious and non-religious gatherings. Religious associations manifested in terms of festivals have made considerable contributions to organized social life in general. Traditionally, *mahaber* are religious gatherings to observe a holy day in honor of, say, one of the Apostles and are observed every month according to the Apostolic doctrine. Usually they are held following the Ethiopian calendar, so on a specific Saint's day a member of a family (whose turn it is) arranges food and drink and invites the members of the association. In many cases, non-member neighbors, friends and relatives of the family are invited as well.[7]

Members of *mahaber* and other invited guests, apart from enjoying the party, normally use the occasion to discuss their personal or social problems in an easy and informal atmosphere. Misunderstandings among the members or in the community in general are dealt with in an open forum or in small groups depending on the issue at hand. If the issue is found to be too serious and complicated, the family priest, referred to as "a father of the soul" and locally referred to as *ye`nefs abat*, and/or an elderly man, known as *shemagle*,[8] mediate and help to reach a decision. The words of the elderly people and priests are generally respected and carry weight. The members also believe it is to their benefit to resolve misunderstandings there and then.[9]

If the case is unresolved in the simple mediating procedure as described above, a committee consisting a number of *shemagle* (council or ad hoc committee) would be formed to look into the matter in detail and assist the priest. If all the arrangements to resolve the conflict(s) failed, the priest will take the matter(s) in hand and pass a decision best sought (with the help of God, according to the priest) to both partners. This decision is irrevocable and called *gezet* (excommunicate) and normally, the conflict ends there.

There are both single sex *mahaber*s and those in which the members are of both sexes. *Mahaber*s, however, are not necessarily and primarily organized for the carrying out of religious observations. For example, outside religiously oriented environments, *mahaber* could be associations of old friends, schoolmates, workers' organizations or professional associations. *Mahaber* could also be based on neighborhood or kinship, but in all forms it is used as a common forum for expressing the members' needs. Such *mahaber*s are more open for adaptability than religiously oriented types.

Socio-economic and Welfare Affiliated Local Organizations

A different type of social organization with some affiliation to community development is widely known as *debo*, (they have different names in different areas, such as *wonfel, jige, woberra* etc. and also exhibit slight discrepancies in function). *Debo* is a traditional form of voluntary-based collective work. For example, a group of people pool their labor resources and/or material belongings (oxen, hand ploughs, sickles etc.) to help a fellow neighbor. *Debo* is usually carried out in harvest season, and it is often organized to build family houses, or for any other matter beyond the capacity of a single family or household to undertake. In general, when a family needs extra labor to accomplish a certain task, a *debo* is called. *Debo* is a temporary, organized body in which the arrangement is made upon the request of a household needing extra labor. The requesting family prepares food and drink for the participants. Apart from lending a hand to a fellow citizen these sorts of occasions were used to discuss matters that concerned the whole neighborhood. The other major example and one that may be more important to our discussion of rural development is a type of welfare association known as *meredaja*. Prior to the 1974 revolution, for example, many welfare associations bore the names of the regions from which the members came (Wollo *meredaja*, Gojjam *meredaja*, Gurage *meredaja* etc.). *Meredaja* could also be professions or other groups pooling their resources together to do something useful to help their fellow countrymen. Such associations were formal organizations with written regulations, having bodies for both administration and accounting and were legally registered. *Meredaja* associations used agenda discussions, invited influential and public personalities from the region in which the welfare association was established, welcomed media coverage of their meetings and discussed issues of development in their regions.[10]

In the 1960s and especially the early 1970s, the members of *meredaja* often discussed the causes of poverty and tried to find solutions to their regional problems. They pooled financial and material resources to construct roads, schools, clinics, etc. In a country like Ethiopia, where open discussion and political parties were totally prohibited, such fora became popular and began to be well-attended. Thus, the organizational capacity and popularity of this forum became stronger day by day and a sort of (healthy) competition among such associations intensified as many people began to openly identify and associate themselves with the organization that stood for the development of their regions. However, the regime of Haile Selassie could not tolerate such activities and finally, many of them were banned.[11]

Traditional Financial Institutions

The other general classification includes local institutions practiced across religious, ethnic or social boundaries such as *equb and eder*—sometimes called informal financial institutions.

There is controversy as to the origin of these local institutions. Endreas Eshete and Pankhurst (1958), for example, more or less argue that *equb* and *eder* are products of the Italian invasion of Ethiopia (1935-1940). The validity of this assertion, however, is questioned by Mekuria Bulcha (1973), by pointing out that the use of other types of voluntary organization had been prevalent in the country (e.g. *debo*) for centuries. Beyond this discussion however, there is consensus that such associations are generally helpful to communities. What, then, are their impacts on communities? We begin by examining *equb*. [12]

Equb normally starts within groups based on strong ties such as kinship, business associates, and schoolmates or within the neighborhood. *Equb* is a rotating fund. It can be a temporary or recurrent saving association. The money received will be used for various kinds of investments ranging from house-building, opening of (local) small-scale business to cottage industries. *Equb* is especially common among large and small-scale businessmen/women and is widely accepted by many government and private employees. The purpose of the poor participating in *equb* is that they are often incapable of saving enough money in their lifetimes to make the necessary investments. So they pool their small savings (by week or by month) together and hand them over to one member on a revolving rota. With some variation from group to group, on average, the practice of *equb* goes like this: the person to receive the collected money is chosen beforehand (according to needs which were discussed and agreed upon), if there is no member that needs the money urgently a lottery is drawn. Many *equb* practice the latter system, and if the person who receives the chance to collect the sum does not need the money, in some *equbs* the sum may be sold to another member who will be deleted from coming draws (*equb* members also receive a certain percent from this sale and use the money for administrative purposes and to cover minor food and drink costs). All members are obliged to pay the agreed sum of money till every member recoups his/her investment (Dejene Aredo, 1993:9-27).

Equb is also an ideal primary forum for economic and social discussion. This is because each gathering usually comprises a small group of people who generally know each other. Their meetings often are short, to the point, and business-like. There are no complicated regulations and many decisions are made on the basis of their near acquaintance and their trust to each other often lies on group pressure.[13]

Eder, one may say, is the opposite of *equb*. In *equb* people gather to improve a fellow member and his family's future through savings that may be used to venture into new investments. In contrast, *eder* is established for the purpose of providing mutual help on the occasion of the final ceremony of one's life—death (remember there is no life insurance in rural Ethiopia). *Eder* is wider than any other local organization where regular fees are paid and all members are obliged to attend funeral ceremonies and must always be ready to help.

There are at least four common types of *eder*, (a) community or village *eder* (people residing in same areas), (b) work-place *eder*, (c) *eder* among friends and (d) family *eder*. Members of *eders*, could also participate in the same *equb* groups (Dejene Aredo, 1993:28-35).

The heart of the above argument is that such local institutional networks that were interwoven into the society for centuries were not given their due respect as agents of transformation in Ethiopia. These local associations had functioned relatively well in the unfavorable conditions that had prevailed but no chance was awarded them to serve the society freely. The point now is, what provisions could be made? And to what effect can they serve society?

LOCAL INSTITUTIONS AS VEHICLES FOR SUSTAINABLE DEVELOPMENT

Under this title I would like to point out the different areas where traditional institutions make positive contributions to the attack on poverty. I will also try to indicate the necessary provisions expected from governments to facilitate local institutions so that they can yield productive results. The discussion hereafter is presented in three steps i.e., (a) traditional or informal institutions, (b) semi-formal institutions and (c) an attempt is made to indicate the link between these institutions and formal ones. I would also like to indicate that terms such as informal and formal are used frequently. While the former concepts indicate local or indigenous institutions and practices the term formal incorporates organizations such as banks, insurance companies and state sponsored institutions.

Traditional or Informal Institutions

The examples presented below reflect the capacities of traditional institutions to adapt and improve methods of work to provide social services (e.g. *mahaber*), facilitate socio-economic development (e.g. *meredaja*) and serve as traditional financial institutions (e.g. *equb* and *eder*).[14]

With regard to strengthening social services, institutions such as *mahaber* (interest group associations) could play a part, though some people doubt that *mahaber* could serve as a vehicle for development because of the relatively high level of food and drink consumption during their social gathering. This, however, seems too simplified an argument—because. Firstly, it is judged from facile observations and does not take into consideration many interest group associations under the same name which are organized for productive purposes in addition to attending festivals. Secondly, *mahaber* is not negative because of much food consumption—remember, at a certain level of development, consumption is an investment, (a) more consumption leads to more production, and people need food to work, etc.

Messfin Kassa's (1973) study for example, reveals the labor sharing aspect of *mahaber* where members pool resources such as oxen and ploughs and work together in harvest seasons. They also help each other in the building of their houses and engage in many other community development activities. The importance of such an organization, apart from the points discussed, lies in its creation of intimacy and closeness among its members. Once the groups are mobilized for the good of the community their contributions are whole-hearted and their cohesion for the common purpose is immense. This again may create a conducive environment for self-help development.

The major contribution of *mahaber* is perhaps in the areas of conflict resolution and as pressure groups. The conflict resolution role may be easier for *mahaber* because of the traditional respect societies pay to elderly people, *shemagle* and family priests, as explained earlier. With their awareness developed, *mahaber* could easily develop into pressure groups aimed at demanding local needs agreed within their respective communities. This is a potentially valuable activity that has not been properly utilized. Thus, under favorable conditions, *mahaber* may be developed into democratic fora where popular dialogue and debate could flourish.

With regard to *meredaja*, for instance, we have stated that they are, to a considerable degree, socio-economic development organizations. They are open to adapt to new technology and improved methods of work to tackle local problems. More importantly, their primary concern is to help rural areas build roads, schools, clinics, etc.

The point to be addressed here is that *meredaja* are development oriented voluntary organizations able to foster many concrete ideas and suggestions to promote further social change and economic development in local regions. These fora may be used for serious discussions of problems of development of physical infrastructure, inter-regional exchange of goods and services, credit opportunities that would liberate local producers from the exorbitant interest rates of the money lenders, serve to run campaigns for health, education and other facilities. In short, they could have been developed into popular mass movements, against poverty. If members of *meredaja* are given the opportunity to freely organize themselves, they may create grass-roots organizations that can respond to the people's demands, formulate their grievances or present local people's complaints against authority. These could develop also into different local pressure-

189

groups (like the Swedish *folkrörelser*). The development of local pressure groups, in turn, is a *political resource* that will enforce more accountability, transparency and stability.

Similar to the above and another possible area where *meredaja* could play a significant role may be if they could be developed into lobbyist groups, advocating for activities in the regions they represent. Because of the pivotal positions the different members of *meredaja* have, like in decision making bodies, in media, and in different government institutions that would enable them to collect more information and assess the possibilities of development of their respective regions. They could also serve as "watch dogs" for their regions. This again seems important in a country like Ethiopia, where neither elected representatives nor any sort of democratic representation from each region was common.

The other major category in the discussion of adaptability and modernity of traditional institutions involves the capacities of traditional financial institutions to serve as vehicles for sustainable development. To illustrate this in detail, I take two examples that were introduced earlier namely, *equb* and *eder*. Let us start with *equb*.

In *equb*, as earlier pointed out, members usually look at business-oriented activities and in many cases the money pooled is meant for productive investments. To create such organizations to encourage small-scale investments and savings in some poor countries (e.g. Grameen Bank in Bangladesh)[15] it took considerable efforts on the part of the governments and foreign development agencies (World Bank, 1990). But in Ethiopia, though they have existed for many decades these local institutions have not yet been properly cultivated and used for societal development.

More generally, there are both negative and positive assessments of *equb*. From the negative side we can name Comhaire (1966), who asserted that "equb can hardly be regarded as a productive institution", and from the advocates of *equb* I may name Mauri (1987) and Baker (1986), who have studied the role of *equb* in Ethiopian societies at different times, and yet arrived at similar conclusions, that *equb* and *eder* are traditional financial institutions, which may have considerable impact on the financial development of the country.

To indicate the relevance of *equb* and to address my point clearly, it may be easier to cite some more examples from Ethiopia. There are *equb* attended by large and small-scale businessmen/women whose members could be as many as two hundred. In Dejene Aredo's (1992) study it is indicated that there are *equb* that have a weekly contribution of birr 500 per person (almost equivalent to a monthly salary of a university graduate) having a weekly collection of total birr 85,000 (p.17). Some people also think that *equb* only take place in towns and cities where there are high money circulations, and where business flourishes. This is not true because *equb* are also utilized in rural areas by poor people (Baker, 1986; Dejene Aredo, 1992).

TABLE 7:1
MONTHLY CONTRIBUTIONS TO *EQUB* AS PERCENTAGE OF
MONTHLY INCOME IN SOME RURAL AREAS,
SELECTED EXAMPLES, 1986

Occupation	Income Per month	Monthly Contribution	Equb as % Income
Tela sellers	11.73	2.75	23.4
Farmers	21.68	4.60	21.2
Pensioners	31.27	2.59	8.3
Employees	77.90	2.31	4.2
Policemen	99.58	2.00	2.0
Teachers	219.17	6.47	2.9

Source: Baker, 1986:166.

As we can see from Table 7:1 the poor local brew, *tela* seller contributes a much higher percentage of income (23.4 percent) in *equb* than any of the other socio-economic groups indicated above. This may demonstrate that *equb* is one way of saving for further investment or consumption which is accepted to the rural poor.

After such explanations one may wonder why *equb* is so popular and people prefer to participate in it? Dejene Aredo's (1992) answer to a similar question is helpful here. After examining different *equb* the author concluded that in *equb* ties of friends or solidarity among members are so strong that defaults are almost unknown; *equb* are more flexible, adaptable to members' needs; *equb* compared to banks have no written paper work or procedure (writing and carrying documents are inconvenient and frightening to illiterate people); credits are offered without or at a lower interest and savings are obligatory and thus help to impose self-discipline on the members.

The other traditional institution that might be helpful for further development of financial institutions is *eder*. As earlier explained, *eder* are non-profit making institutions geared to help a fellow neigh-

191

bors in time of crises such as of death in the family. More generally, the functions of *eder* are economic such as covering funeral expenses, and providing financial support to the mourning family. They can also provide social support, as the members not only accompany the family to the funeral but stay very near to the family for days or weeks offering solidarity and support. In cities and town this human affection and embracing of one family in times of crisis fulfil the role of kinship that has been lost due to migration into urban areas. Over and above this, there is evidence collected indicating that *eder* are also involved in community development activities such as helping in school and road construction (Dejene Aredo, 1993).

Mekuria Bulcha's (1973) study also points out that *eder* organizations have positive roles to play in community development, in social integration processes, social welfare, and as means of social control. Alemayehu Seifu (1968) before the 1974 revolution, and Pausewang (1983) after, have confirmed that these local organizations were (are) expanding rapidly in both urban and rural areas. The latter author especially, notes that this growth is caused by the fact that the different formal systems so far tried by central government have failed to provide poor people with any security of life.

Thus, *equb* and *eder*, apart from their central role in economic development activities may also contribute to democratic working methods through elections of leaders, voting on issues and abiding by the rule of the majority, teach techniques for running meetings, introduce the use of bookkeeping, time discipline, etc. In short, they may way to integrate modernity into traditional sectors.

Semi-formal Institutions

What are the possibilities that these traditional institutions could improve and serve societies better? To begin with, we have to bear in mind that firstly, it is difficult to advise local people to use bank and insurance services not in rural areas. Secondly, such modern or formal establishments demand a minimum of reading and writing skills. This again is impossible, as the overwhelming majority of the peasants is illiterate. Thirdly and most importantly, the socio-economic development of the African countries, including Ethiopia, are dual in character while in some areas there are elements of modern development (e.g. using bank services), the bulk of the rural areas are predominantly engage in traditional practices. For such societies the appropriate approach perhaps, is to advise societies to grow slowly and at their own pace (from traditional first, to semi-traditional or semi-formal and finally, to formal, see also Table 7:2).

TABLE 7:2
ENABLING FACILITIES THAT HELP TRADITIONAL UNDERTAKINGS TO GROW INTO SEMI-FORMAL ORGANIZATIONS, SELECTED EXAMPLES

LOCAL ORGANIZATION	PROVISION (TOP-DOWN)	POTENTIAL FOR DEVELOPMENT
Mahaber	less control more incentives conflict resolve	democratic forum debate circles, & pressure group
Meredaja	less control more incentives	development forum voluntary co-ops, lobbyist group
Equb	training finance support	local entrepreneur saving/credit Assoc.
Eder	training credit source saving/co-ops	insurance social security

As indicated in Table 7:2 and illustrated earlier, the availability of traditional institutions to contribute to the betterment of communities seems clear. What might be emphasized is how this could take place.

The point made above, that small and local activities, for instance, *equb* and *eder*, can develop into semi-formal organizations, is better illustrated with the help of an Ethiopian Air Lines Employee Savings and Credit Co-operative which began as a simple *eder/equb* club in the 1960s. Today the co-operative has over *birr* ten million in capital, 27,000 members and allots credits (up to *birr* 15,000) at low interest rates. The co-operatives' capital per members, at present, is *birr* 3,700, which is ten times the average for the country. The same development is also observed among the employees of the Telecommunications Authority, which today manages twelve million *birr* as capital and provide credits (up to *birr* 12,000) to its members at 1 percent interest rate per month (Dejene Aredo, 1993).

One may think that the above developments are possible because the named saving and credit co-operatives are based on high income earning groups. However, low income employees of the Truck Loaders Union in the rural area, Assella, also provide a success story in its transition from *equb/eder* club to a savings and credit co-operative.

The success of these co-operatives is remarkable especially after 1978, when the government made favorable provisions and legal support for the development of co-operatives. Though the aim of the socialist government was to encourage socialist oriented co-operatives, the savings and credit co-operatives, which were established prior to the revolution made use of these and established a firm basis for operation.

Just to emphasize my point that government provisions may make a difference, I quote an example: the national average annual growth rate of membership of Savings and Credit Co-operatives in Ethiopia prior to 1978 was 10 percent and the average share for participating members amounted to birr 268. After the introduction of legal provisions in 1990, the annual membership increased by 37 percent and deposit per member amounted to *birr* 600 (SACCO, 1990; Yassin Shifa, 1990).

Lastly, it may be important to indicate that many *eder* are adapting better ways of giving services as demanded by the members. For example, some *eder* are not only limited to funeral ceremonies, as they used to be, but have extended their services to providing financial assistance to members, and in some cases they cover medical expenses, loss of property by accident (e.g. fire). One of the leading voluntary organizations in this context is The Ethiopian Teachers Association *Eder* (ETAI) with capital amounting to over *birr* three million, which provides service for nearly half a million of its members (also organized at the national level). This *eder,* today, reimburses for medical care, travel expenses for its office holders, and in so doing has transformed itself into a semi-informal or medium-sized insurance enterprise.

Linkages Between Traditional and Formal Sectors

On some occasions, *equb* money is deposited in banks, but, *eder* use bank deposits to a larger extent. This is because normally, *eder* funds are not often used until an accident occurs. Savings and credit co-operatives use bank services extensively and also deal with large amounts of money. To cite examples, in one study in Ethiopia it is revealed that about 87 percent of the financial assets of *eder* is deposited in banks, and according to the same source, per capita bank deposit of *eder* members in Ethiopian is *birr* 108 while the average for the entire population is only around *birr* 90 (Dejene Aredo, 1993). In addition, traditional or informal activities provide a learning process for participants. It is also a process of accumulating capital, experience, and establishing the necessary contacts with the formal sector (banks, larger enterprises) to launch better investments at a later stage. Inferred from the arguments so far put forward, the ultimate aim of some of the informal institutions seems to be to become formal; and the reason that some stay informal in the initial period is that there is no chance of operating in the formal sector directly.[16]

Many people tend to believe that traditional institutional activities are limited to serving only small pockets in communities and are unable to expand to regional or national level. This is an erroneous assumption. Through horizontal links, i.e. between similar activities and types of organizations, informal activities can integrate their experiences (e.g. the Ethiopian Teachers Association *Eder* is organized at national level). In their vertical links, i.e. contacts with government and semi-government institutions, informal activities could be incorporated with the national interest.

ACTIVITIES OF TRADITIONAL INSTITUTIONS IN SOME SELECTED COUNTRIES OF AFRICA

A question that logically follows from the above presentation is: are these local institutions exclusively an Ethiopian phenomenon or are they prevalent in other African countries? The answer is yes, and below examples are given a of local organizations from some countries of Africa.

In some parts of Africa rotating funds (*equb*) are known by different names such as *esusus, osusus, liekembas, tontines, chilembas*. In countries like Cameroon and Gabon over 28 percent of the population participate in local, rotating fund associations (MacGaffey and Windsperger 1990). In Ghana *equb* like savings groups, *susus*, have evolved into growing credit and savings facility units useful for the development of many communities. *Susus* daily collection, in local currency, amounts to 500 *cedis*, (USD 2) daily, per person. The total sum collected in 1989 was about 2,000 million *cedis*. Because of the large amounts of money they attract, formal banks have started *susus* like activities (*World Bank Report*, 1990:66-67).

Another example of a local voluntary organization with notably positive results is The Rural Saving Development Foundation in

Zimbabwe. It has succeeded in mobilizing neighborhood groups into self-help organizations (like *meredajas*). The organization today has over 250,000 members and a sound savings account. At present it provides services to its members (farmers) to assist in purchasing fertilizers, better seeds and improving their housing conditions (*World Bank Report*, 1990).

In Kenya, *meredaja*-like organization called *harambee*, for example, not only mobilized and led the liberation movement against colonialism, but also in peace time, promoted self-help development projects geared to rural development. Today, *harambee* runs 70 percent of rural schools (including 1,040 secondary schools) and is involved in rural development to provide clean drinking water supplies (Ake, 1990).

Adaptability and Modernity of Traditional or Informal Activities in Other Parts of Africa

Traditional institutions are the breeding ground of what is called the informal sector. Time and again it has been stressed here that traditional practices can adapt to the introduction of new technology and are open to innovations. It is also argued that traditional knowledge and practices are not limited to local level activities, but in fact could serve larger regions and positively contribute to development efforts at the national level.

African peasants and urban poor are withdrawing from the formal and joining the informal sector. Why? As Fantu Cheru (1989) notes, they are forced to move in this direction because they are hindered by financial and bureaucratic networks, from participating in the formal sector and thus the only option left to them is traditional undertakings of a more informal type.

In most African countries, indigenous knowledge and practices as exhibited in informal sectors have already taken the economic upper hand. For example, about 75 percent of sub-Saharan employment occurs in the informal sector. Informal sector economic activity at present is producing between 20-70 percent of GDP in many African countries. According to the *OECD Report*, by the year 2000, approximately 95 percent of the African labor force will be engaged in the informal sector (*OECD Report*, 1991:70).

At present, the informal sector has taken a grip both laterally and vertically in many parts of Africa. A World Bank sponsored study (1990) revealed the wide economic activities of the informal sector. This report estimates between 20 to 80 percent of African economic activities are in the hands of informal actors. With regard to urban jobs, over 50 percent in Dakar and Abidjan and between 60 to 70 percent in Benin and Accra are provided by the informal sector. According to a survey (1983-84) by the Ministry of Agriculture of Ethiopia, it was revealed that the informal sector accounted for 78 percent of the total credit extended to peasants (Dejene Aredo, 1992). The already named and many other reports have illustrated the increased scope of the informal sector in the construction, trade, small scale manufacturing, transportation and maintenance sectors.

Informal sector activities are diverse, ranging from retailing, brooking and money-lending to small-scale manufacturers. The spectrum stretches from one self-employed person through the extended family to activities employing as many as ten people. Informal sector activities are mainly labor intensive, use artisan techniques and involve little capital investment. Women and extended family labor dominate and the enterprises are highly heterogeneous in character and widely distributed in their geographical locations. One *OECD Report* (1991:65) states that the informal sector:

> comprises a vast and otherwise untapped pool of productive and organizational skills, and plays a key role in recycling materials and re-deploying resources that would otherwise remain unused.

The informal sector may be useful in benefiting the poor and those without other resources. They recycle or waste of different types, which would otherwise have endangered the environment, they make use of unemployed family labor caused by shortage of farm land, they effectively use off-the-shelf technologies which otherwise would be wasted.

As the same source confirmed, the informal sector enables the domestic economy to withstand external shocks and to avoid expenditure (less purchase of spare parts, accessories, royalties, etc.) and is vital to sustained long-term economic growth (*OECD Report* 1991:70). Additionally, informal sectors are important generators of capital to re-invest and expand. In this manner, the informal sector is a field for cultivating entrepreneurs, who ultimately may serve national economic growth and ease poverty.

The informal sector provides both economic and social gains to traditional societies. Economic gain because it uses small-scale personal savings for productive investments which otherwise would have been used for celebrations or festivals. Relevant to this study, the informal sector also includes anti-poverty elements. For example, the sector provides employment for marginalized or destitute people and in so doing helps them to gain incomes and to re-integrate into society.

In short, the advantages of the informal sectors are, (a) they are based on local knowledge and practices and are best at recycling and re-use of materials (cost effective and environmental advantage), (b) geared to local consumption and locally oriented, (c) small-scale and therefore manageable and easy to control, (d) and fuse traditional methods of work with modern innovation. As illustrated above, there is no doubt that the fate of Africa's further development lies in this sector.

To sum up, from the discussion held above and the evidence collected, it may be concluded that traditional or local institutions can adapt and transform themselves for the better. For example: voluntary workers and/or agricultural co-operatives could emerge from local organizations. These organizations, in turn, may be used for fostering accountability, transparency, that is to say, democracy. Local saving habits such as saving in kind, with the help of voluntary saving associations, could be transformed into bank savings. Credit facilities, which are part and parcel of the money economy could enable increased investment. By venturing into new or further investment fields, additional income could be generated. Finally, increases of income may be used to alleviate poverty. I, however, recognize that there is not enough power here to effectively minimize poverty in present day Africa, they have to combine their efforts with other enabling factors (described below). But informal activities, on the whole, are basic factors for with in designing strategies to attack poverty.

Enabling and Disabling Factors

Generally speaking, modernity of tradition needs people's initiative (bottom-up) and then, government support through consciously designed policies and provisions (top-down). The modernity or adaptability of tradition is the coupling point of these two efforts. The state, for example, could make provision for training in simple bookkeeping, accounting, auditing, how to handle meetings, to record minutes, development of leadership, which are essential for all organizational undertakings, and obviously, local people have difficulties in obtaining them by themselves.

Government or international development agencies can step in to support local institutions by making provisions in the form of "revolving funds" that will allow the local institutions to create co-operatives especially designed for rural communities. This will help rural people to save and obtain credit at reasonable interest rates. This again would release the poor from paying exorbitant interest rates to local money lenders and at the same time enable them to venture into new but small-scale activities. As experience shows, credit/loan recovery from such groups is remarkable (Tirfe Mammo, 1987b).

To make local institutions facilitators of development, as attempted here, major enabling factors, are provisions and support made by governments. Among these provisions the following could be named as creating an enabling environment to facilitate the use of local institutions—less bureaucratic red tape, more decentralization of power, encouragement and support to horizontal and vertical movements within local organizations and less political control. In order to implement and follow up these provisions, for instance, a national government body responsible only for coordinating and following up the development of traditional institutions may give better results.

Among the disabling factors direct involvement of government in local institutions with the aim of politicizing them. Government policies should protect public property rather than damaging it, as, for example, by forcing local institutions to contribute funds for the waging of civil wars in the name of defending the motherland, a ploy undertaken by the military government of Ethiopia. Such measures discredit government accountability, and most importantly, the trust of the people in the state is undermined.

TOP-DOWN ROUTE: GOVERNMENT INITIATIVES[17]

In presenting top-down efforts, I have to declare from the outset that exhaustive scrutiny of government policies is beyond my capacity. However, the arguments presented below try to elucidate the need for balanced state intervention (as opposed to the excessive interventions described in previous chapters. In order to create a permanent and effective solution to the problems of poverty, I think local initiatives (bottom-up) and government efforts (top-down) ought to be consciously integrated.

Appropriate measures to be taken by governments to assist local efforts are stressed below. These are (a) the increase in food production through effective methods or better technology to check recurrent famine, (b) support of basic human needs and laying the groundwork for the future, (c) creating a conducive atmosphere through establishing internal political legitimacy and stability; and (d) establishing regional co-operation to protect local efforts from external pressures.

Increase in Food Production

The acute problem in Africa today is not only the overall material poverty but lack of food and thus, the provision of food is the number one priority. On average, African food production increases by 1.5 percent while population grows at about 3 percent per annum. Thus, the production of food does not keep in step with the fertility rate. According to FAO (1991) and World Bank (1990) reports, today, 20-30 percent of Africa's population depend on food imports. In this way, fertility and poverty reinforce each other—high fertility causing more poverty. What are the causes?

In most African countries, apart from the socio-political reasons discussed, farming methods or techniques have not been modernized for centuries. For example, in Ethiopia the peasants apply the same farming techniques (a pair of wooden with iron tipped stakes dragged by oxen) as used by their ancestors. These cultivation techniques were developed to feed a population far smaller than today's. Even more extreme is the situation in some countries of Africa where very little help from animals is employed, and the bulk of farming work is carried out by human labor and no of fertilizers. As a consequence of such inappropriate techniques and lack of fertilizers many African countries have been suffering from chronic food shortages for decades.

Improved farming techniques include the introduction of better strains of seeds, popularizing of new farming tools, controlling plant diseases, protection from insect pests, use of fertilizers, etc. It also includes better animal husbandry. Improvement of farming techniques also means to increase yields through better land use, reclamation of unused wasteland and reforestation campaigns.[18] Improved farming techniques requires training in local handicrafts, for both men and women, in order to improve and up-date instruments of production. Intermediate level engineers to improve irrigation systems, build canals and search for ground water are among the immediate needs. Additionally, to improve farming techniques biologists are needed to study better strains of grain and chemists to identify

The Role of Indigenous Knowledge, Traditional Practices

locally available types of fertilizers. Efforts made in these directions may give better results as pilot projects in Ethiopia shown, and as indicated below (Table 7:3).

TABLE 7:3
AVERAGE YIELD PER HECTARE UNDER DIFFERENT
TECHNOLOGICAL MIX (QUINTALS PER HECTARE),
SELECTED EXAMPLE FROM ETHIOPIA

Crop	Without Fertilizer	With Fertilizer & Retarded Techniques	Wiith Fertilizer Improved Techniques
Teff	7.1	11.3	20-22
Wheat	10.5	15.9	32-40
Barley	9.9	15.3	30-40
Maize	14.5	21.2	50-60
Millet	10.0	14.3	25-30

Source: Ministry of Agriculture, 1982.

Many African peasants are too poor to undertake such measures alone. And as we all know there are not enough resources to accommodate these requirements provisions from the government. Therefore, the option left appears to be to mobilize the people's and government efforts in a coordinated manner.

To produce enough food, as earlier pointed out, land must be distributed to the people, and most importantly, farmers must own their plot of land (Dormer, 1972). Farmers must be assisted by the state, and the state must adopt favorable policies to facilitate their efforts to produce enough food and they must be encouraged (with incentives) to supply their grain surplus to the markets. This would help the peasant not only to produce enough food, but also to gain some additional funds to buy essential consumer goods, an additional incentive. However, governments may have not enough resources to do so, and worse still, in some cases governments lack the political legitimacy and accountability to implement such policies.

It is a known fact that the emphasis on peasants and agricultural development will, apart from value of increasing food production to sustain expansion in non-agricultural sectors, absorb labor and increase real income. In many African countries, well over 80 percent of the national income is extracted from the agrarian sector. Thus, it

201

is the peasantry who make a substantial contribution creating employment not only for those involved in agriculture and related activities, but also for those in manufacturing—urban sector (Meier, 1989). The question is, how to mobilize and organize these forces for further productive undertakings.

Another problem area is the development of formal institutions, that is to mean, establishing development promoting establishments and foundations. Such establishments are needed for the analysis of a country's problems, for the formation of locally feasible policies that can contribute to development, for administering programs that lead to improvements, for education and training and for stimulating and building support that could be of help in further innovation and reform. As illustrated in the Ethiopian case, the weakness of institutions to organize, direct, and draw lessons from community efforts, or in short, the failure of such organizations to play roles as executing bodies of development undertakings brought about negative results in the anticipated transformation. Why did it turn out like this?

The *derg* undertook wide-ranging and drastic social reforms such as land legislation, collectivization, nationalization of private farms and extra houses, resettlement and villagization programs. In a short span of time, The *derg* took drastic measures which severely affected over fifty million people in Ethiopia. In so doing, it over-centralized, over-burdened and over-strained existing institutions. The new institutions set up to combat these problems could not cope, not only were they new to the situation, but also ill-equipped materially and lacking in qualified personnel. Shortcomings with regard to institutions that could guide policies, therefore, have diverted Ethiopian social reform onto a negative route which could not have been previously conceived. Thus, the social revolution in which many Ethiopians suffered and sacrificed to secure better living standards ended with severely negative political and socio-economic impacts.

In brief, socio-economic transformation of any African country is difficult unless low-productivity peasant agriculture can be rapidly transformed (Todaro 1981) and peasants start to consume goods and services. In this regard, it has to be stated that the African smallholders or peasants are the kernel, the essential agents, of social change and economic development. The other agents of change, namely the entrepreneurs, the intelligentsia, the state etc, are all facilitators of the primary development agent. The support of one to the other must be carried out in an organized manner through institutions.

Meeting Basic Human Needs

Among development practitioners and international development agencies (e.g. ILO) there are discussions on provision of basic human and material needs. In these discussions there is commonly made distinction between what are human and what are material needs. For the purpose of this study, I have only concentrated on some of the essential or basic needs which make poor people's life worth living. These are: (i) basic education, (ii) health, (iii) shelter, (iv) income generating undertakings, and (v) improved opportunities for women.

(i) Basic Education

Sustained rural development in Africa needs basic education. African education systems as applied so far, were not tailored to suit its society. They were brought from afar to serve in some cases, colonial administration. For example, the education system in many countries, tends to equate education with securing a better office job (inherited from the colonial rule), rather than creating opportunities outside office employment. Therefore, the decolonization of ideas through presentation and practice of the African cultural heritage is vital.

Education ought to build self-confident and upright African personalities. The African education systems should be geared to the improvement of indigenous knowledge and traditional practices. As Riggs (1989) argues, African realities are not Western realities. The Western way of understanding and interpreting things is based on specific experiences and realities. If they can be of any help in the development of Africa, well and good; if they can only help within their context they should be modified and adapted, if not, rejected. In short, major aims of top-down efforts ought to be to improve the quality of standard education in order to facilitate nation-building, harness common identity and establish common symbols—a lack of which the African continent suffers from today.

Generally speaking, educational performance in Africa, at present, faces many problems. There is a significant difference between enrollment statistics and attendance. According to the number of students registered, Africa seems to have made impressive progress, but this differs from actual attendance, performance, or quality of knowledge of the students enrolled. For example, girls' drop-out is more

203

than boys because of early marriage, pregnancy and above all to help their poverty-stricken families. Still worse, in some African countries, there are situations where girls are not encouraged to attend schools (OECD Report, 1991).[19]

The other major issue is that many schools are concentrated in cities and towns, depriving the bulk of the rural student population of the opportunity to take part. This means it is only those who can afford it, rich farmers, local administrators and officers, who send their sons and daughters to school. These students, who have come from the elite and the relatively rich sector of rural society prefer more urban centers. For example, those who can read and write prefer to move to the nearest rural business center, those who finish elementary school may leave for provincial towns; after secondary school attendance, few stay in rural areas and many migrate to the capital and other major cities; finally, those who reach university or college level tend to go abroad.

Despite these problems, education is essential, because it is through education that society's rectilinear is set, it is through education that simple but effective information can be disseminated, it is through education that awareness and consciousness building can be carried out and deepened, and more importantly, it is through education that African traditional knowledge and practices can be integrated with better technology that eventually would enable the continent to attack poverty at its roots.

These arguments are supported by Orivel and Modck (1990). After a series of studies both authors confirmed that the level of performance of a literate person in any work is better than that of an illiterate person. The literate group are receptive and open to new ideas, relatively methodical in their approach and rational towards solving problems both in the short and long term.

(ii) Provision of Health Facilities

Another long-term effort of governments to improve peasant lives, or satisfy basic human need lies in provision of health facilities. To improve the health situation in the rural areas, attention should be paid to local clinics and health stations and identifying remedies for common diseases. Dirty drinking water is the source of much diseases. Improving the life of peasants appears to include increasing the availability of clean drinking water through drilling and development of artificial water storage systems. Fetching drinking water for example, may take half a day's work for many rural dwellers. Child care, inclusive nutritional intake, and sanitary conditions ought to be improved. Using proper latrines protects rural people from the spread of diseases. Training of intermediate doctors (like the barefoot doctors of the Chinese model), training of midwifes, dressers and district nurses is also vital.

(iii) Assistance in Improving Shelter
The housing conditions for African peasants are poor. In many rural areas peasant's huts (tukuls) are constructed out of non-durable thatch and mud. The same is true for grain storage buildings and byres for domestic animals. Additionally, in many rural areas peasants and their domestic animals live under the same roof. According to one study conducted by the Red Cross in Ethiopia, one major source of disease is the sharing of common quarters. The same source reveals that more than 63 percent of the people interviewed lived with domestic animals (Ethiopian Red Cross Society, 1986).

(iv) Income Generating Activities
Income generating activities, to support low and seasonal agriculture income, are essential. During the non-harvest season, the peasants consume what they have and begin to borrow from the money lenders at an exorbitant interest rate just to tide them over to the next harvest period. This situation is repeated year after year. It occurs because there are no other means of earning a living outside of farming and thus many rural people flee to urban areas after harvest season or leave permanently. In the light of this reality, seasonal employment is an essential component in creating supportive income during the non-farming periods.

Seasonal employment can be generated in different rural activities such as mending roads or bridges and school buildings; housing construction; building of dams, canals and irrigation channels; building of feeder roads and erosion controls etc. These may be implemented during non-farming or off-seasons just to absorb the available labor. Additional occupations for peasants in non-farming seasons could also be non-formal education, combined with different training courses such as vocational subjects, home economics, vaccination campaigns (animal and human), family planning etc.

(v) Improved Opportunities for Women
On average, about 20 percent of sub-Saharan households are headed by women. In some countries of Southern Africa as many as

63-70 percent of the men work outside their residential villages (in copper and gold mines) thus, leaving their families for long periods (World Bank, 1990). Though African women struggle hard to change their situation, the weight of poverty falls most heavily on them because of their double workload, lower level of education and smaller income. Focusing on them can reduce poverty. Improving income should incorporate rural women in developing horticulture, animal husbandry, handicrafts, food packing, fish processing, afforestation programs and preparation of different kinds of spices which are in demand in cities.

In order to provide a soft start for long-term socio-economic undertakings some political components of development should also be examined. These are legitimacy and internal and regional stability.

Legitimacy, Internal and Regional Stability

Fundamental aspects of the rule by any state is first to gain legitimacy and then, create stability in its domain. A government need stability and legitimacy, initially for itself, and then as an instrument or means of communication with its subjects. Stability and legitimacy are two sides of the same coin, it is difficult to attain one without the other. The lack (or lag) of one brings down the other and will lead to crisis. We have seen that when the military government of Ethiopia lacked political legitimacy, it was dragged into endless civil wars by which every household was affected.

More generally, internal stability and legitimacy alone is not enough to sustain power in a given country. The state of affairs in many countries have been complicated by the intervention of external interests, which may be regional or international. This has historical background.

It was stated that former colonial powers, in order to sustain their dominance, chopped the large nations of the African continent into pockets of ethnic groups and then recognized them as sovereign states (Chapter One). Mazrui, (1986) states that from the days of the Scramble for Africa (1885-86) to the days of "formal" independence (1950s/60s), Africa was divided into small states, designed not to support small ethnic groups but to keep them strongly dependent on foreign powers. Arguing along the same lines, what Nkrumah (1965) said over thirty years back, holds true even today. He stated that neo-colonialism is based upon the principle of breaking up former large, united colonial territories into several small non-viable states that are incapable of independent development. In many African countries, the ethnic divisions have become sources of conflicts that deepen poverty.

In light of such a discussion, one may ask, what then are favorable conditions that will lead to political stability and economic welfare? One partial answer to the question may be regional co-operation. How? As a result of the divisions discussed above, today over 15 percent of small African nations are landlocked. Is there a better option for these small and landlocked African countries than regional co-operation that would eventually allow them to share available human and material resources and provide an outlet to the sea?

It is a well-known fact that the potential material resources of the world, at present, are enough to provide comfortable lives for all its people. The problem is that the rich wish to be richer, and prefer to die of over-consumption rather than share with the poor. Is there a better option left for the poor than to join together and help each other?

Regional cooperation is advantageous for the poor countries of Africa because it provides them with freedom of movement among their people, easy access to goods and services across borders, it allows them to pool their resources and invest in coordinated projects. Regional co-operation will allow poor African countries to develop their media and transport systems. Cross-boarder relationships creates horizontal contacts between business communities, farmers, governmental and non-governmental organizations etc. and enable them to exchange experiences.

Regional cooperation helps African agriculture to produce specialized and valuable crops. For example, the rift valley regions are rich in cotton, other east African countries produce coffee, maize and meat. West Africa countries have rice and cocoa, while Southern African countries are endowed with diverse agricultural and mineral products. Regional co-operation helps, for example, grain producing countries to acquire minerals from other African countries without paying for them in US Dollars. Regional co-operation will give African countries better terms of trade and therefore commerce among them will encourage African entrepreneurship. One may wonder here how do these countries trade with the rest of world? Even today there are some African countries that import cars and lorries from Europe and Japan in exchange for gold, coffee or ivory (MacGaffey and Windsperger, 1990).

Finally, it is time that Africa formed a common front to stand against the disadvantageous winds blowing in from the industrial countries. The present global economic system whether we call it aid, trade or international relations all appear to be unfavorable to Africa. African countries cannot resist attacks mounted against them while they are separate and divided. They cannot face the severe poverty, which is persistently aggravated by the unfavorable global order. From the ruins of the old political blocks of the world, new blocks are emerging today. To become partners and cope with this trend, Africa must co-operate.

LIMITATIONS AND DELIMITATION OF BOTTOM-UP AND TOP-DOWN ROUTES

The catalogue of provisions indicated above, the number of questions posed, and many of the suggestions made, may not be new. Many of them, perhaps, are essential goals and may even be on the top of the agendas or lists of priorities in many African states. However, the fundamental questions in regard to what has been suggested above are how could all these commitment be attained? Have poor African states enough resources and strength to combat all these negative trends?

The central point to address here is that these efforts could not be attained by governments alone, or by only the people's good will. They also are difficult to implement with the help of massive financial and material support from the developed countries alone, as North/South Commission advocates. The mobilization of forces against poverty must come from all sides. However, the reliable force that could put these efforts in motion is the organized bodies of the poor people themselves through their participation. It needs their will, trust and motivation.

Mobilizing people is not only forcing them to participate in some kind of activity, it also incorporates pooling constructive ideas, finding means and ways of solving common problems, sharing experiences, making joint efforts to acquire financial and other scarce resources. Thus, it is only through coordinated and integrated undertakings that the recommendations made so far might have an impact on poverty. The point I would like to address is that once the people make participatory commitments, governments' efforts towards the same end may also receive people's acceptance and thereafter, external forces may help as catalytic agents to amalgamate the top-down and bottom-up efforts (presented in detail in the next chapter).

With regard to limitations, local organizations and institutions do not always provide a free ride. In fact, there are lots of problems to be aware of. These problems have, at least, two aspects to consider. One is, there are built-in problems, that is to say, problems inherited in the bottom-up and top-down approaches, the other is the problems which will arise in coordinating them.

To begin with the former, the use of some local practices is not an easy task. There are a considerable amount of irrationalities in the application of traditional practices. Sometimes, traditional ways of acting may not serve its purpose. A good example of this is the fact that many local people in Africa affected by incurable and contagious diseases turn to voodoo power rather than searching for information useful for protecting themselves. This however, does not represent all forms of traditional practices but is worth mentioning.

One has also to bear in mind that informal sectors have their disadvantages—unregulated (usually long) working hours, low levels of protection and hard working conditions, harsh and disabling injuries may occur with no insurance to provide compensation, low pay for women, child labor, lack of training and thus poor development of skills.

Concerning coordinating or combining local activities and government efforts there are also problems. For one, there may be a difference of opinion in what, for example, rural people think useful for themselves (bottom-up); while the development planners' directives are based on what is better for the local people judged in the eyes of the state (top-down). This is demonstrated in the Ethiopian case.

Historically, peasants in Ethiopia are used to voluntarily mobilize collective work. They usually worked in groups but always retained possession of what was theirs. Generally speaking, Ethiopian peasant self-respect is based on their own labor and possessions derived from that labor. The term *balebet*, (meaning head of a family) for instance, means one who provides a roof over his family's heads, feeds, clothes and takes care of family members. It has a connotation of self-governing or self-employment. This quality is that which defines the strength of the family and creates legitimacy in the community.

These rural families have local institutions to serve them in times of need. The local institutions, in turn, are rich in ideas of solidarity and mutual understanding and well rooted in people's lives. For many centuries peasants in many regions and communities of Ethiopia were interwoven in social networks provided by these institutions. They had local economic, social and religious organizations useful in their daily activities. However, none of these were given serious consideration in the efforts to transform Ethiopian society—be it during the regime of Haile Selassie or the *derg*. This was because both had erroneously conceived modernization as the graveyard of old traditions and a field in which to sow modern ideas.

After deposing Emperor Haile Selassie in 1974, the *derg* regime aggravated this problem by introducing compulsory programs such as villagization and resettlement schemes, widely known as forced collectivization. This new form of local organization is opposed to the traditional forms. Such enforced displacements more or less disturbed the very basis of voluntary associations and traditional practices oriented towards local problems and primarily based on group membership and kinship. It was seen as the forced disintegration of families which had lived together in a given community for generations and thereby developed common identities and symbols that, I consider, are the pillars of local institutions.

What the military government did instead was to sideline traditional organizations in the name of *socialist collectivization*. When these new practices were applied in collectivized areas (socialist villages) the people felt naked, abandoned and detached from their heritage because of this sudden exposure. For the majority of the peasants it was impossible to replace what they had practiced for centuries with new ideas of which they knew nothing.

To my understanding, collectivization as applied in Ethiopia, had dislocated the people from their environment. Collectivization, in particular, suffocated traditional values concerning the possession of, work with and determination of the fruits of the individual's labor. Being stripped of one's own produce and later having it returned in the form of rations runs completely counter to Ethiopian peasant tradition. This measure was equated with beggar status in the eyes of the peasants. It went against their ethics and degraded their personality before their family. They were no longer self-governing *(balebet or abba-werra)*, and had nothing left to strive for because they did not posses anything and could not influence their circumstances by their own labor any more. The enforcement of such a type of collectivization, contrary to the lifestyle and long tradition of the peasantry, seemed to completely ignore the very essence of Ethiopian peasant social norms and mores.

The Ethiopian Military government failed to consider that the people's history and cultural heritage, indigenous knowledge and experience as practiced by traditional institutions might have been useful for the fundamental transformation of society.

NOTES

1. The attempt hereafter is to indicate areas where contributions of governments, foreign development agents and local people's efforts could be combined to improve the living conditions of the poor.

2. Knowledge of the rural poor extends to identification and recognition of thousands of different types of vegetation. They are familiar with the specific uses of many plants like which of the leaves, the roots or fruits could be used for food, which can be used for building materials and which are suitable for instrument of production.

3. These social scientists agree that rural poor have knowledge that could be useful for promoting development. For detailed discussions of various bodies of rural/local knowledge refer to Brokensha, Warren and Werner's, 1980, Indigenous Knowledge System and Development.

4. Concerning documentation of knowledge, there is no controversy over the advantage of preserving knowledge in written form. Admittedly, if African traditional knowledge had been documented in written form it would have been easier to share experiences with others, and less misunderstandings between peoples would result. The lack of documentation and sharing of experience is a fatal shortcoming for any society.

5. For further discussion with regard to culture and development see, The Challenge to the South, The Report of the South Commission, 1990:131-134.

6. The reader may be aware that though some of the names given below are in Amarinja (referred also as Amharic) there are similar local organizations in different parts of the country baring different local names.

7. *Mahaber*—festivals are common in the local churches every Sunday, known as *senbete* and slightly different form *mahaber* that is normally taking place at home.

8. It is interesting to note that recent peace negotiations in Ethiopia have realised the role of *shemagles* as experienced mediators in

local conflicts as was seen in the 1992 peace conference. For more information see "Seminar on Peace, Reconciliation and Development in Addis Ababa," in *Horn of Africa Bulletin*, Vol:4, No. 5 (September-October 1992), Life & Peace Institute, Uppsala, Sweden, pp. 11-12.

9. Referred to as *yeker le' egzabeher*, which in rough translation means *let all of it remain in the hands of the almighty God.*

10. The word *meredaja* is derived from another word called *meredadat* means "to help" or "support" each other.

11. A strong *meredaja* (association) called *Metcha'na Tulema* (named after Oromo region) was established in the late 1960s and this became very popular among the Oromo ethnic group. At that point Haile Selassie's government became alarmed, and then, the organization was banned, the members harassed and even tortured. This brutal action of the government forced such organizations to go underground and ultimately many of the leading members joined different liberation fronts. Therefore, due to the political repression many useful *meredaja*s diverted their welfare work and became platforms for many of the liberation fronts.

12. For further information on *eder* and *equb* see "Alemayehu Seifu," Eder in *Addis Ababa, A Sociological Study*; Pankhurst and Endreas Eshete, "Self Help in Ethiopia" in *Ethiopian Observer*, December, 1968.

13. Many of the Ethiopians residing in Europe and North America, where there are sufficient banking services, usually have *equb* groupings not only for economic services but also for its social functions including the fostering of group belongingness and the providing of a forum for the discussion of common problems and/or share ideas.

14. At this juncture, it may be essential to support the examples given here with a thorough study of such organizations. In one study of economic development in Liberia, Dieter and Massing (1974) point out that local institutions are very useful during a period of changing economic, social and political conditions (transformation phases). The findings of the study also indicated that during the process of adaptation to changing economic conditions for example, traditional institutions themselves can undergo a structural and functional change in order to adapt to the new conditions.

15. The Grameen Bank activities of group savings and small credit systems are well known for its high recovery and low default rate.

The author of this study has personally visited these activities in Bangladesh.

16. Though one sees the complementary nature of the two sectors there are also differences. As it is pointed out by Santos (1979) "lower circuit" i.e. informal sector, which is mainly characterized by labor-intensive technology, where credit still is non-institutionalized and social relations are direct and personal. On the contrary what he called the "upper circuit"—formal sector, employ capital intensive technology, credit is allotted through banks or financial initiations and social relations are impersonal (1979:12-27). Whatever differences there are, my argument is, there is always a continues flow of exchange of activities from the informal to formal, and visa versa.

17. In dealing with the top-down route we have to keep in mind the discussion we have had on the Ethiopian peasant associations. The peasant associations though were organized with the help of the government, at one time, they had taken initiatives to administer themselves. But this could not continued because of the negative political will from the military government side, and ultimately the major part of the exercise ended up in collectivization (see Chapter Six). Thus, the Ethiopia peasant association may be referred as a typical case where local (village level, rural) efforts are pushed aside to furnish new efforts from above.

18. The other major areas for improvement of farming techniques are the use of biological and chemical innovations like fertilizers, pesticides, insecticides and hybrid seeds, together with better techniques in irrigation and crop rotation. The farming techniques mentioned above increase per capita and total food production and it is possible to produce enough food within a short span of time as has been proved in the Green Revolutions of India, Indonesia and many other Asian countries. The reason that these measures are advocated here is that they are technologically *scale-neutral*, which is to say, they can be applied equally and effectively on large and small farms. They do not necessarily require large capital inputs or mechanized equipment. They are therefore particularly well suited for tropical and subtropical regions and offer an enormous potential for raising agricultural output (Todaro, 1983).

19. Many educated people seem to be dissatisfied and frustrated because education failed to provide work as anticipated. Some argue that since there is what is called "educated unemploy-

213

ment," utilizing any more resources on education is wasteful
and not advisable. Others argue that high level education is not
necessary for Africa because excess education has brought what
is called "education inflation."

Chapter Eight

PARTICIPATION AS A METHOD OF ATTACKING POVERTY

Participation is a very useful device to tackle many of the problems described, and also to round off the major discussion held in this study. For example, in the first part of this study, the main issues discussed were the lopsidedness of development theories and practices hitherto implemented; the problems of debt, dependency and some negative impacts exhibited in Africa via different kinds of international relations (Chapter One to Three). The suggestion made then, was to look for an alternative route which could be more useful to tackle poverty. In the case study of Ethiopia, the attempt was to show the depth and dimensions of poverty, with the help of some examples. Here, the major remedy employed in attacking poverty was a social revolution. However, the force that took power after the revolution imposed unlimited and exaggerated social and political experiments at the expense of small, ordinary people's local knowledge and practices. This experiment finally missed its target of minimizing poverty (Chapters Four to Six). In the last part of this study, in search of options to utilize in the attack on poverty, two approaches were presented, namely top-down and bottom-up (Chapter Seven). Now, I will try to show how participation could be used as one of the tools to attain balance and facilitate, integrate and coordinate efforts exerted by bottom-up and top-down undertakings.

Participation is also used here as an important device to draw together many of the arguments raised in different sections of this study.

GENERAL NEED FOR PARTICIPATION

Participation is a multifaceted concept and difficult to define in a manner that could satisfy all. Generally speaking, however, two points should be remembered throughout the discussion. Firstly, participation can be formal, when it is organized from above say, by governments. It can also be organized informally by the local people from bottom or grass root levels. However, the central discussion here will not be on who organizes, but more specifically, on how the local people influence and control their organizations, and what roles the members of local organizations play. Secondly, though I generally present different forms of participation, the key element of participation, especially at the initial stage, remains political. It is taking part in planning, implementing and evaluating day-to-day activities, which are the concern of local people. Participating thus means sharing power and this makes participation political from the outset.

Participation here entails the creation of opportunities which enable members of a community and the larger society to actively contribute to and influence the development process and to share equitably in the fruits of development (UN, *Ad Hoc Group Report, 1978:5*). It is not about, as Uphoff and Cohen (1977:3) correctly observed, "people" doing just what they are told to do and having no influence on how the benefits of development efforts are distributed"; it is about people's involvement in decision making processes, in implementing programs, their sharing in the benefits of development activities, and involvement in efforts to evaluate their achievements.

Additionally, participation to a great extent is here related to the use of traditional practices in attacking poverty. In this regard, participation implies that local knowledge and experience are not only necessary for the success of rural development activities, but also a vital ingredient in the process of creating development successfully enough to put pressure on poverty.

Many development efforts so far implemented have not been concerned with human and social transformation. Instead, development has been interpreted from the perspective of economic growth. In the eyes of planners, non-economic factors such as culture, religion, tradition, indigenous knowledge and democratic rights did not appear to be important. From the mid-1970s onwards, however, a fundamental departure from the simple top-down development approach was strongly advised. This new school of thought was in favor of the bottom-up approach, which advocated that people should be central to development efforts. This is witnessed in the importance attached to alternative approaches such as self-reliance and basic needs. With regard to the neglect of popular participation in many development activities Oakley, (1991:1-3) argues that,

> The central issue of this search for development alternatives was that development had become capital centered as opposed to people centered; it had by-passed or even marginalized people in its concern to build and construct ... development programs and projects have largely by-passed the vast majority of the rural people; there is a need, therefore, to re-think forms of development intervention to ensure that this neglected majority has a chance to benefit from development initiatives.

This statement is clearly demonstrated in the Ethiopian case where the government designed a development process, and made massive efforts without taking into account how the people would respond to it. The argument hereafter is that if the level of poverty is to be affected at all, the neglect of the people has to be reversed, and balanced through the participation of the people.

Now, it may be wise to confront the common doubt people often have with regard to participatory actions. These doubts are as follows: if participation entails the taking part of ordinary people, say in planning, how could an illiterate peasant to begin with, sit and reason out with knowledgeable economists who speak a different (professional) language? Another doubt, if participation means taking an active part in implementing, what are the ways and means for peasant to be able to take part in it? If participation incorporates the presence of the local people in evaluation, how could the sophisticated techniques of evaluation be explained to an illiterate person? The doubts named above boil down into one important aspect—the *labor input* of rural people is possible, their *their mental capacity* is doubtful.

Local people are capable enough of providing ideas concerning their daily lives. Who can know better than them about their lives and their surroundings? Their physical presence in every undertaking may not be essential, but their felt needs and consent about the matters affecting them are vital. Their needs are expressed by local organizations in which they are represented. When one talks of organization and representation, some people tend to imagine a sophisticated or a Westernized arrangement but this is not necessarily so. The rural people, generally speaking, belong to some kind of association, be it around their local chiefs, village heads or semi-formal traditional organizations like *panchayte* in many parts of Asia, village councils and assemblies in Africa, or different types of rural institutions, like *maheber, merdaja, kebele* and peasant associations, as presented in the case of Ethiopia.

External provision of help may send their remits to such organizations for further suggestions before decision making. The feedback may not even be satisfactory, due to say technical or other reasons, still it is positive to invite local people for a full-scale debate on the unsolved issues to arrive at further clarity. There is enough evidence of how local inhabitants have surprised technical minded engineers and researchers with suggestions on how to solve large-scale problems by small-scale means (Brokensh, 1980). Therefore, participation should not always be taken literally. It can be carried out through members of village councils, representatives or delegations, better still by confronting local people in their village assemblies. The central point is that the people should take part in the decision making process, especially in matters that concern them directly.

One incident from my personal experience may help to illustrate the case in point. Under a participatory evaluation program in Gopalpur in the coastal region of Orissa, India, I discussed with local fishermen the low enrollment of students in one of the schools in the area, built by a donor development assistance program. The fishermen told me that the school enrolment was low because of the poverty of the parents but that they had a proposal to overcome this problem. For instance, had the money (donor assistance) spent on building the school been initially dispersed as loans to the parents, at a reasonable interest rate to equip them with better nets and boats, the money with interest could be paid back in two years to build the school. During these two years the students could also have gone to their "temporary shelter,' which was used as class rooms. After two years, as they reasoned out, when the permanent school opens, more students will enroll because of the better income generated by better catches effected by sailing into deep-sea areas with better boats and nets. Therefore, with the same amount of money two basic problems of the village namely, generating more income (less time to spend in search of catch by the children) and school building might have been undertaken. However, this did not cross the minds of the local authorities. The decision-making body could perhaps not imagine that local fisherfolk were able to construct such rational and premeditated socio-economic reasoning. Asking for advice, providing information and creating a conducive atmosphere for dialogue may actually pay back with better results.

PARTICIPATION AS A RURAL DEVELOPMENT STRATEGY

Participation can also be interpreted as a guideline or method for rural development strategy (Rudqvist, 1986). The term strategy implies here a method or an effort to establish or shape better conditions of life for the rural poor. Participation in rural development as a way out of poverty, is based mainly on mobilization. Mobilization of the poor and their available resources is the key element for the entire exercise. Such a statement, however, raises many doubts—mobilization by whom, for whose benefit and for what purpose?

Mobilization of the people can be initiated by governments, non-governmental organizations, by the local people themselves, etc. The essential point is, after the people have received the support they need to organize, they have to be free from impositions. In short, the bottom line of mobilizing the poor implies that they confront their daily problems using mainly their own local knowledge and practices. This does not imply that they should not be assisted, the implication is rather, if there are provisions to be made, they should be made on the terms of the poor.

The most common type of participation in rural development as stated above, is through the mobilization of the people. However, mobilization in everyday life takes different forms. For example, mobilization is often used to implement a certain task or a series of activities already designed by, say, central or local government. In this type of participation, or rather mobilization, the people are instrumental in carrying out certain work that has already been decided upon by others. This kind of participation takes place in the form of physical labor such as building schools, houses and bridges, digging wells, etc. Participation in such activities is often measured by labor input, not by feelings or opinions about the activity undertaken. This kind of participation, might be called *passive participation*.

In contrast to the above type, we have a kind of participation where the people concerned take part in generating ideas i.e. contribute their mental capacity. The people may take part from the initiation of the development program and follow it through to its conclusion. It is characterized by the active involvement of the group concerned based on their common understanding of the problems and their readiness to work together for the common good. These efforts may lead to self-reliance, self-confidence, and the empowering of the local people. This will enable the participants to face and solve their own problems. This kind of self-esteem mobilization may be referred to as *active participation* (active and passive are here referred to as levels of participation). Therefore, when participation is discussed, it is essential to clearly state, in which context participation takes place and for what purpose the mobilization of the people is undertaken.

With regard to rural people's participation to date, there are two dominant interpretations that development practitioners intensively argue either for or against. On the one hand, participation is seen as a "means," while on the other, it is seen as an "end" for achieving development objectives (Rudqvist, 1986).

Participation used as a means is described as inputs such as physical labor and many other forms of local community involvement, but is mainly based on matters decided over the heads of the participants. This kind of participation, I may say, varies in level— ranging from pure coercion and force to the consultative variety. We also find a process where the members of a community participate voluntarily and meaningfully in resolving their problems. Meaningful participation involves the people taking part in development efforts accepting and believing in the project—this is referred to as participation as an end. Participation as an end is believed to have an impact on the economic life of the individual and the community as a whole and result in independent administration, initiative taking, problem identification and problem solving.

As explained above the passive types of participation may also be explained as a means and the active ones as an end. However, participation as an end in itself cannot be an end, as the name suggests, and as many of its proponents argue. Based on the assumption that development is a continuous upward spiral of change, which never ends, what is an end today may be the beginning of the next stage of development tomorrow—that is to say, today's end may serve as the means to a higher level of development in the future. A situation where participation can lead to an end *per se* (i.e. not spiral to the next) is an ideal goal and difficult to ascertain.

Participation as a Method of Attacking Poverty

The important issue here is to note that participation *only* in physical labor or *only* in mental exercises may not produce positive results to reduce poverty (taken separately both are passive participation). However, the combination or integration of both efforts (mental and labor) may make the participants more active and their undertakings more meaningful.

Does rural participation strategy help people as explained above, or is this merely an assumption? To answer this question I will cite selected examples, where participatory efforts succeeded in integrating people's efforts (bottom-up) with government efforts (top-down). A sixteen country rural development participation comparative analysis (Uphoff and Esman, 1974:2-4) indicated that the different participation methods applied in these countries have positively affected "both agricultural productivity and social welfare measures." The comparative analysis also confirmed that "effective systems of participatory local organizations link rural development communities to national centers' of decision making and implementation" (of development activities). This wide study confirmed a strong correlation between rural development and participation. The question is, in what manner is this correlation established? Which factors were improved?

Summarizing the participatory experience of these sixteen Asian countries in one monograph, Uphoff and Esman, (1974) pointed out the areas where participatory activities gave positive results. The achievements were, improvements in agricultural activities, of technology and of welfare, rural security, employment, equality in income distribution and political participation. The more strongly organized participatory activities gave better results than the less organized. This also supports the argument that participation and organization of the people are closely related to each other.

There are a number of evaluations undertaken by ILO, FAO, and different bilateral development agencies where popular participation in project activities also exhibits positive results. Additionally, some evaluations carried out by the author in different community development projects, confirm positive results for participation used as a rural development strategy. These are: (a) Universalization of primary education through non-formal education centers in Orrisa, India, (b) Link workers approach in Tamil Nadu, India and (c) Participatory integrated rural development in Matara, Sri Lanka which have repeatedly confirmed the positive use of the participatory approach in rural development (Tirfe Mammo, 1987a and 1989).

Let us first take the extent and contribution of the participatory approach in the non-formal education scheme. The program was initially the result of the community's own expressed need for schools for their children, not a project thrust upon them by outside agencies. The local people selected the construction site and the whole village co-operated in building the school. Not only labor but also building materials were local. The village elected committees for supervision and maintenance of the schools. Most importantly, they also participated in the development of curriculum. In this development of curriculum for example, the local people provided vital information on rituals, local knowledge and practices in farming and fishing equipment, seasonal changes and orientation in the community's social, political and economic environment. They even decided upon the school time, since conventional school hours (i.e. from eight to four) could not apply in these rural areas as children are part of the labor force.

The positive results of such participatory activities are not only that the school enrollment increased, but also the teaching materials were built on the local knowledge and practices. This made the children aware of their surroundings and this in turn may result in them tackling and solving their problems based on these local objectives.

Concerning the participatory link workers approach in Tamil Nadu, (establishing day-care center for village children) it was observed that in villages where the extension officers were trained to work with the people (i.e. gave the village people more chance to decide), the facilities were utilized more than in villages where the officers had done most of the planning themselves. In the participatory integrated rural development in Sri Lanka, (i.e. coir making project), the salient features were sensitization of rural development catalysts called village cadres or social animators. These social animators were advised to live as simple a life as possible and were also trained in the role of the counselor rather than the order giver. Village leaders, local level government officers etc. were also invited to participate in training to be able to implement a rural development project identified by the people.

In both cases, as later on revealed, that asking the local people before implementing policies, made the work easier to implement, and also easier to follow-up.[1]

INTEGRATION OF BOTTOM-UP AND TOP-DOWN EFFORTS

The major issue in relation to what has been discussed is the process of integration between ordinary people's participatory activities, on the one hand, and government's efforts on the other. It is argued that the people's effort could best be utilized when they are combined with positive inputs from government and vice versa. The dilemma often discussed here is that government impositions are not always acceptable to the beneficiaries, and people's effort without government goodwill often encounter problems. In this process, the balance may be found when the participants themselves take the initiative and come forward with suggestions as to how such a provision is to be made.

In order for common people to state their demands and for their voices to be heard, it is essential for them to be organized. Organization, in turn, cannot yield anticipated results if the members do not share responsibilities and participate whole-heartedly to fulfill the desired objectives. In such efforts, external assistance (be it government and/or foreign) may be essential. However, this again should be based on the request and the consent of the people. Unless government entry finds balance, as discussed earlier, it may lead to unlimited interference and neglect of the beneficiaries (see the Ethiopian case). To move such undertakings into balance the participation of the people appears vital.

In reference to the imbalances created by the top-down approach, participation through mobilization, has to do with empowering the powerless, weak, poor and even destitute groups. Empowering is defined as an organized effort to increase control over resources by the hitherto excluded sectors of societies (*OECD Report*, 1991:45).

However, participation to the extent of empowering the poor, by-passing the relevant government, seems to be unrealistic. Normally governments cannot easily be avoided. What should be done instead is, as Hulme and Turner (1990) suggest, to influence governments and re-orient bureaucrats into becoming more local problem-oriented and co-operative in the overall fight against poverty, using participation of the people as their essential instrument.

Thus the magnetic field that attracts both and realizes the necessary dynamic development in society is, in fact, participation. Without it, neither government agencies, nor people's efforts will bear fruit. A good example of this is the Ethiopian peasant organizations, which undertook many positive development activities, but were finally dismantled by the *derg* (Chapters Five and Six).

The use of a participatory approach is not only limited to balancing local people's and government efforts. It also extends to areas of integrating traditional with modern knowledge. As argued earlier, indigenous knowledge and traditional practices are preconditions for development. These preconditions are more fruitful if combined with better technology. However modernization should not suffocate traditional knowledge and marginalize common practices. The introduction of the new ought to be built on the old, and in order to apply this, modern practices have first be demystified and simplified to enable the people not to only learn, but also to critically understand, and use their new knowledge. In this context, participation creates a development process where the learning of new skills and the sharing of old experiences go hand-in-hand. This process is exhibited in the informal sector discussion (Chapter Seven).

In the search for balance between the top-down and bottom-up approaches, it is implied that governments have to step down to co-operate with the people (with their partner) in order to influence poverty in a positive direction. But this working together calls for government accountability, transparency, open dialogue and tolerance. But, at present, there is a lack of political participation, or democracy. Democracy is the lubricating agent that enables participatory activities to work smoothly. Participation is based on democracy and its essence is voluntary choice, it cannot be otherwise.

Levels of Integration Between Top-down and Bottom-up

The points discussed in the preceding chapters seek to find balance between top-down (TD) and bottom-up (BU) efforts. In line with this, the following illustration is presented (Diagram 7:1).

The situation in level (A) where TD and BU efforts have no relationship is difficult to find in practice today. The example that may illustrate this phenomenon was the colonial rule of Africa (Chapter One) where the colonizers' primary interest was to extract resources without obligation to improve living conditions in their colonies. The illustration here, is to show the starting point of TD and BU efforts that may lead to the ideal goal, which the efforts of government and people integrate to a satisfactory level.

Level (B), starts by illustrating situations where not enough provisions are made from TD to support BU efforts. At this stage, little or no efforts were made to mobilize indigenous knowledge, traditional practices and local institutions to combat poverty, and thus, the common fields or *the shared space* (Santos, 1979) is narrow. Level (C) tries to show relatively improved situations where TD supports BU efforts—attempts to utilize traditional knowledge and practices with the participation of the people concerned. Level (D) is employed to illustrate conscious polices adapted to use traditional practices and local institutions with the help of active participation of the parties involved.

FIGURE 8:1
LEVEL OF INTEGRATION BETWEEN TOP-DOWN AND BOTTOM-UP

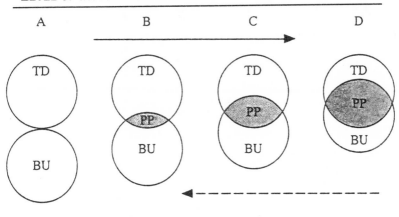

_____Forward direction
----------- Reverse direction

From this illustration, it is assumed that the readers can easily judge that when more provisions and better local efforts are made, the shared space or the common field widens. In contrast, weak efforts from both sides minimize the shared space. Still worse, if any unpredictable and negative development occurs, the overall level of development could also reverse.

Political Participation

The present movement calling for more political participation in some countries of Africa is the continuation of the struggle, which should have taken place just after independence. In light of this, the struggles (or the debates) for democracy that have surfaced in many African countries are definitely welcome. However, the issue to be addressed here is that the route to such political participation or democracy must be thoroughly discussed, explained and defined so that there is concrete basis for believing that such actions will be sustained for a longer period of time and become a tradition.

If Africa desires to attain sustainable political participation, the target set ought to be a minimum level of freedom and basic human rights to fully utilize its indigenous knowledge, traditional practices and local institutions on which African societies may base further development. *The Report of the South Commission* (1990:12) puts this argument in its right context by stating that:

> "The form of democracy—its machinery—must be appropriate to the nation's history, size and cultural diversities. Other nations do not necessarily provide models which can be directly transplanted. Political systems need to be understood by the people they serve and suited to their own value systems. What is vital is that governments should be, through nationally appropriate mechanisms, accountable to the people and responsive to their freely expressed views."

To place emphasis on the question stated above, the African path to genuine political participation appears to be via accountability and transparency of the state, and through mobilizing and organizing the broad masses into democratic fronts. This also requires further explanations.

African people need to express their ideas and participate in decisions that concerns their lives and the lives of their children. Often we hear arguments that political participation or democracy can only be fully utilized by the educated and by the affluent members of society who can express their feelings through the media and in assemblies. This is only partially true. Political participation or democracy is a relative phenomenon and differs in degree, but it is necessary to societies, rich as well as poor.

I further argue that the poor need political participation even more than the wealthy. The vast groups of illiterate rural peasants of Africa need to take part in improving their own and their children's lives as much metropolitan, affluent groups do. The peasantry, through their village organizations can exercise and learn more democratic methods of action. They are capable of maintaining and making use of democratic rights. The right of free expression, to state one's own ideas and felt needs in whatever form is a question of necessity rather than choice.

The most practical aspects, which can bring sustainable democratic tradition to any society are dialogue and tolerance. The harm created by the lack of political participation, as illustrated in the Ethiopian case, has brought about fatal consequences. In denying dialogue and tolerance, and in the absence of a forum to ventilate differences of opinions, the *derg* isolated opposition groups and finally even forced ordinary people to take antagonistic positions. Under such circumstances, many of the opposition forces searched for their ethnic basis, first to protect themselves, and finally got organized and challenged the military government.

In order to organize and fight the *derg*, ethnic groups had to find new symbols and identities to profile themselves. In this process national symbols and common identities, which had been inculcated into the minds of the people for many centuries, were pushed aside to accommodate new ones. To some of the ethnic groups this method of struggle worked perfectly and was ultimately able to topple the military government and assume its place (e.g. Tigray Liberation Front). Some have even managed to establish a new state from part of the old Ethiopia (Eritrea). In the aftermath of this confused economic, political and social order, today, Ethiopians are once again in desperate search for common identities and symbols. And this could (only) be materialized by looking into their traditional and cultural heritage that may bring the nation together.

Sustainable Participation

In many African countries at present, it is the government in power that dictates the level of political participation that the people need. It may be one of the possible options for obtaining democracy. Political participation (democracy) is not a condition that is obtained only through decrees and made use of immediately. It is not a prefabricated product. Real political participation is born from both economic and political struggles and hard work. Through this political and economic participation the beneficiaries get a grip on the essential factors of life. Thus, sustainable democracy is a product of government's political will and people's struggle to obtain and sustain it. In other words, the sustainability of participation is strongly related with the integration of top-down and bottom-up approaches.

If democracy is to take root in African societies, we have to look at the transformation of the African people from the present state of socio-economic misery to a qualitatively better standard of living. However, the paradox is this improved standard of living is unobtainable without integrated efforts in the present, to obtain better result in the future. This in turn, very much depends on democracy, rule of law and social stability.

Based on the strong relationship between democracy and economic development as instruments of attacking poverty, what Bangura (1992:39), states summarizes my points:

> The establishment of stable and sustainable democracy requires sustainable changes in the form accumulation; the promotion of an acceptable level of welfare that will allow the majority of the people to have confidence in the capacity of democratic institutions.

There are some important questions, however, which still remain unanswered like, how to strike the balance? In what proportion should the dosage of top-down and bottom-up efforts be determined? Who is the determinant force? What are the processes of integration? In short, what are the connecting points?

The answers to these questions are difficult to put forward in terms of measurements and it is also difficult to judge or determine from the outside.

However, it is possible to say, the more people support themselves the better. But this cannot always be expected to happen, as poor people often lack resources to manage all their needs by themselves, and therefore outside assistance (local and/or foreign) becomes essential if not determinant. Thus, a balanced outlook seems to be—the more the people demand their rights (political, economic, social etc.) combined with positive support, co-operation and goodwill from the state, the better the results obtained. The more serious the people are in their intentions of changing their situation, the better foreign assistance can help them in unblocking bottlenecks.

The moment judgement is passed from afar, the determination of what is good or bad for the people becomes more or less arbitrary. This again should not be taken as building a wall between the beneficiaries and the benefactors—what is simply suggested here is that action taken concerning a certain activity to help a given community has to be carried out in consultation and then with the active participation of the people concerned.

Lastly, another major point needs to be stressed—in suggesting the fusion between traditional practices and modern technology, the problem remains of how to bring this about. The fusion of modern technology that may help a certain traditional practice is primarily determined by its efficiency to solve the immediate problems of the people who need that technology, in other words, by its capacity of integration into traditional technology (its adaptability) and by its functional use to serve the people (its practicality or applicability). Finally, the gauge that indicates the degree of acceptability of the new idea (modernity) is only to be seen if local people use the adapted technology to solve their day-to-day problems.

COMPONENTS OF PARTICIPATION

In its broader perspective, participation presupposes the sharing of political and economic power and therefore, the *decentralization* of political as well as economic power to the local level are basic necessities to facilitate participation.

Participation could not be dreamed of without a minimum *organizational framework*. It is through an organized body that people can consult each other, search for alternative solutions and work together to overcome their problems. Participation, like any other development activity, requires an efficient information network. Rural people need technical information, say, about improved farming techniques, soil conservation, taking care of forests, seed storage, etc.

Participants *need basic education*. This helps poor people build awareness and run the administrative work. Training in bookkeeping, accounting, auditing etc. would help the people to document their work, register and exchange experiences, and run their daily routines more efficiently (these were also identified as some of the factors that contributed to the set-backs of the Ethiopian peasant associations see Chapter Six).

Participation, as a development strategy, means to incorporate and make use of the *indigenous knowledge* prevailing in a country, to transform the local people from passive recipients to active producers, to create opportunities for the rural poor to make their voices heard in decision making processes and also to ensure that they retain their share of the produce of their labor.

The most importat groundwork for participation is to prepare the participants psychologically, to modify their *expectations*. To make them aware, from the beginning, of the fact that participation is not a short cut to material rewards as the goals could be farther away than they expect. The work can be tedious and often difficult to quantify in terms of hard data. Decades of work for example, may result only in awareness building without giving material benefit. But once the groundwork is laid, positive results of one type or another are bound to come.[2]

Thus, accepting participation as a rural development strategy underlines a major diversion from the old approach (only top-down) and an embarkation on a new approach (bottom-up). The old argues that rural people are ignorant, idle or apathetic, non-receptive and bound by backward tradition. The new approach starts from the premise that people are resourceful, knowledgeable and hardworking (Oakley, 1991). The new strategy emphasizes indigenous knowledge, traditional skills and practices of the ordinary people. The fundamental assumption of participation, as reasoned here, is that it is an input to development activities geared towards bringing about self-reliance, self-confidence and substantial and balanced socio-economic development that finally help to reduce the level of poverty.

For a short period (1975-1978/79), as earlier recounted, the implementation of participatory rural development was practiced in the peasant association of Ethiopia. In this reform, efforts were made to ensure that peasants directly undertook local administration work, accomplished the most difficult task of implementation of land legislation and organized rural institutions including rural jurisdictional tribunes etc., but finally the whole exercise gave poor results. One obvious reason is that it failed to create a democratic environment in which the people could participate freely. A concrete lesson that we may draw from this is, among others, that lack of will on the part of the government (top-down) caused the failure of the Ethiopian peasant organization's efforts (bottom-up). To overcome such failure, what might be said here is that the interference of a state should consciously be limited and carefully fused with the efforts of the local people.

The application of participatory development in Africa has bright prospects. Participation in day-to-day African life is not something new, the African people participate in each others affairs not because they are instructed to do so but because as Ake (1990:25) puts it, "it is an inter connected whole to Africans." As earlier noted the economic and social life of African societies (non-formal activities) largely depend on the extended family. Members of extended families, regardless of age and physical powers, participate in many branches of work and share the benefits. Thus, participation or participatory action on local levels is one of the traditional methods of executing social activities in Africa. In this case, the right option, per-haps is that the state must strive to find appropriate entry points (see examples given in Chapter Seven) and help the people in their every day struggle against poverty. However, to avoid the mistakes like that of Ethiopia, it is advisable to base development efforts on the felt-needs and consent of the people. Finally, if any effort to attack poverty takes place in Africa, participation of the rural people is not only desirable but also necessary.

CONCLUSION

At the beginning of this study, I made a brief assessment of pre-colo-nial Africa in order to provide some examples of how certain African countries were capable of using their indigenous knowledge and tra-ditional practices for development. In this respect, I gave an account of African performance in small-scale manufacturing, handicrafts, commerce etc. However, with the advent of colonialism, the situation changed and Africa was forced to serve colonial powers.

With regard to the post-colonial period, one of the central issues in this study is that problems of economic development and social change in Africa stem from external as well as internal forces. Internal forces weakened political participation or democracy, open dialogue and above all neglected local knowledge and traditional practices. As a way out, the use of indigenous knowledge and traditional practices are extensively discussed and more openness, or transparency and accountability on the part of the states are suggested.

Discussing development strategies applied in many countries, an attempt is made to point out certain weaknesses. In so doing, I have selected the widely accepted (in many aid programs) Rostow (1960) development model, which, I think, was representative of the devel-opment practices that took place, at least up to the early 1980s. Rostow model implies a stage theory of development namely, *tradi-tional society, pre-conditions for take-off, take-off, the drive to maturity and finally, the stage of mass consumption.* Be it Rostow's stage theory, or other similar schools of thought, development is often presented as linear. Such theories advocate the *new,* or modernization, in the place of the *old* or tradition of a given society. In questioning these assump-tions, I try to emphasize the danger behind this "new syndrome" and instead make an attempt to investigate the pros and cons of traditions and build the blocks of change on the base of prevalent local knowl-edge, practices and resources.

231

Here I would like to stress that the use of indigenous knowledge and traditional practices should not be exaggerated beyond their capacity. For example, while it is stated that local practices are useful for further development, it does not mean that they are enough *per se.* What is consistently argued is, this available local knowledge and practices should be improved, molded and lifted to a specialized and competitive level.

Contemporary development practitioners advocate imported knowledge and practices. I argue that it is much better to revitalize local knowledge and practices as preconditions for further development, before importing new ones.

While many of the conventional theories set up aims for quantitative results (e.g. economic growth measured in GNP terms, Chapter One), this study, especially in relation to the African situation and in this particular period, simultaneously stresses the development of qualitative efforts such as fostering political participation or democracy, dialogue, and re-examination of ones cultural heritage, upgrading the positive aspects of it, and revitalizing it. These are supposed to lay the ground for further socio-economic development.

In short, the emphasis given in this study with regard to the processes of preparing the ground for further development are for the individual to acknowledge traditional values and cultural heritage. This also includes demystifying faulty premises, building self-confidence, accepting one-self and finding ways and means to improve conditions of life within the framework of the given resources. This is what I call *basic steps.*

Once the basic steps are laid, then it will be possible to set forth on the use of local resources both material and local knowledge. Here it is important to identify knowledge and practices useful for further developmental purposes. Consciousness and goal orientation, strengthening and inculcating indigenous knowledge and practices useful to serve societies in the fight against poverty is one important aspect. This may be referred to as a step towards *mobilizing local resource and setting targets.*

Adaptation of better technology to support indigenous efforts; search for better technology that the local people can easily understand and use—sustainable or adaptation of traditional practices are other important aspects. After fulfilling these preconditions it may be possible to be ready for the decisive assault, to fight aggressively against poverty.

Participation as a Method of Attacking Poverty

The alternative theory illustrated in this study, opposed to the hitherto orthodoxy, is that Africa is poor because its development efforts so far have caused it to neglect its base, namely its indigenous knowledge and practices. By neglecting its roots, it suppressed the self-confidence needed to venture out into new ideas, and this enforced inaction eventually contributing to the continent's poverty. As part of the discussion on these problems it has been suggested that the route to reduction of African poverty is not through the adoption of a series of blueprints of the experiences of the industrial countries, but through the expression of the felt needs and aspirations of the local people based on locally available knowledge and resources.

International development actors, development assistance agencies especially, financial institutions and international trade agreements are critically reviewed. The examination of them focuses, among others aspects, on indebtedness, dependency and what is called transfer of technology plus the cynical equal exchange opportunities in international trade among unequals, which all ultimately deepen African poverty. As a remedy to these negative international relations, close cooperation among African states is recommended. With regard to aid, it is suggested that external assistance ought to be catalytic.

To illustrate, exhibit and verify many of the arguments forwarded in this study I chose Ethiopia as a case study. This case study is designed: a) to avoid and differentiate this study from speculative ones by furnishing concrete examples, (b) to support many of the arguments made in the general African context, and (c) to show that internal efforts (not affected by direct colonialism), did not either bring about prosperity or stability to the majority of Africa automatically. On the African continent, only Ethiopia and Liberia were fortunate enough, not to be directly colonized, but their social development is not very different from the colonized countries. In Ethiopia, for example, the main negative attributes of underdevelopment are identified as related to centuries of feudal exploitation, followed by unselective modernization or rather Westernization. With the advent of this

Westernization, indigenous knowledge and traditional practices were pushed aside and/or even neglected altogether.

Furthermore, in this case study, I point out how negative resource allocation and misuse of power by the political elite deepened poverty and how the people reacted against it in the form of social revolution. However, the outcome of the revolution did not bring betterment as the people expected. This is because the lopsided policies adopted finally enabled the military officers to assume the role of the former Crown, which they had severely criticized before seizing political power.

The focus on Ethiopia also elucidates how a genuine social revolution led to negative results, mainly due to lack of political participation or democratic tradition and open dialogue on one hand, and through the introduction of forced collectivization on the other. In the latter case, the neglect of small-scale peasant initiatives and dependence on imported large-scale efforts run contrary to the local people's experience and everyday reality. While the Ethiopian peasants' lives are built around family, clan and village relations, the *derg* attempted to transform them almost overnight into socialist citizens. Such radical discourses, as could be expected, over-stretched the peasants' capacity. The peasants were not prepared at all for any of those government's measures. The lesson one may draw from this incident is that introduction of new technology or modes of life, need not only a long span of time but also that they should be voluntarily accepted (adapted) by the users (beneficiaries) of this technology or new form of social organization.

Problems manifested as political crises often lead to internal instability, and deepened poverty. Such crises in many parts of Africa mainly stem from lack of legitimacy and stability created by internal as well as external forces. The lack in legitimacy reinforces instability and vice versa. As it is clearly indicated in the Ethiopian case, the central government barred the intelligentsia from political participation, which finally led these groups into opposition based on their ethnic origins. As a counter-position to such negative development, it is argued here that ethnic problems should be brought to the surface and be subject to open public discussion rather than swept under the carpet. The debate should focus on one hand, recognizing the rights of every ethnic groups to express itself, and on the other stress the advantages of living together as equal partners.

Moreover, regional co-operation was also recommended to counter internal and external instability. Apart from internal political participation, regional co-operation, to the extent of free movement of capital, labor and services, perhaps could minimize instability through making common efforts towards common goals. This may have more impact (a) to protect small and infant internal efforts, like local business and handicrafts and allow them to mature without strong pressure from overseas and (b) to mitigate the artificial differences once injected by colonial powers.

In search of options, in the last part of this study, I tried to discuss the underestimated reality of the African informal sector. The participatory aspect of the informal sector, how this sector helps many family members, kinship groups, close friends etc. and in so doing, also helps their communities is stressed here.

Additionally, the informal sector, as reasoned in this study, assists the formal sector in many ways. It creates labor market mobility, facilitates adaptability and turns activities done at home into useful consumer articles for communities. In the latter process, i.e. by employing family members and encouraging self-employment, the informal sector reduces unemployment and generates income. As Santos (1979) so perceptively observed, it is the informal sector that meets the demands of the middle class's conspicuous consumption of many modern goods through imitations.

The major conclusion from the discussion of the formal and informal sectors is that since the present economic condition of many poor countries of Africa could not provide necessary resources such as credit and employment, and could not produce or import and meet the demand for consumption items, it is the informal sector that partially satisfies the demand. If this is believed to be the situation, the informal sector should gain acceptance, necessary provisions and should be included as one of the vital strategies with which to attack poverty.

Many ideas are expressed when arguing on top-down or bottom-up routes. However, after weighing many facts, the remedy I suggest gravitates towards searching for a balance. This is because, more generally, development and social change are subjects with many dimensions, differing in depth and scope. They differ from place to place, from people to people, from culture to culture, and thus no ready-made formula applicable to all is possible. Instead, what may be said, however, is that neither government nor people's efforts in attacking poverty could be successful without democracy, participation of the people concerned, peace and political stability with an open dialogue between the participants.

Participation in development, it is clear should not be limited to only taking part in physical labor, such as the carrying of stone and wood, leveling of roads etc. The important point is that decision making must be decentralized, the participants must be allowed to be an active partner in all stages of development efforts—from initiation to implementation, and finally, to evaluate decisions that affect their lives.

Deviation from this standard, therefore, creates frustration in attaining the objectives of transformation. Pateman (1975) seems correct in pointing out that participation increases the freedom of the individual by enabling he/she to be his/her own master. It also enables collective decisions to be more easily accepted by the individual members of a community. Participation increases the feeling among individuals that they belong in their community and that the community is a safe and free environment.

What is clearly emphasized here is that the goals of development set for the poor cannot be attained without considering for the views of the poor. If development agencies and local governments would like to improve the conditions of the poor, they have to play the role of a physician who first questions the patient as to the nature of his illness, pain and other symptoms; and thereafter begins to assist. This approach is conspicuously absent in the programs put forth by development agencies and governments today.

Another major conclusion to be drawn from this study is as a sort of response to many problems raised herein—that terms like balance, integration, fusion (mix) and coordination are central. During the course of my writing, I sometimes argued with myself, "what is development, after all, but a question of balance", at other times I argued against this "middle path" and searched for a radical way out. But finally, reality has forced me to make a compromise and settle for balance.

For instance, though I strongly question the application of foreign aid, at present, foreign assistance is unavoidably an ingredient in the development process of many African countries. Traditional knowledge and practices, which I warmly advocate, give better results if they are appropriately supported by better knowledge. The method I support, namely, a bottom-up approach could not be effectively implemented without proper support from the top-down. Therefore, for rural developmental issues discussed in this study, searching for the right mix and then striving to attain planned balance is the essential lesson that may perhaps be learned.

Finally, as a project for further inquiry it is necessary to look into the capacities of local institutions as vehicles for sustainable rural development and their capacities for adapting innovations. Such a study is essential as, considering what has been illustrated so far, positive factors for development, such as indigenous knowledge, traditional practices, participation etc. are already incorporated into local institutions.

NOTES

1. For further discussion see Tirfe Mammo, 1987, People's Participation in BOBP (FAO) extension Activities, *BOBP News*, Issue No.9; and see also Tirfe Mammo, 1987, Women in Participatory Fisheries Development, Stockholm University, Department of Social Anthropology Publishing, Biståndsantroplogen, Issue No.9.

2. A report by International Development Research, Canada, undertook a study of examining participatory development efforts in various poor countries of Africa, Latin America and Asia. The findings imply that participatory work has positive impacts on the participants. For further information see "With Our Own Hands, Research for Third World Development," Canada's Contribution Through The International Development Research Center, 1970-1985.

Glossary

amhara	Northern Ethiopia people and dominant ethnic group in terms of language and cultural activities and political power.
abe'lig	Relationship established between the baptizer family (godfather/godmother) and that of the baptizer.
akne abat	Indigene of an area usually applied in *rist* system of northern Ethiopia.
asrat	Land tax (one-tenth of the produce) tithe tax .
awraja	Administrative unit below the province level. The Ethiopian traditional administrative hierarchy starts from *tekelay gizat* or *Kifle ager* (province) to *awraja*, then *woreda* and finally to *chika* (the lowest administrative unit. The administrator (of *chika*) was referred to as **chika shum**. The lowest administrative unit today is **kebele**—it means neighborhood organizations, in urban as well as rural areas.
balager	People living in a countryside, peasants.
bale'abat	Local gentry, whose father was *akne abat*. This should not be confused with **mekuannent**, which also meant local gentry, but they could be war-lords. The term **mekuannent** is derived from **mekonenn** meaning an officer. The other similar term is **mesafint**, local gentry belong to the ruling local families, or members of the imperial family.
birr	Ethiopian currency.

239

debo	Collective work, mutual aid and joint action during ploughing, weeding, harvesting, etc. called also *wofara, wonfel,* etc.
derg	Committee, name of the Military Government.
edir	Voluntary organization to provide mutual help incase of death.
equb	Savings association.
etiopia tikdem	Amharic slogan meaning "Ethiopia First."
Ethiopian Calender	About eight years less than Gregorian Calender.
Hectare	2.47 acres.
hebretesbawinet	Ethiopian version of egalitarian socialism.
kegnazmach & gerazmach.	Commander of the right and left brigades, respectively. Another similar term is **dej'azemach,** which could mean a General.
maderia	Possession of a plot of land instead of salary to support oneself.
mahaber	Association.
meret la'rashu	Land to the tiller—land reform.
ras	Supreme aristocratic title—it can be commander-in-chief, administrator of a province or duke. In the last case, one must be a member of the royal family, called also *leul ras.*
shimagle	Elder person, traditional arbitrator in case of conflict.
teff	Ethiopian staple crop (Eragrostis teff).
quintal	100 kilogram.

Bibliography

Ethiopian authors are listed under their first names.

Adedeji, A., (ed), 1981, *Indigenization of African Economies*, Hutchinson University, Library for Africa, London, Sydney, Johannesburg.

——, 1990, *Preliminary Assessment of the Performance of the African Economy*, Addis Ababa.

African Contemporary, Annual Survey and Documents from 1975-1990, Holm & Meier, New York.

Africa South of Sahara, 1989, Europe Publications Limited, London.

Ake, C., 1990, "Sustaining Development on the Indigenous," in World Bank, *The Long Term Perspective Study of Sub-Saharan Africa, Institutional and Sociopolitical Issues*, Vol. 3, Washington, D.C.

Alemayehu Seifu, "Eder in Addis Ababa," *Ethiopia Observer*, Vol. VII No. 1, 1968, Addis Ababa, Ethiopia.

Alemayehu Lirenso, 1990, "Villagization: Policies and Prospects," in Pausewang, Brune, Fantu Cheru and Eshetu Chole, (eds.), *Ethiopia: Rural Development Options*, Zed Books, London and New Jersey.

Alemneh Dejene, 1987, *Peasant, Agrarian Socialism and Rural Development in Ethiopia*, Westview Special Studies on Africa, Westview Press, Boulder and London.

Aliboni, R., 1983, "The Ethiopian Revolution, *Armed Forces and Society*," Vol. VII, No. 3.

Alula Abate and Tesfaye Teklu, 1979, "Land Reform and Peasant Association in Ethiopia—Case Study of a Two Widely Different Regions," World Employment Research, Working Paper.

Alula Abate and Fassil Gebre Kiros, 1980, *Agrarian Reform: Structural Change and Rural Development in Ethiopia*, ILO Pub. Geneva.

Andargachew Tirnuneh, 1993, *The Ethiopian Revolution, 1974-1987*, Cambridge University Press, Cambridge.

Amin S., 1974, *Accumulation on a World Scale*, Vol. II, Monthly Review Press, New York.

——, 1977, *Imperialism and Unequal Development*, Monthly Review, New York .

Arnold, Guy 1985, *Aid and Third World: The North/South Divide*, Sussex.

Asmaron Legesse, 1963, *Gada: Three Approaches to the Study of African Society*, New York.

Ayittey, G, 1990, "Political Indigenous African System: An Assessment," in World Bank, *The Long Term Perspective Study of Sub-Saharan Africa, Institutional and Sociopolitical Issues*, Vol. 3, Washington, D.C.

Bahru Zewede, 1991, *A History of Modern Ethiopia 1855-1974*, East African Studies, James Currey, London; Ohio University Press Athens; Addis Ababa University Press, Addis Ababa.

Baker, J., 1986, *The Rural-Urban Dichotomy in the Developing World, A Case Study from Northern Ethiopia*, Norwegian University Press.

Bangura, Y., 1992, "Authoritarian Rule and Democracy in Africa: A theoretical Discourse," in Gibbon, P., Y., Bangura, A., Ofstad, (eds) *Authoritarianism, Democracy and Adjustment*, The Scandinavian Institute of African Studies, Uppsala.

Balsvik, R., 1985, *Haile Selassie's Students, The Intellectual and Social Background to Revolution, 1952-1977*, East Lansing, Michigan African Studies Center.

Basic Documents of the Ethiopian Revolution, POMAA, 1977, Addis Ababa.

Beckman, B., 1992, "Whose Democracy? Bourgeois Versus Popular Democracy," in Rudebeck (ed), *When Democracy Makes Sense*, Akut, Uppsala.

Befekadu Degefe, 1981, "Ethiopia" in Adedeji (ed), *Indigenization of African Economies*, Hutchinson University Library for Africa, London, Sydney, Johannesburg.

——, 1990, "Profile of the Ethiopian Economy," in World Bank, *The Long Term Perspective Study of Sub-Saharan Africa, Country Perspectives*, Vol. 1, Washington, D.C.

—— and Tesfaye Tafesse, 1990, "The Marketing and Pricing of Agricultural Products," in Pausewang, Brune, Fantu Cheru and Eshetu Chole, (eds.), *Ethiopia: Rural Development Options*, Zed Books, London and New Jersey.

Bergman G., 1975, "Fakta om Etiopiens Jordreform," *Rapport från SIDA*, No. 4, Stockholm.

——, 1976, "Agriculture in Ethiopia, An Overview of the Agricultural Sector with Comments on Some Problem Areas," (Report), *SIDA*, Stockholm.

Berri, L. Ya , (ed), 1977, *Planning a Socialist Economy*, Progressive Publishers, Moscow.

Bibliography

Blomström, M., B., Hettne, 1984, *Development Theory in Transition, The Dependency Debate & Beyond: Third World Responses* Zed Books, London.

Bierstedt, R., 1963, *The Social Order, An Introduction to Sociology,* McGraw-Hill Book Company, New York.

Bondestam, L., 1975, *Feodalismen Skall Krossas: Om Inledningen till Revolutionen i Etiopien,* Berlingska Boktrykeriet, Lund.

Bottmore, T., & R., Nisbet, 1978, *A History of Sociological Analysis,* Heimann, London.

Brainard, L., & R., Dummett 1975 (eds.), *Problems of Rural Development, Case Studies and Multi-disciplinary Perspectives,* The Netherlands.

Brietzke, P., 1976, "Landreform in Revolutionary Ethiopia," *Journal of Modern Africa Studies,* xx London.

Brokensha, D. Warren, D. M., Verner, O., (eds.), 1980, *Indigenous Knowledge System and Development,* University Press of America.

Brune, S., 1990, "The Agricultural Sector," in Pausewang, Brune, Fantu Cheru and Eshetu Chole, (eds.), *Ethiopia: Rural Development Options,* Zed Books, London and New Jersey.

Bukharin, N.,1973, *Imperialism and World Economy,* Monthly Review Press, New York.

Cabral, A., 1969, *The Revolution In Guinea,* The African Research Group, Cambridge, Mass.

Cassen, R., and Associates, 1986, *Does Aid Work,* Clarendon Press, Oxford, England.

Challenge to the South, The, 1990, The Report of the South Commission, Oxford University Press, Oxford, New York.

Chambers, R., 1983, *Rural Development, Putting the Last First,* Longman, London, Lagos, New York.

——, (ed), 1989, *Farmers First, Farmers Innovation and Agricultural Research,* Intermediate Technology, London.

——, and Howes, M., 1980, "Indigenous Technical Knowledge: analysis, Implications and Issues," in Brokensha, D. Warren, D. M., Verner, O., (eds.), *Indigenous Knowledge System and Development,* University Press of America, Lanham.

Clapham, C., 1969, *Haile Selassie's Government,* Longmans, London.

Cohen, D., 1981, *The Political Economy of Africa,* London.

Cohen, J., and Weintraub, 1975, *Land and Peasants in Imperial Ethiopia: The Social Background to a Revolution,* Van Gorcum, The Netherlands.

———, "Revolution and Land Reform in Ethiopia: Peasant Association, Local Government and Rural Development," *Rural Development Occasional Paper,* No. 6, Cornell University.

———, 1976b, "Rural Development Issues Following the Ethiopian Landreform," *Africa Today,* Denver.

———, and Koehn, 1977, "Rural and Urban Land Reform in Ethiopia," *African Law Studies* No. 1, 1977.

———, and Isaksson L.I., 1986, "Villagization in the Arsi Region of Ethiopia," Report Prepared by SIDA Consultants to the Ethio-Swedish Mission on Villagization in Arsi Region, Swedish University of Agricultural Sciences, International Rural Development Center, Uppsala.

Colonialism, Old and Modern, 1966, Central Department of Oriental Literature, Moscow.

Comhaire, 1966, "Wage Pool as a Form of Voluntary Association in Ethiopia and other African Towns," in *Proceedings of the Third International Conference of Ethiopian Studies,* Institute of Ethiopian Studies, Addis Ababa.

Curtain, P.D., 1969, *The Atlantic Slave Trade,* University of Wisconsin Press, Madison.

Davidson, B., 1984, *The Story of Africa,* Mitchell Beazlie, London.

———, 1989, *Modern Africa, A Social & Political History,* Longman, London and New York.

Dawit Wolde Giorgis, 1989, *Red Tears: War, Famine and Revolution in Ethiopia,* The Red Sea Press, New Jersey.

Declaration of Political Policy of Socialist Ethiopia, 1975, Addis Ababa.

Declaration on Economic Policy of Socialist Ethiopia, 1975, Addis Ababa.

Dejene Aredo, 1993, *The Informal and Semi-formal Financial Sectors in Ethiopia: A Study of Iqqub, Idder, and Savings and Credit Co-operatives,* African Economic Research Consortium (AERC), Nairobi.

Dessalegn Rahmato, 1982, "Agrarian reform and rural development (1975-1982)," Paper Presented at the Seventh International Conference of Ethiopian Studies, Lund.

———, 1984, *Agrarian Reform in Ethiopia,* Scandinavian Institute of African Studies, Uppsala.

Development Co-operation, 1991 Report, OECD, Paris.

Diamond, L., 1987, "Class Formation in the African State," *Journal of Modern African Studies,* Vol. 25, No. 4.

Dieci, P., Viezzoli, C., (Eds.), 1992, *Resettlement and Rural Development in Ethiopia,* Franco Angeli, Milano.

Bibliography

Dieter and Massing, 1974, *Traditional Organizations and Economic Development, Studies on Indigenous Cooperatives* in Liberia, Praeger Publishers, New York, Washington, London.

Dorner, P., 1972, *Land Reform and Economic Development*, Harmondsworth, Middlesex.

Dumont, R., 1966, *False Start in Africa*, The Trinity Press, Worcester and London.

Ehrmann, H., 1965, *Democracy in a Changing Society*, Pall Mall Press, London.

Eisenstadt, S.N., 1966, *Modernization Protest and Change*, Inglewood Cliff, Prince Hall, Inc. New Jersey.

Eisenstadt, S.N., 1970, *Social Change and Development*, Reading in Social Evolution and Development, Pergamon Press, Oxford.

Emmanuel A., 1972, *Unequal Exchange*, Western Printings Service Ltd., Bristol.

Eshetu Chole and Teshome Mulat, 1988, "Land and Settlement in Ethiopia, A Review of Development" in Oberai, A., (ed) *Land Settlement Policies and Population Disruption in Developing Countries*, New York.

———, 1990, "Agriculture and Surplus Extraction," in Pausewang, Brune, Fantu Cheru and Eshetu Chole, (eds.), *Ethiopia: Rural Development Options*, Zed Books, London and New Jersey.

"Ethiopia," *Africa Guide*, 1975-1990.

Ethiopia, 1980, A Country Study, Washington.

Ethiopia: Country Presentation, UN Conference on the Least Developed Countries (LDC), 1981, Paris

"Ethiopia," *New Africa Year Book*, (various), London.

"Ethiopia": in *Economic Development Documents of International Monetary Fund* (IMF) (various)

Ethiopia: Statistic Abstract, (various), Addis Ababa.

FAO, *Year-book, Production*, 1991, Vol. 45, Rome.

FAO, *The State of Food and Agriculture 1991*, Rome, 1992.

Fanon, F., 1974, *The Wretched of the Earth*, Penguin Books, Middlesex.

Fantu Cherru, 1989, *The Silent Revolution in Africa, Debt, Development and Democracy*, Zed Books, London and New Jersey.

———, 1990, "The International Context," in Pausewang, Brune, Fantu Cheru and Eshetu Chole, (eds.), *Ethiopia: Rural Development Options*, Zed Books, London and New Jersey.

245

Fassil Gebre Kiros, 1982, "Mobilizing peasantry for rural development: The Ethiopian experiment," Paper Presented on the Seventh International Conference of Ethiopian Studies, Lund, Sweden.

Fonues-Sundell, M., 1980, "Agrarian Reform and Rural Development: Theory and Practice," *Rural Development Studies,* No. 6, Swedish University of Agricultural Sciences, International Rural Development Center, Uppsala.

Frank A.G., 1967, *Sociology of Underdevelopment and Underdevelopment of Sociology,* Buffalo University of New York.

Galbratith, J.K., 1979, *The Nature of Mass Poverty,* Harvard University Press, Cambridge, Mass. and London.

Gebru Tareke, 1991, *Ethiopia, Power and Protest: Peasant Revolt in the Twentieth Century,* Cambridge University Press.

Ghartey, J.B., 1987, *Crisis, Accountability and Development in the Third World,* Blackmore Press, London.

Gibbon, Bangura and Ofstad, 1992, (eds.) *Authoritarianism, Democracy and Adjustment, The Politics of Economic Reform in Africa,* The Scandinavian Institute of African Studies No. 26, Uppsala.

Gilpin, A., 1977, *Dictionary of Economic Terms,* Fourth Edition, Butterworts & Co., Ltd., Boston.

Gladwin, H., 1980, "Indigenous Knowledge of Fish Processing and Marketing Utilized by Women Traders of Cape Coast, Ghana,",in Brokensha, D. Warren, D.M., Verner, O., (eds.), *Indigenous Knowledge System and Development,* University Press of America, Lanham.

Godelier, M., 1987, "Introduction: The Analysis of Transition Process," *International Social Science Journal,* Vol. 114, UNESCO, Paris.

Gorbachev, M., 1987, *Perestroika: New Thinking for Our Country and the World,* Fontana/Collins, Glasgow, London.

Greenfield, R., 1965, *Ethiopia: A New Political History,* Pall Mall Press, 1965, London.

Gupta, K.R, 1976, *GATT and Underdeveloped Countries,* Atma Ram & Sons, Delhi.

Gutto, S.B., 1988, "Social Revolutions—the Preconditions for Sustainable Development and People's Power in Africa. A contribution to the Anyang' Nyong'o and Mkandawire," *Africa Development,* Vol. XXX, No. 4, Dakar.

Bibliography

Gyenge, Z., 1976, *Ethiopia on the Road of Non-Capitalist Development*, Institute for World Economics of the Hungarian Academy of Sciences, Budapest.

Göricke, F., 1979, *"Social and Political Factors Influencing the Application of Land Reform Measures in Ethiopia,"* Publications of the Research Center for International Agrarian Development, No. 10, Saarbrucken.

Haque, W., "Quarter Century of (anti) Rural Development," *Development Dialogue*, 1972:2, Dag Hammarskjöld Foundation; Uppsala.

Haile Yesus Abegaz, 1982, *The Organization of State Farms in Ethiopia After the Land Reform of 1975*, Socio-economic Studies on Rural Development, Saarbruken.

Harbeson, J., & P., Brietzke, 1975, *Rural Development in Ethiopia*, Department of Political Science, University of Wisconsin, Madison.

Harbeson, J., 1988, *The Ethiopian Transformation: The Quest for the Post-Imperial State*, Westview Special Studies on Africa, Westview Press, Boulder & London.

Hettne, B., 1982, *Development Theory and the Third World*, The Swedish Agency for Research Cooperation with Developing Countries, (R2:1982) Schmidts Boktryckeri AB, Helsingborg.

——, 1990a, *The Globalization of Development Theory*, Institute for World Economics of the Hungarian Academy of Science, Budapest.

——, 1990b, *Development Theory and Three Worlds*, Longman, London.

Himmelstrand, U., 1987, "Introduction: Exogenous Factors in Economic Analysis," *International Social Science Journal*, Vol. 113 pp. 293-300, UNESCO, Paris.

——, 1993, "Perspective, Controversies & Dilemmas," in Himmelstrand, U., Kinyajui, K., Mburugu, E., (eds.), *African Perspectives on Development*, James Currey, London Study of African Development.

Hirschman, A. O., 1958, *The Strategy of Economic Development*, Yale University Press, New Haven.

Hobsbawm, E., & T., Ranger, 1983, *The Invention of Tradition*, Cambridge University Press, London .

Holmberg, J., 1977a, *Integrated Rural Development, A Discussion of this and its Implications of Swedish Aid, Farm Management and Productions Economics*, Department of Economics and Statistics, The Swedish University of Agricultural Sciences, Uppsala.

———, 1977b, *Marketing for Small Farmers Development—A Case Study from Ethiopia*, Swedish University of Agricultural Sciences, Uppsala.

Howes, M., & R., Chambers, 1980, *"Indigenous Technology Analysis, Implications and Issues"* in Brokensha, D. Warren, D.M., Verner, O., (eds.), *Indigenous Knowledge System and Development*, University Press of America Inc., Lanham.

Hulme, D., & Turner, M., 1990, *Sociology and Development, Theory, Policies and Practices*, Harvester Wheatsheat, London, and New York.

Hult, T., 1972, *Dictionary of Modern Sociology*, Littlefield, Adams & Co., Totowa, New Jersey.

Hunton, W.A., 1957, *Decision on Africa*, New York.

Huntington, S.P., 1968, *Political Order in Changing Societies*, Yale University Press, New Haven.

Hyden, G., 1968, "The problems of democracy in Africa," Seminar Paper, Jyväskylä.

———, 1980, *Beyond Ujamaa in Tanzania, Underdevelopment and Uncaptured Peasantry*, Heinemann, London.

———, 1983, *No Short Cuts to Progress, African Development Management in Perspective*, Heinemann, London, Ibadan, Nairobi.

———, 1990, "The Changing Context of Institutional Development," in World Bank, *The Long Term Perspective Study of Sub-Saharan Africa*, Institutional and Sociopolitical Issues, Vol. #3, Washington, D.C.

Iliffe, J., 1983, *The Emergence of African Capitalism*, The Macmillan Press Ltd., London.

Inikori, J.E., 1979, "African Slave Trade from the Fifteenth to the Nineteenth Century," in *General History of Africa Studies and Documents*, No. 2, UNESCO, Paris.

———, 1992, "Africa in World History: the Export of Slave Trade from Africa and the Emergence of the Atlantic Economic Order," in *General History of Africa Studies and Documents*, No. V, UNESCO, Paris.

International Trade, Statistical Year-book, Volume II, 1990 - 1992, UN, Department of Economic and Social Development, Statistic Office, New York.

Irving, G.W., 1935, *An Introduction to Economic History*, Macmillan and Co. Limited, London.

Kessing's Contemporary Archives, (various), London.

Bibliography

Kidane Mengisteab, 1990, *Ethiopia: Failure of Land Reform and Agricultural Crisis*, Greenwood Press, New York and London.

Krisch, Göricke, and Wörz, 1989, *Agricultural Revolution and Peasant Emancipation in Ethiopia*, Studies in Applied economics and Rural Institutions, Saarbrucken.

Lakew Yebza, 1974, *Local Government Administration in Ethiopia*, Addis Ababa University, Institute of Development Research (IDR), Addis Ababa.

Lazarsfeld, P., et. al, 1967, *The Use of Sociology*, Basic Books, New York.

Lenin, V.I., (translated 1968), "Imperialism the Highest Stage of Capitalism," in *Selected Works*, Vol. I, Progressive Publishers, Moscow.

Lewis, W.,A., 1950, "Economic Development with Unlimited Supplies of Labor," *The Manchester School of Economics and Social Studies*, Vol. XXII, Manchester.

Lindberg, S., 1992, "Peasants for Democracy? Farmers' Agitation and the State in India," in Rudebeck (ed.), *When Democracy Makes Sense*, Akut, Uppsala.

Lipsky, G., 1967, *Ethiopia: Its People, Its Society, Its Culture*, Survey of World Culture, Hraf Press, New Haven.

Lipset, S., 1960, *Political Man, The Social Base of Politicians*, Grand City, New York.

Long, N., L 1977, *An Introduction to the Sociology of Rural Development*, The Chaucer Press, London.

MacGaffey, J., and, Windsperger, G., 1990, "The Endogenous Economy," in World Bank, *The Long Term Perspective Study of Sub-Saharan Africa*, Institutional and Sociopolitical Issues, Vol. 3, Washington, D.C.

Magdoff, H., 1969, *The Age of Imperialism*, Monthly Review Press, New York

Makonen Getu, 1987, *Socialism, Participation, and Agricultural Development in Post-revolutionary Ethiopia*, (ACTA) Stockholm Studies in Economic History, Almqvist and Weiksell International, Stockholm.

Malowist, M., 1992, "The Struggle for International Trade and its Implications for Africa," in *General History of Africa Studies and Documents*, No. V, UNESCO, Paris.

Mao Tse-Tung, 1975, *Selected Works*, Vol. II, Foreign Language Press, Peking.

Markakis, J., 1975a, *Ethiopia: Anatomy of A Traditional Polity*, Oxford University Press, Addis Ababa, Ethiopia.

———, 1975b, *Peasant, Nomads and Students in Ethiopia*, Ch'ludaba, Accra.

———, 1981, "The Military State and African Socialism," *African Political Economy*, Leeds, UK.

Marx, K., 1957, *The Eighteenth Brumaire of Louis Bonaparte*, New York.

———, and Engels, F., 1969, "Manifest of the Communist Party," *Selected Works*, Vol. I, Progress Publishers, Moscow.

Mazrui, A., 1986, *The Africans, A Triple Heritage*, BBC Publications.

M'bokolo, E., 1992, "From the Cameroon Grasslands to the Upper Nile," in *General History of Africa Studies and Documents*, No. V, UNESCO, Paris.

Meier, G.M., (ed.), 1964, *Leading Issues in Economic Development*, Oxford University Press, New York.

Meier, G., 1989, *Leading Issues in Economic Development*, Oxford University Press, Oxford, New York, Toronto.

Mesfin Kassa, 1973, "The Relevance of Multipurpose Farmers' Co-operatives in the Landholding System of Damot Awraja, Gojjam," Seminar Paper, Addis Ababa.

Mekuria Bulcha, 1973, "Eder: Its Role in Development and Social Change in Ethiopian Urban Centers," Senior Essay, School of Social Work, Haile Selassie I University, Addis Ababa, Ethiopia.

———, 1988, *Flight and Integration, Causes of Mass Exodus from Ethiopia and Problems of Integration in the Sudan*, Scandinavian Institute of African Studies, Uppsala, Sweden.

Mobounije, A., 1982, *The Development Process; A Special Perspective*, Hutchinson & Co. Ltd. London.

Mohammed Hassen, 1990, *The Oromo of Ethiopia: A history 1570-1860*, African Studies Series 66, Cambridge University Press, Cambridge, New York and Sydney.

Mamdani, M., 1989, "The IMF and Uganda," *African Events, June 1989*, Uganda.

Moore, B, 1967, *Social Origins of Dictatorship and Democracy*, Beacon Books, Boston.

Moore, W. E., 1963, *Social Change*, New Jersey.

Mauri, A., 1987, "The Role of Financial Intermediation in the Mobilization and Allocation of Household Saving in Developing Countries: Interlinks Between Organized and Informal Circuits: The case of Ethiopia," Paper presented on International Experts Meeting on Domestic Savings Mobilization, East West Center, Honolulu.

Bibliography

Mustapha, A. R., 1992, "Structural Adjustment and Multiple Modes of Livelihood in Nigeria, in Gibbon, Bangura and Ofstad," 1992, (eds.) *Authoritarianism, Democracy and Adjustment, The Politics of Economic Reform in Africa,* The Scandinavian Institute of African Studies No. 26, Uppsala.

Myrdal, G., 1977, *Asian Drama: An Inquiry into the Poverty of Nations,* H. Wolff, New York.

Nedegwa, P., 1985, *Africa's Development Crisis,* Heinemann, Nairobi.

Negarit Gazeta, (various) Ethiopian Government Official Policy (legislative) Declarations or Proclamations, Addis Ababa.

New Africa Year-book, (various), London.

Nkrumah, K., 1965, *Neo-colonialism: The Last Stage of Imperialism,* Thomas Nelson Ltd., London.

———, 1970, *Class Struggle in Africa,* Panaf Books Ltd., London.

North South: A Programme for Survival, 1980, Pan Books Ltd. London.

North South: Common Crisis, 1983, Pan Books Ltd., London.

Nyerere, J., 1967a, "Rural Development in Tanzania after the Arusha Declaration," Unpublished document of Nordic Taganyika Project, from Styrelsessammanträde den 13 November, 1967 (5/67), Bilaga 1, Stockholm.

———, 1967b, *Socialism and Rural Development,* Dare es Selaam.

Nyong'o, A., 1988a, "Political instability and prospects for democracy in Africa," *Africa Development,* Vol. XIII. No. 1.

———, 1988b, "Democracy and Political Instability: A Rejoinder to the Comments by Thandika Mkandawire," *Africa Development,* Vol. xiii, No. 3.

Oakley, P., and Marsden, D., 1985, *Approach to Participation in Rural Development,* International Labor Office, (ILO) Geneva.

———, 1991, *Project with People, the Practice of Participation in Rural Development,* ILO, Geneva.

OECD Development Co-operation, Reports, 1990-1994, Paris.

Onimode, B., 1988, *A political Economy of the African Crisis, Institute for African Alternatives,* Zed Books Ltd., London and New Jersey.

———, 1992, *A Future for Africa, Beyond the Politics of Adjustment,* Earthscan Publications Ltd., London.

Ortner, S., 1984, *Theory in Anthropology Since the Sixties, Comparative Studies in Society and History,* Cambridge, London.

Ottaway, M., 1975, "Land Reform and Peasant Associations: A Preliminary Analysis," *Rural Africa,* No. 28, East Lansing.

———, 1977, "Land Reform in Ethiopia 1974-1977," *African Studies Review,* Vol. 20 No. 3, University of South Carolina.

————, (ed), 1990, *The Political Economy of Ethiopia*, New York, London.

Palmberg, M. (ed), 1978, *Problems of Socialist Orientation in Africa*, The Scandinavian Institute of African Studies, Uppsala, Sweden.

Pankrust, Alula, 1990, "Resettlement: Policy and Practice" in Pausewang, Brune, Fantu Cheru and Eshetu Chole, (eds.), *Ethiopia: Options for Rural Development*, Zed Books, London and New Jersey.

Pankhurst and Endreas Eshete, 1958, "Self-help in Ethiopia," *Ethiopian Observer*, Vol. II, No. 11.

Pankhurst, R., 1961, *An Introduction to The Economic History of Ethiopia, from Early Times to 1800*, Sidgwick and Fackson, Ltd., London.

————, 1990, *A Social History of Ethiopia*, Institute of Ethiopian Studies, Addis Sbaba University, Ethiopia.

Parsons, T., 1951, *The Social System*, Free Press, Chicago.

————, 1960, *Structure and Process in Modern Society*, Free Press, Chicago.

Pateman, C., 1975, *Participation and Democratic Theory*, Cambridge University Press, Cambridge.

Patman, R., 1981, "State and Class," *American Journal of Sociology*, Vol. 87, No. 1.

Pausewang, S., 1979, *Land Tenure, Social Structure and Landreform*, (Revised), Bergen, Norway.

————, 1983, *Peasant, Land and Society: A Social History of Land Reform in Ethiopia*, Weltforum Verlag, München, Köln and London.

————, 1988a, "Alternatives in Rural Development in Ethiopia," *Development Research and Action Program*—DERAP Working Papers, [A 380], Bergen, Norway.

————, 1988b, "Local democracy and Central Control," *Development Research and Action Program*—DERAP Working Papers [A 382], Bergen, Norway.

————, Fantu Cheru, S., Brune, & Eshetu Chole (Eds.), 1990, *Ethiopia: Rural Development Options*, Zed, London.

Petras, J., 1977, *"State Capitalism and the Third World," Development and Change*, The Institute of Social Sciences, The Hague, Vol. 8.

Phillips H., 1969, *Guide for Development: Institution-Building and Reform*, Praeger special studies in International Economics and Development, Frederick A. Praeger, Publishers, New York, Washington, London.

Picket, J., 1991, *"Economic Development in Ethiopia: Agriculture, the Market and the State*, Development Center Studies, OECD, Paris.

Bibliography

"Popular Participation as a Strategy for Promoting Community Level Action and National Development," 1981, Report of the Meeting of the Ad Hoc Group of the Experts held at United Nations Headquarter from 22 to 26 May, 1978, UN, New York.

Poulantzas, N., 1976, *Political Power and Social Class,* Low and Brydone Printers Limited, London.

Redfield, R., 1974, "The Folk Society," *American Journal of Sociology* (52:292-308), xx.

"Report of NGO Consultation on Participation in Fisheries Development," 1987, Bay of Bengal Program (FAO), Madras, India.

Richards, P., 1980, *Community Environmental Knowledge in African Rural Development,* in Brokensha, D. Warren, D.M., Verner, O., (eds.), *Indigenous Knowledge System and Development,* University Press Of America Inc., Lanham.

Rodney, W., 1972, *How Europe Underdeveloped Africa,* Love and Malcomson, London.

Rostow, W.W., 1960, *The Stages of Economic Growth: A Non-Communist Manifesto,* Cambridge University Press, London.

Rudebeck, L., 1990, *Conditions of People's Development in Post-colonial Africa,* Working Group for the Studies of Development Strategies (AKUT), University of Uppsala, Uppsala.

———, 1992, (ed), *When Democracy Makes Sense,* Studies in the Democratic Potential of Third World Popular Movements, Working Group for the Studies of Development Strategies (AKUT), Uppsala University, Uppsala.

Rudolph, L., and Rudolph H., 1967, *The Modernity of Tradition, Political Development in India,* The University of Chicago Press, Chicago & London.

Rudqvist, Anders, 1986, "Popular Participation—Theoretical and Methodological Points of Departure," (mimeo), Development Study Unit, Dept. of Social Anthropology, University of Stockholm, Stockholm.

———, 1987, "Popular Participation: Levels and Dimensions," (mimeo), Development Study Unit, Dept. of Social Anthropology, University of Stockholm, Stockholm.

Rubenson, S., 1976, *The Survival of Ethiopian Independence,* Heinemann Educational Books, Nairobi.

Savings and Credit Co-operation Development Office (SACCDO), 1990, *The Saver,* No. 1.

Sandbrook, R., 1982, *The Politics of Basic Needs, Urban Aspects of Assaulting Poverty in Africa*, Heinmann, London, Ibadan and Nairobi.

———, 1985, *The Politics of Africa's Economic Stagnation*, Cambridge University Press, London, New York and Sydney.

Santos, Milton, 1979, *The Shared Space, The Two Circuits of the Urban Economy in Underdeveloped Countries*, Methuen, London and New York.

Sartori, G., 1987, *The Theory of Democracy Revisited, Part One: The Contemporary Debate*, Chatham House Publishers, Inc. New Jersey.

Scott, M., and Gormley, 1980, "The Animal of Friendship (Habbanaae): An Indigenous Model of Sahelian Pastoral Development in Nigeria," in Brokensha, D. Warren, D.M., Verner, O., (eds.), *Indigenous Knowledge System and Development*, University Press of America Inc., Lanham.

Shanin, T., 1973, "The Nature and Logic of the Peasant Economy," *Journal of Peasant Studies*, Vol. 1, No. 1.

Shivji, I.J., 1975, *Class Struggle in Tanzania*, Tanzania Publishing House, Dar es Salaam.

Shumpeter, J., (1936), 1981, *Capitalism, Socialism and Democracy*, Counterpoint, London.

Smelser, N.J., 1959, *Social Change in the Industrial Revolution*, London.

Smith, D., 1983, *Violence, Morality and Political Change, Theoretical Traditions in the Social Sciences;* The Macmillan Press Ltd., London.

Solodovnikov, V. & V., Bogoslovsky, 1975, *Non-capitalist Development: An Historical Outline*, Progress Publisher, Moscow.

Stavalastoga, K., 1976, *Social Differentiation*, Social Science Series, Van Rees Press, New York.

Stöhr, W., and Taylor, F., 1981, (eds.) *Development from Above or Below, The Dialectics of Regional Planning in Developing Countries*, John Wiley & Sons, New York and Toronto.

Survival International, 1986, *Ethiopia's Bitter Medicine: Setting for Disaster*, Mount Pleasant, London.

Swanson, R., 1980a, *Development Interventions and Self-Realization*, in Brokensha, D. Warren, D.M., Verner, O., (eds.), *Indigenous Knowledge System and Development*, University Press Of America Inc., Lanham.

Swanson, R.,1980b, *Development Innovations and Self Realization Among the Gourma*, in Brokensha, D. Warren, D.M., Verner, O., (eds.), *Indigenous Knowledge System and Development*, University Press of America Inc., Lanham.

Bibliography

Sweezy, P., 1970, *The Theory of Capitalist Development,* Monthly Review Press, New York.

Taddesse Tamerat, 1972, *Church and State in Ethiopia 1270-1527,* Oxford University Press, Ely House, London.

Tatek, (various), *Journal of Ethiopian Students in Europe,* Stockholm, Paris (in Amharic).

Tedros Kiros, 1992, *Moral Philosophy and Development: The Human Conditions in Africa,* London.

Teglachen, (various) *Journal of Ethiopian Students in Europe,* Stockholm, Paris (in Amharic).

Tekeste Negash, 1987, *Italian Colonialism in Eritrea, 18882-1941, Policies, Praxis and Impact,* Almqvist & Wiksell International, Stockholm.

——, 1990, *The Crisis of Ethiopian Education: Some Implications for Nation-Building,* Department of Education, Uppsal University, Sweden.

Tekle Sadek Mekuria, (1981, Ethiopian Calender), *Emperor Tewodros,* (in Amharic), Kuraz Publishing Agency, Addis Ababa.

——, (1982, Ethiopian Calender), *Emperor Yohannes,* (in Amharic), Kuraz Publishing Agency, Addis Ababa.

——, (1983, Ethiopian Calender), *Emperor Menelik,* (in Amharic), Kuraz Publishing Agency, Addis Ababa.

Tenker, Bonger, 1994, *The Current Political and Economic Conditions in Ethiopia,* (in Amharic), London.

Tesema, Ta'a, 1994, "Traditional and 'Modern' Cooperatives Among the Oromo," Seminar paper.

Thomas, C.Y., 1978, "Class Struggle, Social Development and the Theory of the Non-Capitalist Path," in Palmberg, M. (ed), 1978, *Problems of Socialist Orientation in Africa,* The Scandinavian Institute of African Studies, Uppsala.

Tirfe Mammo, 1987a, "People's Participation in BOBP's Extension Activities," in *BOBP News,* No. 9, 1987, Madras.

——, 1987b, "Study in Income, Indebtedness and Savings Among the Fisheries Folk of Orissa," India, in FAO's Working Paper, BOBP/WP/55, Madras.

——, 1991, "Ethiopia: Tasks of the Transitional Government in the Initial Period of Economic Recovery," in *Some Problems of Transformation in Ethiopia,* Paris.

Titze, U, 1985, *Artisanal Marine Fisherfolk of Orissa,* Balubazar, Cuttack.

Todaro, Michael, 1983, *Economic Development in the Third World,* Longman, New York and London.

"Towards Another Development" 1975, Prepared on the Occasion of the Seventh Special Session of the United Nations General Assembly, *Development Dialogue*, Dag Hammerskjöld Foundation, Uppsala.

Trimingham, J.S., 1976, *Islam in Ethiopia*, Frank Cass and Company Ltd., London.

Tönnies, F., [1887] 1957 *Community and Society,(translated by Loomis, C.)* Michigan State University.

Uphoff, N., and Esman, M., 1974, *Local Organization for Rural Development: Analysis of Asian Experience*, Development Committee, Center for International studies, Cornell University, Ithaca.

———, and Cohen, G., 1977, *Rural Development Participation: Concepts and Measures for Project Design, Implementation, and Evaluation*, Rural Development Committee, Center for International Studies, Cornell University, Ithaca.

Upper Mille and Cheleka Catchment, *Disaster Preventation Program*, Ethiopian Red Cross, 1986, Addis Ababa.

UNDP, *Human Development Report, 1990-1994*, New York and Oxford.

UNESCO, 1978, *The General History of Africa Studies and Documents*, No. 2. Paris.

UNESCO, 1990, *Statistical Year-Book*, Paris.

Vadney, T.E, 1987, *The World Since 1945*, Penguin Books Ltd., London.

Wallerstein, I., 1974, *The Modern World-System, Capitalist Agriculture and the Origins of the European World-economy in the Sixteenth Century*, Academic Press, Inc., London, New York and San Francisco.

Waterstone, Albert, 1974, *Development Planning: Lessons of Experience*, The Johns Hopkins University Press, Baltimore and London.

WCARRD, Ethiopia: Country Review Paper on Ethiopia, World Conference on Agrarian Reform and Rural Development, Secretariat, 1979, Rome.

Weber, M. [1920], 1961, *General Economic History*, (Translated by Frank H. Kright), New York, pp.

Weber, M., 1978 *Economy and Society*, Vol. I, University of California Press, Berkeley, Los Angeles and London.

WHO, 1990, *World Health Statistics*, Annual, Genéva.

Wiking, S., 1983, *Military Coups in Sub-Saharan Africa*, Scandinavian Institute of African Studies, Uppsala.

Wolf, E., 1966, *Peasants*, Foundations of Modern Anthropology studies, University of Michigan.

World Bank, 1980, Economic Memorandum on Ethiopia.

Bibliography

———, 1990a, *The Long Term Perspective Study of Sub-Saharan Africa*, Vol. 1 Country Perspectives, Washington D.C.

———, 1990b, *The Long Term Perspective Study of Sub-Saharan Africa*, Vol. 3., *Institutional and Sociopolitical Issues*, Washington D.C.

———, 1993, *Annual Report*, Washington D.C.

———, World Tables, (various), The Johns Hopkins University Press, Baltimore and London.

World Development Report on Poverty, 1990, Oxford University Press, Oxford, New York, Toronto and Delhi

World Statistics in Brief, 1991, UN Statistical Pocketbook, New York.

World Population, 1992, UN, Department of Economic and Social Development, New York.

Yassin Shifa, 1990, "The Development of Savings and Credit Co-operatives in Ethiopia," Senior Paper, Departments of Economics, University of Addis Ababa.

Young, F., 1986, *Interdisciplinary Theories of Rural Development*, Department of Rural Sociology, Cornell University, Greenwich, Connecticut.

Index

Ethiopians are listed under their first names

abat(s), 92, 108, 184
Abidjan, 197
absentee landlords, 88, 90-113
accountability, 6, 26, 69-72, 141,
    174, 182, 183, 190, 198, 199,
    201, 224, 226, 231
Accra, 197
acculturation, 90, 93
accumulation, 59, 159, 228
    of capital, 159
Addis Ababa, 36, 91, 92, 104, 130,
    139, 154, 168, 177, 212
afar, 208, 228
Africa, 3, 5-11, 17-27, 29-55, 59,
    61-80, 105-113, 126, 127, 133,
    149, 158, 167, 176, 177, 180,
    195, 196, 198, 200, 203, 205-
    209, 212, 214, 215, 218, 224-
    226, 230, 231, 233-235, 237
Africanization, 27, 38, 39
agrarian, 17, 113, 118, 129, 130,
    132, 135, 137, 142, 143, 145,
    150, 151, 166, 201
    reform, 17, 113, 132, 136, 138,
    142-170
agricultural, 7, 17, 19, 20, 38, 45,
    46, 58, 59, 66-68, 74, 85, 87,
    98, 99, 101, 128, 129, 131-133,
    135, 142, 149, 151, 152, 156,
    221
    development, 59, 131, 151,
    159, 160, 165
Ake, 8, 43, 180, 196, 230
Alemayehu Seifu, 192, 212
Alemneh Dejene, 17, 129, 144, 150,
    158

Algeria, 42, 49
alliance, 36, 60, 122, 123, 125, 126,
    138, 162, 165
Alula Abate, 142
amarinja, 93, 109, 211
Amin, Idi, 8, 39
Amharic, 136, 138, 139, 211
Anatomy, 109
Annenkov, 22
Apostles, 184
Arab, 10, 22, 47, 103
arable land, 9, 31, 88, 98, 99, 102,
    108, 120, 129, 142, 143
arash, 89, 90
Arnold, 54, 55
Arssi, 88, 91, 121, 132, 143, 144,
    150, 153, 158
artisan, 59, 128, 197
Arusha, 45
Asante, 78
assistance, 6, 29, 37, 38, 42, 51, 53-
    55, 57, 62, 69, 77, 161, 165,
    165, 194, 205, 218, 223, 228,
    233, 236
    development, 6-28, 37, 53-57,
    62, 69, 76, 77, 218
Atlantic Slave Trade, 5, 6, 7, 8, 9,
    10, 11, 18, 21, 24, 25, 94
authentic, 72, 76
Authenticity, 47
authoritative, 182
authority, 38, 89, 94, 146, 189, 193
autonomy, 13-28, 73, 135
awareness, 73, 117, 120, 129, 189,
    204, 229, 230
    political, 129

Awash, 160
aweraja, 121
Axum, 20-28
Ayittey, 19-28

Bahru Zewede, 99
balager, 93
Bale, 88, 98, 99, 109, 110, 121, 132, 139, 144, 155
bale'abat, 92, 93, 108
balebet, 209, 210
Balsvik, 100, 101, 117
Bangladesh, 190, 213
Bangura, 228
barter, 19, 79
bazaar, 19, 20
Befakadu, 158
Begemder, 107, 121, 132, 144
Belgium, 28, 49
beneficiaries, 21, 88, 101, 223, 227, 228, 234
Benin, 78, 197
Berbers, 10
Berlin, 23, 28
bilateral, 66, 221
birr, 130, 134, 149, 157, 168, 191, 193-195
Blomström, 45
bogus results, 114, 125, 135
Bondestam, Lars, 103, 104
bourgeois (ie), 39, 40, 43, 47, 48, 50, 51, 76, 78
breakthroughs, 95
Bretton Wood, 57
Britain, 10, 23, 28, 40, 63, 64, 99
Brokensha, D., 211
Buganda, 20
bureaucracy, 47, 158

cadres, 124, 127, 134, 135, 146, 147, 155, 160, 222

Cameroon, 49, 195
Campaign, 115-117, 137, 149, 152, 169
capitalism, 8, 11, 17, 19, 20, 39-43, 46, 47, 76, 122, 158, 164
Caribbean, 32, 45
Casablanca, 36
catalogue, 12, 33, 40, 178, 208
catalytic, 77, 209, 233
centralism, 127
Chad, 33
Chambers, Robert, 15, 178, 180
charter, 65
cheka, 120, 137
China, 24, 27, 41, 50, 51, 110, 151, 161
civilization, 5, 10, 17, 19, 24, 78
clan, 34, 79, 167, 234
Clapham, 95, 109
classes, 51, 86, 93, 97, 98, 101, 103, 122
classical, 17, 37, 43
clergy, 89, 90, 101, 102, 104, 105
clique, 79, 125, 162
Cocoa, 31, 45, 68, 69, 168, 207
Coffee, 31, 68, 69, 102, 158, 168, 207
Cohen, 107, 129, 130, 133, 134, 143, 144, 151, 153, 165, 216
Colchester, 155
collectivization, 114, 128, 132, 135, 141, 142, 146, 202, 210, 213, 234
colonialism, 5-9, 11, 18, 20, 22-25, 29, 35, 41, 71-73, 84, 95, 196, 205, 231, 233
Commission, 57, 62, 65, 75, 78, 162, 169, 208, 211, 226
commodities, 18, 24, 68, 102
communal, 76, 98, 107

Index

communities, 39, 85, 91, 174, 176, 183, 184, 186, 189, 193, 195, 199, 207, 210, 221, 235
compensation, 104, 152, 209
complementary, 173, 176, 213
concentration, 64, 153, 155
conflict, 138, 165, 185, 189
Congo, 42, 71
consciousness, 75, 204, 232
constitution, 89, 96, 97, 114, 139
constraints, 12, 96
continuity, 40, 181
conventional, 13, 14, 48, 134, 222, 232
cooperatives, 128, 131, 149, 154
Coptic, 87, 89, 93, 109
Corporals, 127
Corporation, 104, 131, 157
corruption, 40, 45, 71, 72, 115
cottage, 187
cotton, 19, 22, 24, 31, 68, 160, 168, 207
coup, 15, 94, 100, 101, 105, 110, 111, 114
crown, 87, 89, 114, 234
Cuba, 126, 138, 149, 164
currency, 57, 138, 195
customs, 175

Dahomey, 20, 78
Dakar, 197
Davidson, 10, 19, 20, 23, 26, 78
Dawit, 133, 134, 137, 139, 154, 155, 166, 167
debo, 184, 185, 186
decentralization, 199, 229
decolonization, 27, 29, 203
deepening, 11, 53, 55, 69, 70, 84
deforestation, 156
dejazemach, 92

Dejene Aredo, 187, 190-193, 195, 197
demilitarized, 72
democracy, 13, 39, 41, 43, 46, 47, 50, 51, 71, 74, 146, 198, 224-228, 231, 232, 235
demystify, 232
Denmark, 79
dependency, 17, 41, 45, 55-57, 59, 66, 69, 75, 215, 233
Dessalegn Rahmato, 129, 146, 166
destitute, 32, 33, 102, 198, 223
devaluation, 57, 61
development, 3-18, 2-27, 32-42, 44, 46-51, 53-57, 59, 62, 65, 69-72, 74-78, 83, 94-97, 105, 106, 114, 115, 122, 123, 125, 128-129, 135, 137, 139, 141, 145, 148, 149, 151, 155, 156, 158-162, 165, 166, 173-175, 177-181, 184-185, 188-196, 198, 199, 202,203, 204, 206, 197, 109, 211, 212, 215-226, 228-235
dictatorship, 15, 51, 71, 127, 135, 164, 166
Dieci, P., 134, 154
disputes, 23, 121, 125
Djibouti, 23
doctrinaire, 46
Dorner, P., 17
Dutch, 78

Echat, 137, 138
ecological, 98, 134, 167, 177
economy, 8, 9, 21, 24, 26, 38, 39, 45, 158, 60, 63, 88, 91, 96, 103, 117, 148, 149, 150, 159, 197, 198
eder, 183, 184, 186, 187, 188, 190-195, 212

educational, 31, 35, 13, 103
egalitarian, 27, 86, 113, 114
egalitarianism, 124
egoism, 115
Egypt, 42, 47, 78
egzabeher, 212
ekul-arash, 90
elderly, 167
elite, 6, 25, 27, 34, 39, 40, 43, 72, 73, 78, 79, 92, 93, 101, 105, 110, 150, 204, 233
  political, 6, 72, 73, 78, 233
embargo, 103
emirates, 85
Emperor Tewodros, 85
employment, 58, 65, 69, 102, 103, 150, 151, 173, 196, 198, 202, 203, 205, 209, 213-214, 221, 235
empowering, 220, 223
Endreas Eshete, 186, 212
Engles, Frederick, 18, 42
Enlightenment, 115
enrollment, 31, 203, 218, 222
entrepreneurial, 156, 158, 160, 177
entrepreneurship, 20, 156, 207
environment, 14, 33, 78, 150, 153, 154, 180, 189, 197, 199, 210, 222, 230, 236
equb, 178, 183, 184, 186-188, 190-195, 212
equity, 43, 71, 118
Eritrea, 26, 73, 85, 98, 99, 102, 106, 164, 227
erosion, 63, 156, 167, 205
Eshetu Chole, 133
esusus, 195
ethics, 8, 44, 210
Ethiopia, 4, 9, 10, 12, 19, 20, 23, 26, 33, 40, 42, 43, 45, 47, 49, 51, 56, 59, 73, 78, 83-93, 95, 96,

98, 100-110, 113-120, 122-130, 132-134, 136-144, 150-151, 153, 156, 161-163, 165, 167-169, 176, 177, 183, 184, 186, 187-190, 192, 194, 197, 199-202, 205, 206, 209-213, 215, 218, 227, 230, 231, 233, 234
ethnic, 23, 34, 39, 45, 48, 69, 70-74, 97, 108, 115, 118, 119, 153, 186, 206, 207, 212, 227, 234
European, 5, 8, 19-24, 26, 28, 40, 48, 49, 64, 65, 73, 76, 77, 106, 109, 125, 161, 178
evolutionary, 116, 120, 132, 136, 137, 138, 143, 146, 149, 156, 162, 165, 175
exodus, 102, 105
expansionist, 10
exploitation, 24, 45, 97, 106, 115, 118, 233
extraction, 63, 91
extravagances, 101
Exxon, 78

famine, 7, 30, 33, 74, 97, 98, 102-105, 133, 134, 136, 143, 144, 151, 165, 166, 200
Fantu Cheru, 30, 58, 59, 196
farm, 67, 84, 90, 91, 128,. 130, 131, 132, 135, 143, 152, 153, 157, 160, 177, 197
fascist, 10
Fassil Gebre Kiros, 129, 139
fertilizer, 129, 201
feudalism, 12, 84, 110, 117, 120, 122
Finland, 79
fisherfolk, 177, 219
fitawrarie, 92
folksongs, 177
forestry, 177

Index

forum, 95, 110, 161, 162, 184, 185, 186, 187, 193, 212, 227
foundation, 11, 18, 42, 43, 109, 121, 127, 148, 181, 195, 202
fragmentation of land, 143
France, 23, 28, 40, 50, 63
functionaries, 108, 145, 167
Fund, 49, 53, 57, 186, 195

Gabbar, 88, 90, 91, 92, 106, 107, 108
Gabon, 63, 195
Galbraith, 15
Gambia, 23
Gamo Goffa, 121, 132, 144
Gebru, 91
Gebru Tareke, 89, 95, 98, 99, 100, 109, 110
gentry, 84, 87, 89, 92, 93, 98, 99, 100, 101, 108
German, 23
gerraazmach, 92
Ghana, 9, 19, 20, 31, 36, 42, 44, 45, 59, 63, 195
Gibbon, 58, 59
Gibe, 85
globalize, 69
Gode, 155, 167
Godelier, 14
Gojjam, 91, 98, 99, 107, 110, 121, 132, 134, 143, 144, 158, 168, 186
grant, 77, 138
grass-roots, 71, 127, 189
Greece, 64
Gross, 32, 78
groundnuts, 22, 31
guerilla, 154
Guinea Bissau, 76
Gulf, 60
gult, 86-89, 108
Gurage, 177, 186

Haile Selassie, 87, 88, 94-101, 103, 106-110, 116, 125, 162, 186, 210, 212
handicrafts, 35, 59, 178, 200, 206, 231, 234
Harar, 85, 88, 92, 107, 121, 130, 132, 139, 144
Harbeson, 103, 104, 116, 119, 127
Hausa, 23
hibersebawinet, 47
Holmberg, 166
horticulture, 162
hostilities, 162
household, 59, 98, 118, 120, 121, 128-134, 142, 145, 150, 151, 157, 179, 185, 206
Humera, 155, 160
Hyden, 17

Ibo, 20
ideology, 16, 44, 70, 71, 89, 110, 114-116, 124, 137, 141, 160, 161, 162
Iliffe, 19
Illubabor, 88, 91, 107, 132, 134, 135, 144
Imperialism, 122
incentives, 49, 151, 156, 193, 201
indebtedness, 55, 62, 233
India, 10, 24, 213, 218, 221
indicators, 29, 31, 34, 107
indigenous, 3-13, 15-20, 24, 27, 30, 35, 38-40, 42, 47, 53, 55, 65, 70, 72, 76, 77, 83, 108, 165, 173, 175, 176-181, 183, 188, 195, 203, 211, 216, 224, 226, 229-233, 236
indigenous knowledge, 3, 4, 6-12, 15-18, 20, 27, 30, 38, 40, 47, 65, 70, 77, 165, 173, 175-178,

180, 181, 183, 196, 203, 211, 224, 229-233, 236
indigo, 19
Indonesia, 213
industrialization, 5, 6, 38, 40, 48, 65, 75, 76, 96
infrastructure, 45, 189
innovations, 4, 15, 178, 181, 196, 213, 236
intelligentsia, 47, 50, 73, 97, 105, 110, 114, 122, 125, 126, 148, 161-164, 166, 169, 202, 234
intervention, 4, 40, 49, 94, 125, 156, 199, 206, 217
intrigues, 109
irbo-arash, 90
irrigation, 177, 200, 205, 213
Islam, 27
Israel, 149
Italy, 10, 23, 28, 94
Ivory Coast, 38, 45, 168
Iyassu, 96, 109

Japan, 8, 30, 33, 207
Jenne, 19
Jimma, 85
judicial system, 26, 96, 97
junta, military, 125
jurisdiction, 120, 121, 145

Kaffa, 85, 88, 91, 107, 121, 132, 134, 135, 144
Kano, 19
katikala, 178
Kebele, 120, 121, 137, 152, 157, 218
kegneazamach, 92
Kenya, 9, 38-40, 56, 168, 196
Kessing Archives, 126
kibbutzim, 149

Kidane Mengisteab, 107, 119, 129, 130, 131, 142
Kikuyu, 39
kingdoms, 9, 20, 72, 85
kinship, 86, 87, 93, 107, 155, 185, 186, 192, 210, 235
kolkhozes, 149
Konso, 85
Koran, 47
kulaks, 150

laissez-faire, 65
land holding, 35, 88, 102
landless, 17, 90, 106, 118, 143, 144, 162
landlord, 17, 85, 86, 88, 90, 91, 92, 95, 99, 101, 102, 107, 108, 117, 118, 119, 137, 144, 148, 156, 159, 166, 168
leadership, 20, 41, 43, 47, 50, 51, 71, 125, 126, 138, 141, 148, 161, 162, 163, 183, 198
legislation, 96, 107, 113, 116, 117, 118, 119, 121, 128, 141, 142, 144, 145, 160, 162, 165, 202, 230
Lenin, 163
liberalization, 57, 61
Limmu, 85
Lipsky, 94, 109, 110
literacy, 32, 34, 148
Liverpool, 21, 22
livestock, 35, 153
London, 21
Lozi, 19
lucrative, 22, 61, 65, 160, 168
Lund, 139

MacGaffey, 195, 207
Madagascar, 56, 73, 78
Maderia, 86, 89, 92

Madinga, 19
Magdoff, 77
magnitude, 21, 22, 116, 133, 163
Mahdist, 78
maheber, 218
Makonen Getu, 168
maladministration, 72, 151
Malawi, 38
Malerid, 138
Mali, 19, 36, 38, 42
malnutrition, 22, 30, 31
manufacturing, 21, 35, 38, 39, 62,
    63, 68, 96, 159, 178, 197, 202,
    231
Mao Tse-Tung, 50, 51
Markakis, John, 87, 88, 90, 106,
    108, 109
Markato, 177
Marx, Karl, 18, 22, 42, 163
Mazrui, Ali, 8, 30, 72, 206
medieval Europe, 89
Mediterranean, 19, 24
Meier, 202
Meison, 124, 138, 161
Mekuria Bulcha, 74, 186, 192
Menelik, Emperor 85, 87, 96, 109
Mengistu, Haile Mariam 78, 137,
    138, 139, 155, 166, 167
meredaja, 184, 185, 186, 188, 189,
    190, 193, 196, 212
meret la'rashu, 103
Meroe, 10, 20
mesafent, 93, 108
Metcha'na Tulema, 212
metropolitan, 226
Mexico, 78
misappropriation of land, 95
mobilization, 48, 70, 71, 115, 116,
    129, 174, 208, 219, 220, 223
    of peasants, 204
Mobutu, 78

modernization, 6, 7, 16, 17, 25, 27,
    33, 34, 48, 49, 76, 94, 95, 96,
    109, 179, 210, 224, 231, 233
monopolistic, 158
monopoly, 141, 156, 157
Morocco, 30, 36
Moscow, 41
Mozambique, 23, 42, 56
multinational corporations, 6, 11,
    38, 53, 62
muskets, 22
Muslims, 91, 99
mystification, 71

Namibia, 63
Nasser, Gamal, 42
nationalization, 27, 41, 43, 50, 72,
    130, 131, 156, 158, 159, 160,
    164, 165, 168, 202
nech-lebash, 92
neftenga, 92, 93, 108
Negarit Gazeta, 118, 122, 123, 129,
    142
Negritude, 47
neopatrimonialism, 38
nepotism, 71, 72
Netherlands, 77
Niger, 19, 23, 58, 63
Nigeria, 19, 23, 38, 45, 63, 78
Nile, 10, 20, 24
Nkrumah, 29, 44, 50, 54, 70, 206
Nordic, 79
Norway, 79
Nubians, 10
Nyerere, 35, 45, 46

Oakley, 217, 230
Ogaden, 23, 26, 85, 98, 99, 126, 167
oil, 31, 61, 63, 65, 68, 102, 103, 160
oligopsony, 72

Onimode, 30, 36, 44-46, 62, 63, 67, 68, 69, 82
Oriental, 41
ornaments, 22
Oromo, 85, 106, 119, 212
Ottaway, M., 103, 124, 164
Ottoman, Empire, 10, 85
ownership of land, 107, 142
ownership of oxen, 129

Paleolithic, 175
panafricanism, 36, 70
Pankhurst, Richard 10, 19, 26, 27, 84, 212
Pankrust, Alula, 133, 134, 135, 154
parishioners, 89
parliament, 96, 114
participation, 7, 12, 14, 15, 40, 66, 71, 73, 100, 105, 127, 146, 147, 162, 165, 174-175, 208, 215-221, 223
pastorals, 134
Pateman, 236
patrimonial, 86
Pausewang, S., 103, 118, 137, 146, 192
peasant, 35, 42, 85, 86, 89-91, 95, 98-100, 102, 105, 106, 118, 120-122, 128, 131, 135, 141-143, 145-150, 152, 154, 155, 166, 182, 201, 202, 204, 205, 209, 210, 213, 217, 218, 223, 229, 230, 234
periphery, 8, 61
Philippines, 64
philosophy, 46
physician, 236
Picket, 157, 158, 168
Poland, 149
politburo, 124, 126, 127, 137

Portugal, 28, 64
pragmatic, 39
Privatization of these lands, 87
proclamation, 113, 115, 118, 119, 122, 128, 129, 137, 138, 142, 145, 157, 161, 165
of land proclamations, 115
proletarian, 51, 164, 166
Provisional, 114, 124, 162, 168

qualifications, 62
quintal, 130, 131, 149, 168, 201
quota, 158, 168

racism, 5
ras, 92, 94, 96, 109
reclamation, 134, 200
reconciliation, 212
reforestation, 200
reform, land, 17, 88, 90, 108, 113, 116-119, 121, 135, 137, 143-145, 165, 166
refugees, 74, 148, 166
regionalism, 69, 85
rehabilitation, 104, 133
relationships, 27, 48, 72, 86, 93, 95, 207
representation, 89, 127, 190, 218
repression, 125, 212
republic, 50, 51, 126, 128, 139
Resettlement Program, 133-135, 149, 153-155, 167
retrogressive, 95
revisionist, 169
revolution, 12, 18, 27, 41-45, 47, 48, 50, 51, 86, 87, 90, 93, 94, 97-107, 113-120, 122-125, 135, 136, 138-139, 141, 143, 144, 145, 147-149, 151, 153, 155-157, 159-161, 163-167, 169,

Index

185, 192, 194, 202, 213, 215, 233, 234
rhetoric, 27, 43, 49
rist, 86-88, 91, 107
Rodney, 8, 19
Rostow, 37, 231
Rudebeck, 76
Russia, 47, 126, 169

Sahara, 21, 167
Sandbrook, R., 20, 38, 39, 40, 44, 64, 72, 76, 168
schism, 169
scientific, 27, 44, 136, 137, 180
Scott, 178
Scramble for Africa, 23, 28, 206
semon land, 89, 90
Senegal, 23, 38, 47, 50
serfs, 98
Setit Humera, 160
settlement program, 155
shemagle, 184, 185, 189
shemane, 178
Shoa, 91, 107, 121, 132, 144, 154
Siberia, 155
Sidamo, 88, 91, 92, 121, 132, 144
Sierra Leone, 23, 63
Singapore, 8
Sino-Soviet conflict, 169
siso, 90, 109
socialism, 9, 11, 17, 18, 27, 70, 83, 113, 114, 122, 124, 126, 136, 137, 155, 161, 164, 169
socialization, 93
societies, 4, 5, 7, 11, 13-17, 20, 33, 34, 35, 37, 42, 43, 48, 49, 60, 62, 70, 72, 74, 75, 76, 86, 120, 129, 133, 166, 175, 176, 178, 179, 181, 183, 189, 190, 192, 197, 223, 226, 227, 230, 232
sociological, 93, 212

Solodovinikov, 42
Somali, 23, 28, 42, 56, 74, 99, 126, 133, 138, 139, 162, 164
sovereignty, 29, 164
Soviets, 126, 161
Spain, 28, 64
Stalin, 163
strategy, 3, 109, 126, 131, 151, 162, 219, 221, 229, 230
stratification, 89
strike, 103, 104, 228
structural change, 14
subsistence economies, 76
Sudan, 31, 42, 60, 68, 78, 148, 166, 167
superstructure, 162
Swanson, 178, 181
Sweden, 33, 79, 139, 149, 212
symbols, 73, 203, 210, 227
synthesis, 46

Tanzania, 9, 23, 42, 45-47, 56-58, 120, 149, 151
taxi drivers, 103
technocrats, 59
technology, 16, 17, 21, 53, 62, 64, 65, 77, 83, 174, 180, 189, 196, 200, 204, 213, 221, 224, 228, 229, 232, 233, 234
teff, 94, 131, 157, 168, 201
Tekeste Negash, 26
Tendho, 160
tenure, land, 89, 91, 107, 165
territorial integrity, 139, 162
Tigray, 73, 91, 93, 99, 106, 107, 108, 109, 121, 139, 154, 227
Timbuktu, 19
Tirfe Mammo, 84, 199, 221, 237
tithe, 90
Todaro, M., 37, 50, 63, 77, 151, 202, 213

traditional, 3, 4, 6-13, 15-18, 20, 27, 33, 37, 38, 40, 47, 69, 70, 75-77, 89, 96, 99, 109, 131, 135, 144, 160, 165, 173-181, 184-186, 189-199, 203, 204, 209-212, 216, 218, 224-233, 236, 237
transformation, 4, 10-17, 25, 34, 35, 38, 40, 44, 54, 62, 77, 97, 113, 118, 119, 123, 126, 128, 129, 132, 134, 135, 141, 142, 146, 148, 165, 183, 188, 202, 211, 212, 216, 227, 236
tribal, 20, 99
Trimingham, 20, 85
tukuls, 205

Uganda, 39, 60, 78
Ujaama, 46
undemocratic, 72
underdevelopment, 7, 12, 14, 15, 24, 32, 37, 72, 76, 233
unemployment, 102, 103, 150, 151, 213-214, 235
unification of Ethiopia, 85
Uppsala, 212
urbanization, 94
utilization, 9, 13, 14, 55, 145

vaccination, 205
vacuum, 40, 123
vertical, 122, 195, 196, 199
viceroy, 92
villagization, 46, 128, 132, 135, 139, 149, 151-155, 202, 210
voluntary, 132, 153, 158, 182, 224

Walayeta, 85
Wallerstein, 8
Weber, 16
welba, 129

welfare, 17, 60, 184-186, 192, 207, 212, 221, 228
Westernization, 4, 17, 25, 33, 70, 83, 93, 94, 178, 180, 233
wielding, 127
Wolf, R., 86
Wollega, 85, 88, 91, 107, 121, 132, 134, 135, 143, 144
Wollo, 88, 91, 107, 121, 132, 139, 144, 154, 186
wonfel, 185
Woreda, 120, 121
Workers' Party, 43, 128

Yam, 85
Yemen, 138
Yoruba, 20
Yugoslavia, 149

Zaire, 30, 47, 78
Zambezi, 19
Zambia, 47, 58, 168
Zanzibar, 21
zemecha, 115, 116, 137, 169
Zimbabwe, 49, 63, 196